THE POLITICS OF PROPERTY

Labour, Freedom and Belonging

Laura Brace

EDINBURGH UNIVERSITY PRESS

For my parents, and especially my father who, like the proper
liberal he is, believes in the nationalisation of the land

© Laura Brace, 2004

Edinburgh University Press Ltd
22 George Square, Edinburgh

Typeset in Goudy by
Koinonia, Manchester, and
printed and bound in Great Britain by
CPI-Bath

A CIP record for this book is available from the British Library

ISBN 0 7486 1534 2 (hardback)
ISBN 0 7486 1535 0 (paperback)

The right of Laura Brace
to be identified as author of this work
has been asserted in accordance with
the Copyright, Designs and Patents Act 1988

Contents

Analytical Table of Contents

Acknowledgements

I want to start by acknowledging the support of the University of Leicester in funding my trip to Australia in 1999 to attend the 18th Annual Conference of the Australia and New Zealand Law and History Society on 'Land and Freedom'. The conference was organised by Andrew Buck and Nancy Wright, and I thank them for their hospitality, and for providing the inspiration for this book in its present form. The University of Leicester also granted me study leave in 2000, which proved invaluable for putting the book together, as did the help and advice of Andrew Reeve and Simon Tormey.

During 2001 and 2002, I was involved in organising an ESRC-funded Seminar Series on the theme 'Beyond Contract? Borders, Bodies and Bonds'. This proved to be that rare thing: an academic experience that really was about sharing ideas and expertise, thinking through the intersections between theory and practice and between disciplines, and struggling with how to analyse class, race and gender together. I would like to thank the organisers, Julia O'Connell Davidson, Jacqueline Sanchez Taylor, Bridget Anderson and Nirmal Puwar, our core participants, in particular Vanessa Pupavac, Donna Dickenson, Jo Doezema and Raia Prokhovnik, and our speakers, especially Charles Mills and Norman Geras, all of whose ideas and approaches I found enormously engaging and productive for thinking about property. In the same spirit, I would like to thank those who participated in and attended the PSA panel in 2001, where I gave a version of my paper 'The Tragedy of the Freelance Hustler: Hegel, Gender and Civil Society' and the participants in the 'Citizenship and its Futures' seminar at Northampton in December 2000, with Carole Pateman. The papers, responses and discussion at both events enabled me to think more clearly about the wider questions of freedom and belonging that underpin this book.

I would like to thank Julia O'Connell Davidson and John Hoffman for all their help and support, especially in reading chapters and providing me with critical, challenging and useful feedback. Nicola Carr was an encouraging and sympathetic editor, and Ros Hague was a welcome travelling companion through Hegelian theory. In the course of writing this book, I have incurred debts that go well beyond the intellectual. I am immensely grateful to Sam Haigh, Phil Leonard and Julia O'Connell Davidson who have not only given me practical support, but have also proved themselves to be fellow creatures and elementary humans of whom Winstanley would be proud. Finally, my heartfelt thanks to Matt Clark for surviving, and for reminding me that the honourable labour of working the allotment was sometimes more important than the drudgery of writing this book.

CHAPTER I

Property: Race, Gender and Class

The idea of property has a complex legacy that has filtered through the ideas of key political thinkers from John Locke to Karl Marx and beyond, and through the ideologies of liberalism, conservatism and socialism. It is a concept that has got caught up and entangled with other ideas along the way, and in particular with structures of power and with social and political relations. Private property has been understood as a distribution of freedom and unfreedom. It is, as C. B. Macpherson pointed out, not to do with the ownership of things but with relations between people. This distinction between property as a bundle of things and property as a bundle of rights is important, and as Brendan Edgeworth argues, distinctively modern.[1] Envisioning property as a relation between people and as a bundle of rights involves emphasising in particular the rights to use and enjoy, to exclude others and to alienate. Edgeworth quotes from the eighteenth-century jurist, William Blackstone, at the start of Volume II of the *Commentaries on the Laws of England*: 'Property is that sole and despotic dominion which one man claims and exercises over the external things of the world, in total exclusion of the right of any other individual in the universe.'[2]

This modern conception of property as sole and despotic dominion, with a particular emphasis on exclusion, is the subject of this book. It is a conception of property as an economic resource, and it connects all forms of property to the ideas of freedom, natural right and independence. Modern freedom, caught up with private property, is then about not being a slave, being secure from interference and being in a position to expect the quiet enjoyment of a private life. The doctrine of natural rights suggests that all rights are proprietary, and that all ownership is based on outright freehold.[3] This idea of property as immediate, personal and sovereign carries particular cultural significance, and is 'inextricably part of the way we understand the world'.[4] Property is made to look stable and secure, anchored in individual dominion, and 'the relational, mediating and dynamic side of property is often repressed'.[5] This book is an attempt to address the relational side of property, and to draw out its volatility by emphasising the despotism of the dominion involved, investigating the meaning of 'total exclusion' and the identity of the 'one man' who makes the claim.

Theorists have often been ready to treat property as an economic concept, and so to concede that it might intersect with political concerns where property meets class. In a British political tradition, thinking critically about property has always meant thinking about political economy and about class relations in particular, dividing the world into the propertied and the propertyless. The bourgeoisie owned the land and the means of production, and they required a landless labour force willing to work for wages. In America, the political tradition is different and structured by the legacy of slavery and a theoretical preoccupation with race rather than class. Property is centrally about who can own property, and who can be property, and the answer turns out to be racially inscribed. The separation of land and labour in America meant the dispossession of the Native Americans and the forced appropriation of black African labour. This often means that whiteness is equated with ownership and blackness with non-ownership, and property and race are expected to define each other. Both these forms of analysis risk assuming that in the transition from feudalism to capitalism, absolute private property has triumphed over every other form of property rights. Edgeworth reminds us that flexible and limited property rights persisted throughout the nineteenth century, and draws attention to the remarkable complexity and competing conceptions of property forms and practices.[6] It is important to the themes of this book that there was no single moment when absolute ownership was ushered in, and every other form of property hustled out. Property is a site of struggle: despotic dominion is not achieved without a fight.[7] The alternatives to outright freehold may be repressed, but they do not necessarily disappear.

The connections between property and race disrupt the idea that Blackstone's 'one man' is universal and the assumption that everyone has the same despotic dominion and right of total exclusion. As Joseph William Singer points out, 'many of the most cherished truisms of property theory turn out to be questionable when we find out that they seem

– 2 –

not to apply, or to apply in different ways, to white women and women and men of color.'[8] Defining property as legal relations between people with respect to things risks taking our attention away from intangible interests and obscuring the ways in which legal rules contribute to gender and racial inequality. By assuming that each individual is sovereign over herself and free to exclude others, we neglect 'the value people may place on the kind of power relations in which they stand to others'.[9] This book is centrally concerned to undo such neglect. Property is an important mechanism for placing value on power relations, expressed through notions of honour and dishonour, distinction and degradation.

Aue

Some of the most valued kinds of power relations are those expressed through gender. As soon as we begin to claim that property and self-ownership are about the capacity to exclude others, or to exercise a kind of mastery over ourselves, gender is being invoked at some level. As Margaret Davies argues, gender is heavily inflected with the thought of property, and property is deeply gendered.[10] Property relationships are forged at the intersection between the social and the natural, where the boundary between self and other is expected to be fixed in nature, but where what counts as natural and real is constantly shifting. To some extent, seeing property as a set of legal relations makes it unstable, contingent and in constant flux. At the same time, the volatility of property is offset by its 'strong connection with the essential, the authentic, the permanent, the territorial and the individual'. Property has not left behind the symbolism of despotic dominion and masculine control of the feminine other.[11] It is not just that the boundary between self and other is imagined as the boundary between male and female, but also that the creation of independent selves is imagined as the production of masculine and feminine identities. The question of who can own property has historically been answered in terms of gender as well as of race and class, and women have campaigned and struggled to be recognised as persons with equal rights, including the right to own property, and to vote. Property is a moral and political space as well as an economic relationship and it needs to be understood and analysed in terms of gender, race and class.

gender.

3 aspects.

– A COMPREHENSIVE APPROACH –

Laura Underkuffler distinguishes between two approaches to property. The absolute approach to property rests on two basic assumptions: first, the idea that property is something that is objectively definable apart from social context, and second, 'that it represents and protects the sphere of legitimate, absolute individual autonomy'.[12] This conception of property as despotic dominion is the legacy of a particular strand of liberalism based on possessive individualism and a negative conception of freedom, where being free and autonomous means having the capacity to exclude others from an impregnable internal fortress. This approach to selfhood and property crystallises a Hobbesian world-view within which individuals are by nature equal, rational, self-interested and competitive. In pursuing their individual appetites and aversions they can expect to find themselves in conflict with one another. The inherent danger of these absolute conflicts is that one person's absolute autonomy will come to rely on extinguishing the autonomy of another individual. Power becomes a zero-sum game. The only way to prevent these conflicts of power from escalating out of control is for each individual to recognise every other individual as equally rational and self-interested, and as ultimately separate from them. Property becomes a means of separation between individuals.

The territorial understanding of self encourages a self-identity based on a fixed and unbreachable boundary between self and other. This creates particular relations of honour and status between individuals. People tend to see all others as external to their own identity, and as possible threats to their own integrity. At the same time, they are, in Jean-Jacques Rousseau's terms, afflicted by the unremitting rage of distinguishing themselves. In a situation where other people are competitors and potential enemies, people begin to live outside themselves and to seek glory from self-aggrandisement and gaining power over others. Property relationships arising from a territorial self-identity and social relations of rage are bound to be centrally concerned with the exclusion of others. The possessive character of this kind of individualism means that it is this capacity to exclude that is understood to be what makes a man human. The centrality of exclusion creates a particular cluster of relations based on race, gender and class, fixing a boundary between male and female, black and white, rich and poor.

In contrast to this despotic dominion, Underkuffler points to an alternative, and more comprehensive, construction of property including rights to freedom of conscience, freedom of expression, physical liberty and the ability to use intelligence and creative powers. This more comprehensive approach does something different with the notions of equality and rationality, and with the idea of self-determination. It builds on the liberalism of Locke's conception of property as lives, liberties and estates, including the notion of property in the person. Such a conception of property cannot be divorced from its social and political context, and autonomy is connected to consent, morality and self-development. In this version of liberty and liberalism, property became that which without a man's own consent cannot be taken from him. This notion of property is tied to a notion of human beings, and in particular men, 'as masters of themselves'.[13] Self-mastery is central to idealist conceptions of property and underpins the idea that property is intrinsically connected to personality and self-determination. The distinction between despotic dominion and self-mastery turns out to be important for liberalism and for connecting self-ownership to gender, and is discussed in more detail in Chapters 5 and 9.

The connections between property, liberty, consent and self-government mean that the comprehensive approach to property is a rights-based theory, where a 'right can be defined as that which fulfils an individual need or individual interest that is considered to be of sufficient moral importance to justify the generation of duties for others'.[14] This sense of moral importance has to be rooted in some concept of human well-being and tied to the development of human personality. In generating duties for others, property has to be recognised by others and so becomes collective as well as individual. Individual property rights require a collective context for their exercise and realisation – even a right to exclude requires others to exclude. Private property 'is held by virtue of communal relations', and this suggests that individuals can never be fully private or separate from others.[15] The collective plays an integral role in supporting and restraining the concept of property itself, and this raises the possibility that the self owes its identity to the community, rather than holding itself in splendid and despotic isolation. For Rousseau and G. W. F. Hegel, for example, freedom 'needs a mixture of endowment and anchorage'.[16] The balance between endowment and anchorage, freedom and belonging, is central to the approach to property taken in this book, not only in its discussion of Hegel, but also in the final section, where we consider the connections between self-ownership, slavery and the land.

Property tied to self-realisation, and so to a more positive view of freedom, requires the co-operation of others in the property-owning community. It is within this more comprehensive approach to property that we can begin to discuss whether property exchanges always take place between equals and across a market run by impersonal rules of supply and demand within which each individual is a self-interested and rational actor. Collective concerns cannot be separated from issues of relative power and the social relations inherent in any definition of property. As the Chartists argued in the nineteenth century, property requires the public realm of social relations and membership of the imagined community before it can function in the private. For them, the property that supported rights and duties was 'the property of membership' embodied in notions of skilled and fair labour.[17] Skill was articulated as a property owned by those who worked within the rules and practices of their trade, and so within the bounds of membership of a skilled community. Political exclusion was then explained as 'the people being deprived of their rightful property in honorable labor'.[18] This conjunction of ideas brings together all the major themes of this book: honour as opposed to degradation; righteous labour as opposed to drudgery, and belonging as opposed to exclusion.

– PROPERTY AND PERSONHOOD –

An approach to property that sets out to protect the lives, liberties and estates of independent, self-governing individuals rests on a set of interpretations about what it means to be independent and autonomous. Lockean individuals are expected to lead their own life, without being dependent on anyone else. They take responsibility for themselves, for their labour, their conscience and their reason. They own themselves. The question then arises of what happens when people do not fully own themselves – those who are understood in some way to belong to someone else, for example, or who are regarded as hopelessly dependent on another's will. Rights-based theories such as the comprehensive approach to property require rational, independent agents able to perceive their own self-interest and respect the equal rationality and justifiable claims of others. There is not much room for those who are characterised as irrational, vulnerable or uncivilised. Traditional property theory is predicated on taking personhood for granted 'and thus excludes the differential experience of those who have ceaselessly had to fight to have their personhood recognized in the first place'.[19] The fight to have personhood recognised is not straightforward, and black and female subjectivities find themselves in a double bind: 'Subjects assume value...only in so far as they are bearers of rights; and they are properly vested with rights only in so far as they are imbued with value.'[20]

This raises the possibility of subjectivities who are not imbued with value or vested with rights. Charles Mills argues that the concept of personhood has to include the concept of a 'subperson' – not an inanimate object, and not entirely outside the imagined moral community, but not fully a person.[21] Such a subperson is defined in contrast to those who own themselves. Subpersons are assumed to have less mental capacity, no real history and no real contribution to make to civilisation. Crucially, they are individuals 'who in general can be encroached upon with impunity'.[22] White people were then defined as white on the basis that they had the capacity to exclude others, and to exercise despotic dominion over themselves. Whiteness itself was a probationary category with permeable boundaries of belonging and identity. Those who were properly white, who confirmed their status as white by being virtuous, hard-working and productive, deserved the benefits that accrued to them from their whiteness. Whiteness was a moral category, more like masculinity than maleness, a 'natural' identity that had to be socially reproduced. Racism, like patriarchy, plays on the slippage between the two, eliding the social and the natural, crystallising whiteness into an identity, a status and a property in membership. The assumptions, privileges and benefits that accompany the status of being white have become a valuable asset in need of protection and of exclusion: 'whites have come to expect and rely on these benefits and over time these expectations have been affirmed, legitimated, and protected by law'. As a set of 'settled expectations', it becomes possible to identify 'a property interest in whiteness'.[23] Being white, and being able to exclude others from whiteness, involved being able to prevent yourself from becoming property, to protect yourself from the threat of commodification. Owning whiteness as property means never being owned as property by others, and so whiteness becomes the characteristic of a free human being. The presumption of freedom arose from being white and 'whiteness became a shield from slavery, a highly volatile and unstable form of property'.[24]

Race, in this account, 'will in general be the marker of entitlement or dispossession, civilization or barbarism, normative inclusion or normative exclusion, full or diminished personhood'.[25] Property is directly implicated in this process of marking and the construction of race. As self-ownership is central to personhood, it follows that property relations help to structure inclusion and exclusion, and notions of civilisation and barbarism. Property is central to the project of colonialism, defined by Ania Loomba as 'the conquest and control of other people's land and goods'.[26] The colonial system extracted wealth for the empire through the seizure of bullion and the expropriation of land through slavery and colonial labour. White, Lockean persons who owned themselves (and exercised despotic dominion over themselves) emerged 'not merely in contrast to but to a certain extent on the backs of non-white subpersons thousands of miles away'[27]– and not only non-white subpersons, and not only those thousands of miles away. Slaves and landless labourers were regarded as having only a qualified self-ownership. Their labour was stigmatised as inefficient and their rationality and moral autonomy as limited. They were regarded as being incapable of honourable labour, and so they were deprived of their property in membership and understood to be without endowments or anchorage. In such a situation, slavery and despotic rule became legitimate modes for dealing with barbarians, even for liberals like John Stuart Mill, who subscribed to a notion of liberty tied to self-development. For him and others, the divisions between barbarianism and civilisation were bound to ideas about human progress.

The interconnections between eighteenth-century Enlightenment notions of progress, nineteenth-century liberalism and colonialism put the empire and race at the centre of ideas about property, and about modernity itself. Mills argues that conquest, colonialism and African slavery are internal to the West, and integral to European modernity. They are part of the ethical and intellectual heritage of the West in general and of the American polity in particular. Full self-ownership for white persons includes a share in the benefits of the qualified self-ownership of non-white subpersons. The racial contract Mills describes is 'in effect an agreement to divide among themselves (as common white property) the proceeds of nonwhite subordination'.[28] In terms of the discussion of property rights, however, this cannot be the end of the story. It leaves unanswered the question of how that common white property is divided, and makes inexplicable subordination and qualified self-ownership based on gender and class rather than race.

This does not mean that we can ignore the racial contract, but we do need to pay more nuanced attention to its terms. Under colonialism, the formation of identities was 'played out in the definition of entitlement to welfare and to property rights, both within the metropole and on the periphery.'[29] Dominion, endowment, anchorage and membership were all mediated through property rights in land, persons and labour. The volatility and flux of property meant that these property rights were constantly renegotiated and contested. Property, like race, was shape-shifting and fluid. For example, the English used their own ideas about 'proper' land use and ownership to displace Native Americans, marking them as wandering, transient and potentially troublesome. The persistent mobility of the original inhabitants was coded as resistance to 'the English colonial agenda of fixity and social place'. The New England settlers imposed their notions of property by enclosing the land, turning its products and the land itself into commodities and bringing it into a new market-driven economy.[30] Private property in land solidified, crowding out competing conceptions, and in the process, the 'Indian power to define the terms for possessing the land' vanished, and in turn the Native Americans themselves were constructed by the colonial power as vagrant, marginal and about to disappear. They were excluded from belonging, and figured as fugitives and exiles in their own land. Chapter 2 explores this process in more detail, and the whole book is concerned with those who are unable to define their own terms of possession, and so are regarded as marginal and invisible.

As fugitives and exiles, the Native Americans were constructed by the settlers as savage, wild men who 'existed outside civil society, and yet … constantly threatened to enter and disrupt this society'.[31] The only way to keep them at bay, to police the boundary effectively, was through the despotic dominion of exclusive property. Civility required property not only to fix a place in the landscape, but to fix a sense of self, a boundary between self and other and between male and female, black and white, rich and poor. The ultimate confirmation of the wildness of the savage was cannibalism, the threat that they could turn against and devour Europeans, and in the process breach the boundary between self and other. Again, this is not about a straightforward division of the spoils of blackness among the white population. Bentham argued that poverty was the primitive condition of the human race and the savage was made savage by being forced to live a life of day-to-day subsistence. The boundary between civil society and the rest of human society was crucial to maintaining the racial and sexual as well as the social contracts, but, again, it was not unbreachable. The equation of savagery with subsistence and civilisation with private property keeps resurfacing throughout the book, in the thoughts of Jeremy Bentham and Marx, and in the ideas of slave owners and of colonists in Rhodesia. The ways in which society is constructed as civil, civilised and civilising are crucial to the ideas of all the thinkers examined in this book, and to the ideologies of liberalism, socialism and conservatism.

– CONCLUSION –

The liberalism that stresses property in the person over the more absolute possession of possessive individualism works through identity, reputation and property, and so honour, labour and belonging, in different ways. Self-identity requires a more social and collective context, and so reputation is more about recognition and the acknowledgement that relations with others may be constitutive of individual identity and of a civil society based on collective concerns. Property relations then have to be concerned with more than straightforward exclusion and take account of complex social relations of power. Race, gender and class have to be understood as more fluid and less fixed, as social rather than natural categories and as connected to wider discourses about colonialism, civilisation and progress.

Property as a moral space tied to integrity and self-government generates duties for others and connects the individual and the collective. This ensures the continuing mythological importance of the concept of property: it becomes part of the story of land and labour, of civilisation and progress, of conquest and colonialism, and of the self and other. The idea of property is always entangled with moral, social and political rights – it can never only be about economic rights. In the same way, property is never simply about class; it is tangled up with race and gender as well. It is this entanglement that makes it crucial to focus on the history of property, its fluidity rather than its fixity. It is important not to expect to find property relationships only in specific places (like the market) or between particular individuals (like equal economic actors). By exploring the tangle of property, class, race, gender and selfhood, we can begin to understand why some people in Nigeria, for example, are not regarded by the multinational pharmaceutical companies as capable of giving properly informed consent to medical treatment. The same cluster of relationships, differently constituted, can help us to see the importance of the idea of slavery in current debates about trafficking, or the role of colonialism and conquest in issues of land redistribution and justice in South Africa and Zimbabwe.

This book works through the complex relationship between property and power relations by exploring the dualisms of honour and degradation, labour and drudgery, and belonging and exclusion. Its particular focus is on the connections between freedom and belonging that are forged in theories of property. In Chapter 2, the different attitudes of Gerrard Winstanley and Locke towards the earth as a common treasury bring out their contrasting notions of freedom, labour and belonging. In Chapter 3 William Godwin and Bentham draw the boundaries around civilisation and savagery in new ways, and Godwin's arguments make clear that despotic dominion over the self relied on the 'slavery and sweat' of others, and not just their total exclusion. Chapter 4 shows how Hegel and Marx develop these ideas in the context of industrialisation and the problem of poverty. Hegel's definition of poverty as exclusion from the physical and ethical benefits of society, which cuts individuals off from advantages such as skills, education and access to justice and estranges people from themselves and one another, encapsulates how honour, labour and belonging are inextricably linked. Property requires both endowment and anchorage, and the balance between the two is worked out through the ideologies of liberalism, socialism and conservatism and the different theories of property which inform them. For liberals, the idea of property is central to the construction of the individual and to notions of justice. In the chapter on socialism, we return to the questions of honourable labour and of poverty as exclusion. Conservatism takes us back to belonging, to anchorage and independence, and in particular to the boundaries of civil society.

In Chapter 8, slavery raises the issues of degradation, drudgery and exclusion in their starkest terms. Slavery is treated here as part of the ideology of property, and as both an abstract idea and a practice it makes clear that freedom is inextricable from belonging. Some of the connections between freedom, personhood and the idea of 'despotic dominion' are worked out in Chapter 9 in terms of gender as a valued power relation. Fugitives, hustlers and exiles are excluded from civil society and the market on the grounds of gender as well as race, and it is important to consider how 'perhaps we may at once have and be property'.[32] The final chapter explores how notions of property, belonging and freedom have worked themselves out in the colonial and postcolonial contexts of Ireland and Zimbabwe, bringing us back to questions about subsistence, access to the soil, land and labour first explored in the ideas of Locke and Winstanley.

– NOTES –

1. Brendan Edgeworth, 'Post-Property? A Postmodern Conception of Private Property', *University of New South Wales Law Journal* 11, 1988, p. 88.
2. Ibid. p. 89. The quotation comes from Sir William Blackstone, *Commentaries of the Laws of England*, 11th edn (London: T. Cadell, 1791), Vol. II, p. 2.
3. Alan Ryan, *Property* (Milton Keynes: Open University Press 1987), p. 69.

4. Kenneth R. Minogue, 'The Concept of Property and Its Contemporary Significance', in J. Roland Pennock and John W. Chapman (eds), *Nomos XXII: Property* (New York: New York University Press, 1980), p. 24.

5. Margaret Davies, 'Queer Property. Queer Persons: Self-Ownership and Beyond', *Social and Legal Studies* 8:3, 1999, p. 328.

6. Edgeworth, 'Post-Property?', pp. 91–2, 101.

7. Donna Dickenson, *Property, Women and Politics* (Cambridge: Polity Press, 1997), p. 80.

8. Joseph William Singer, 'Re-Reading Property', *New England Law Review* 26, Spring 1992, p. 713.

9. G. A. Cohen, *Self-ownership, Freedom and Equality* (Cambridge: Cambridge University Press, 1995), p. 80.

10. Davies, 'Queer Property. Queer Persons', p. 330.

11. Ibid. p. 342.

12. Laura Underkuffler, 'On Property: an Essay', *Yale Law Journal* 100: 127, 1990, p. 133.

13. Ibid. p. 138.

14. Ibid. p. 139.

15. Davies, 'Queer Property. Queer Persons', p. 341.

16. Ryan, *Property*, p. 125.

17. Margaret R. Somers, 'The "Misteries" of Property: Relationality, Rural-industrialization, and Community in Chartist Narratives of Political Rights', in John Brewer and Susan Staves (eds), *Early Modern Conceptions of Property* (London and New York: Routledge, 1996), p. 67.

18. Ibid. 'Misteries', p. 69.

19. Charles W. Mills, *Blackness Visible: Essays on Philosophy and Race* (Ithaca, NY and London: Cornell University Press, 1998), p. 9.

20. David Theo Goldberg, *Racist Culture: Philosophy and the Politics of Meaning* (Oxford: Blackwell, 1993), p. 37.

21. Mills, *Blackness Visible*, p. 6.

22. Ibid. p 7.

23. Cheryl I. Harris, 'Whiteness as Property', *Harvard Law Review*, Vol. 106, 1993, p. 1713.

24. Ibid. p. 1720.

25. Mills, *Blackness Visible*, p. 127.

26. Ania Loomba, *Colonialism / Postcolonialism* (London and New York: Routledge, 1998), pp. 2, 71.

27. Mills, *Blackness Visible*, p. 128.

28. Ibid. p. 135.

29. Martin Daunton and Rick Halpern (eds), *Empire and Others: British Encounters with Indigenous Peoples, 1600–1850.* (London: UCL Press, 1999), p. 6.

30. Jean O'Brien, '"They Are So Frequently Shifting Their Place of Residence": Land and the Construction of Social Place of Indians in Colonial Massachusetts', in Daunton and Halpern (eds), *Empire and Others*, p. 206.

31. Loomba, *Colonialism / Postcolonialism*, p. 57.

32. Davies, 'Queer Property. Queer Persons', p. 345.

CHAPTER 2

Locke and Winstanley: Land and Labour

This chapter explores fundamental questions about the relationship between property, dominion and freedom as they arose during the seventeenth century, both in theory and in practice. It aims to begin an examination of the origins of the modern liberal idea of property, together with its discontents. This means exploring the contested connections between property and liberty, and in particular ideas about the right to own land, the possibility that human beings could claim dominion over the earth and its products. Improvement ideas, developed in the seventeenth and eighteenth centuries, represented a particular mode of ownership and control, easily converted into the doctrine of 'vacant lands' that was applied to the frontiers of the British colonies and used as a justification for the dispossession of indigenous peoples and the expropriation of their land. The struggles over enclosure and dispossession in seventeenth-century England raised the question of whose labour counted as honourable, and how that righteous labour was distinguished from the drudgery of others. Some forms of labour underpinned a sense of belonging, and grounded membership of the imagined community. Those who owned property were figured as industrious, rational and civilised, while those who owned their labour and were forced to sell it were figured as undisciplined and lazy. In these constructions, we can trace some of the ideas underpinning 'the West's mandate to conquer the earth'.[1] In the process of conquering the earth, some were bound to become excluded from the physical and ethical benefits of society, cut off from skills, education and access to justice, and estranged from themselves and one another. The poor and the conquered were differentially incorporated into civil society and the state. Ideas about labour and about belonging were inextricably entangled in each other, and they operated together to make private property a fraught and contested moral and political space.

In the seventeenth century, one of the central ways of understanding property was through the discourse of 'improvement', the idea that property should be improved, sustained and made productive and useful – rather than hoarded or stewarded, or stored up as treasure. It was a notion that contested both aristocratic notions of property and the idea that the earth was a common treasury, opposing itself to the wastefulness of aristocratic estates and forests, and of the common lands. The idea that the earth could be owned or land sold as a commodity became the subject of debate. The enclosure movement gained momentum during the seventeenth century, and critics challenged the loss of common lands and the removal of ordinary people's access to the soil. The defence of the common lands invoked concepts of stewardship, and of communal and customary ownership to counter enclosure and the commercialisation of the land. The defenders of the commons stressed the importance of the earth as a common treasury, held on trust for the preservation of all humankind. Rather than defending an individual right to appropriate and own the earth as private property, some radicals, such as the Diggers, talked about establishing an equal and universal right to cultivate the earth for subsistence. Access to the soil and to subsistence were fundamental to freedom. For the Diggers, private property undermined rather than promoted equal rights, and the intensification of private ownership through processes such as the commercialisation of agriculture involved shutting the poor out of the earth and promoting self-preservation over common preservation. At the heart of the contest, was the question of how far human identity was associated with this inevitably conflictual version of self-preservation as self-interest, mediated through the market. Was the mercenariness of humankind part of the 'hard core' of human nature? How far did membership of the imagined community of the commonwealth depend on industry, rationality and property ownership?

John Locke is at the centre of this chapter, and also in many ways at the core of the book. He took property to be the basis for self-preservation, and his theory made self-ownership 'integral to survival'.[2] This meant that, for Locke, property was part of the hard core of human nature, and so each individual had a natural right to property. He began from the proposition of a state of nature, humanity's original state, that was 'a *State of perfect Freedom* to order their Actions, and dispose of their Possessions, and Persons as they think fit, within the bounds of the Law of Nature, without asking leave, or depending upon the Will of any other Man'.[3] In this state of nature, there were no natural hierarchies. It was a state of equality as well as of freedom because all individuals were owners of themselves and of the fruits of their labours. This was because, for Locke, in his famous formulation: 'Every Man has a *Property* in his own *Person*. This no Body has any Right to but himself. The *Labour* of his Body, and the *Work* of his Hands, we may say, are properly his.'[4] When these owners of themselves laboured on a resource, they put something of themselves into it, and so made it theirs. By mixing their labour with it, they then had the same sort of entitlement to the resource as they originally had in respect to their person and labour.[5] Under these conditions, private property could legitimately exist outside political society, apart from government and positive law.

Locke used 'property' in a wide sense, to include life, liberty and estates but, as Jeremy Waldron argues, the sense of the term was always the same: 'that *without a Man's own consent* it *cannot be taken from him*'.[6] This gave property its political, moral and psychic dimensions. Civil societies and governments were established, according to Locke, expressly in order to preserve property. Individuals took their property in their person, their labour and their right to own resources with them out of the state of nature and into political society. They had a natural right to self-preservation and to own themselves, which could not be taken from them without their own consent. These rights were natural 'in the sense that the force of these rights obtains and can be recognized as valid by moral and rational people quite apart from any provisions of positive law'.[7] Their force came from the sense that property was rooted in the hard core of human nature, that it could not be taken away without causing significant damage, and was central to individuals' sense of themselves as persons. Individuals as 'creators of their own actions' needed their property to sustain their morality and rationality, and so their membership of the imagined community.[8] The structure of Locke's argument, and the centrality of owning a property in the person, underpinned specific conceptions of honour, labour and belonging that emerged out of struggles over land and labour in the seventeenth century. Locke was responding to a changing world of cultivation and profit that was bringing the idea that the earth was a common treasury, held in common by all humankind, under considerable pressure. To explore some of the roots of this pressure, we need to go back from the Second Treatise, written in 1698, to the mid-seventeenth century.

– Land and Labour –

In seventeenth-century England, the pattern of landholding was changing. During the fifteenth century, demographic collapse left vacant many former customary peasant holdings which were then appropriated by the landlords and annexed to their demesnes. This reduced the area of land available for potential peasant proprietorship in the future. Landlords were in a position to engross the customary holdings, consolidate their estates and enclose more common land, confirming their sense that land was private property, and a source of private profit. Christopher Hill points out the extent of the commercialisation of agriculture during the seventeenth century. Between 1605 and 1661 the consumption of corn in London increased by 230 per cent, exerting pressure to cultivate the commons, wastelands and royal forests.[9] Landowners with capital used consolidation and enclosure of lands and the engrossment of smaller farms to develop more intensive and efficient production of commodities for the market. Economies of scale and labour-intensive farming methods required capital, and the new, more commercial farming methods promoted the interests of ambitious improvers, those prepared to invest in expensive schemes and projects to increase their profits.[10] The principal investors in and beneficiaries of the drainage of the fens, for example, were members of the court circle, the nobility and the gentry. The peasantry were disconnected from this kind of enterprise, and so from the process of farming, and eventually from the land itself. The owners of the great estates became great employers of wage labour to work their land. Owners were entrepreneurs and investors who expected profits and returns on their capital, but made no investment of their own labour. Land and labour were uncoupled from one another.

In 1650 the English economy was in crisis. The Civil Wars had decimated manufacturing and trade and the successive bad harvests had led to high prices and people starving in the streets. In this atmosphere of collapse and crisis Parliament established the Council of Trade in August 1650. The Council was instructed to discover the means to stimulate manufacture and domestic trade and to investigate how to set the unemployed and underemployed poor to work, and how to distribute wealth throughout the country. The concerns of the Council were part of a wider world-view, one which wove together economic, cultural, political and religious concerns. They reflected a more receptive attitude to new ideas consistent with Puritan ethics and an increased confidence in the capacity of the human intellect to solve economic and social problems. These attitudes were central to theories of property and human nature, and this confidence in the capacity of the human intellect reemerged in Enlightenment debates about property and justice, and in socialist ideas about the abolition of property, and was contested in the ideas of their conservative opponents.

The belief in the possibility of the complete return of man's dominion over nature permeated the atmosphere of the 1650s and informed the improvement discourse which drove the commercialisation of agriculture. For the improvers, their improvement was part of the story of the creation. God had made all creatures, plants, fruits, trees and herbs serviceable to mankind, who was expressly created 'to husbandize the fruits of the earth'.[11] Those involved in husbandry and improvement felt themselves engaged in a tremendous project to convert the desolate wastes into fruitful fields and the wilderness into comfortable habitations. This idea of transformation underpinned both the communism of Gerrard Winstanley and the liberalism of Locke. Wild and vacant wastelands were regarded 'like a deformed Chaos' which brought discredit to the common- wealth and needed to be made productive by righteous labour.[12] Improve- ment of the fruits of the earth by human ingenuity was regarded as 'little lesse then an addition of a new world'[13] gained above the natural fruitful- ness of the earth. This sense of renewal was central to the improvement context, and so was the language of colonialism.

Improvers felt strongly that land held in common fields was often spoiled through lack of good husbandry, and as a result could have little worth. This, to them, constituted the sin of wasting God's workmanship. Nature provided a valuable treasury, but people would not be able to reverse the Fall unless they were prepared to labour and improve. Paradise was made paradise through dressing and keeping, and gardens were only perfect so long as they were cultivated.[14] Adam Moore made explicit the distinction between enclosed and common lands.[15] He characterised the commons as a desert where there was no private property, and no rights to sale and disposal. He contrasted this desert to the garden of enclosure, where everyone had the right to exclude others from their property, and to dispose of it at their pleasure. The time had come to convert the desert into a garden by distributing land to private owners 'which being appro- priated to their particular uses, will then be cleansed and purged of the former deformities'.[16] Land which had not been appropriated was being carefully constructed as vacant, deserted, a space with limitations that needed to be overcome, conquered and transformed by the human capacity to solve economic and social problems. The distinction between enclosed and common lands hinged around the differential opportunities they offered for improvement and accumulation. Common lands could not involve enterprise or initiative because they were subject to more restrictive ownership than enclosed lands. For the improvers, paradise was emerging from the desolate wastes through the commercialisation of agriculture and new methods of cultivation.

– DIGGING THE LAND –

The implications of the improvement discourse were disputed by a range of thinkers, and in particular by those who defended the traditional and customary rights of the poor against a narrowing definition of what counted as genuine property rights. Traditionally, the poor had not had to resort to working for wages from the improving landowners. The commons and wastes, small farms, rural crafts and trades had all provided them with options other than waged employment.[17] Pastoral areas had often been successful because common pastures were used as a community asset and supplemented by additional work opportunities in fishing, thatching, mining, nail-making or weaving. Attitudes towards the commons were central to notions of property. Winstanley, among others, argued that both the common lands and the common woods ought to have provided a livelihood for all, including the poor. The rich freeholders had tried to make a profit from the commons by over-stocking them with sheep and cattle, punishing the poor 'if they cut wood, heath, turf or furzes in places about the common where they disallow'.[18] Winstanley protested, in particular, against those who intended to cut down the common woods and trees for their private use. He declared the hope that 'all woodmongers will disown all private merchandise, as being a robbing of the poor'.[19]

Winstanley responded directly to the assumptions of the improvers, and in particular their insistence that paradise would emerge through the mechanisms of enclosure and more intensive agriculture. He argued that the present system of ownership meant that England was not properly cultivated. There was enough land available to maintain ten times the population, and yet the poor were left to starve. One third of the land was left as barren waste which the landlords would not allow the poor to improve for themselves. Winstanley believed that the property rights of the lords of the manor in the commons should have been abolished, to allow the poor to use the wastelands to their own advantage. For Winstanley, the laws of property formed part of what he termed 'kingly power'. By this he meant power relations based not on consent, but on force. Property was not that which without a man's consent could not be taken from him, but the act of taking. Kingly power was despotic. It was the law of the conqueror, and it took away the rights of the poor: 'The power of the sword does not only kill and rob; but by his laws, made and upheld by his power, he hedges the weak out of the earth, and either starves them or else forces them through poverty to take from others, and then hangs them for so doing.'[20]

Winstanley aimed to reclaim both the righteousness of labour and access to the soil, bringing land and labour back together. Landlords had initially gained land from their fellow creatures by oppression, murder and theft, but it was unrighteous, alienated wage labour and drudgery that allowed them to maintain their tyranny. Winstanley wanted to organise a national strike of wage labour so that rich men could no longer 'live at ease, feeding and clothing themselves by the labours of other men, not by their own'.[21] His point was that the poor should work for themselves and not for the rich. Winstanley drew parallels between ancient Israel and 1640s England. Through rejection of wages and the establishment of communal cultivation, the modern Pharaohs would perish: 'By withholding their labour, common people can force landowners to work.'[22] Once wage labour had been abolished, peasant proprietorship would become the only viable form of land ownership.

For Winstanley, communal cultivation of the commons was the key to reform. Collective cultivation of the waste land could give the poor the advantages of large-scale agricultural methods, and more intensive cultivation could feed the increasing population. Winstanley was the leader of the Diggers, a radical movement which grew out of the economic hardship caused by the Civil War. Diggers established a self-sufficient community on the common lands of St George's Hill in Surrey in April 1649, four months after Charles I had been executed and the monarchy abolished. They called themselves 'True Levellers' because they aimed to create equality by ending private property and wage labour. Their digging experiment involved cultivating the commons, and so invading the property rights of landowners. They sowed the common land there with carrots, parsnips and beans: 'The work we are going about is this, to dig up George Hill and the waste ground thereabouts and to sow corn, and to eat bread together by the sweat of our brows.'[23] Their community aroused enormous local hostility. They were subjected to organised raids by mobs of local poor people and to legal harassment by the richer sort. By April 1650 they had been forced to disband.[24]

Digging was a practical, a symbolic and a political action. It was a way of showing how the poor might reclaim the earth and use it as a common treasury. Winstanley proclaimed digging as an act of justice, righteousness, love and charity. The poor had been shut out of the earth, and the cultivation of St George's Hill was about taking some of it back, physically invading what was also a moral and psychic space. The digging experiment was about bearing witness: 'their intention was to live now as all will live after the restoration [of Christ]'.[25] The digging experiment was in part about reasserting the original, harmonious dominion of humankind over nature, regaining paradise, getting back behind the Fall. The idea of the Fall was central to Winstanley's theory of property, and he saw private property as its cause rather than its consequence. No man owned the apples in the Garden of Eden, and ownership rested with God. God bestowed the fruits of the earth on men for *use* rather than appropriation, and any attempt to instigate a system of private property transgressed God's 'intended principle of usufruct'.[26] The principle of usufruct involved the right to use and enjoy God's property without having the right to change its character. Humans were entitled to the enjoy the fruits of the land, its produce, without turning it into a commodity or making it alienable. Once this principle was broken, at the Fall, covetousness began to rise up in Adam and 'to kill the power of love and freedom within him'.[27] Cain lifted himself up above Abel, consenting to the serpent of covetousness and falling from righteousness: 'And in that time began particular propriety to grow in one man over another.'[28]

The Fall, then, in Winstanley's thought, had three stages. First, the elder brother, termed by Winstanley the first Adam, ate from the tree of knowledge and imagined that he deserved a larger part of the earth, and to be esteemed and acknowledged as superior by the rest. The others consented to these inventions and so mankind fell from its original unity and equality to be full of divisions: 'one member of mankind is separated from another, which before were all one, and looked upon each other as all one …'[29] This sense of separation from each other was the first step of the Fall. The original order meant an 'evenness' existed between men and men, between men and creatures and between man and his maker. It was an evenness that had been destroyed by their 'climbing power of self-love'. This created tyranny: husbands, parents, masters and magistrates all acted as oppressors, not recognising their wives, children, servants and subjects as fellow creatures with 'an equall priviledge to share with them the blessing of liberty'.[30] This sense of dissociation created by private property and the damage this does to the social instinct resonates throughout the anti-property literature, from Winstanley through Godwin and Proudhon to Marx. It contrasts directly with the more conservative view of private property as a condition of humanness, a way of ensuring rather than destroying 'evenness'.

The second step of the Fall, for Winstanley, was the break into outward action, the separation from the earth. The stronger brother enclosed parcels of the earth and called those enclosures his own property 'and the younger brother lets it go so'.[31] He ruled over, imprisoned, oppressed or killed his fellow creatures and so was 'a destroyer of the Creation, and an actor of the Curse'.[32] The curse was exploitation, not labour itself. The curse on Cain sent him into exile and made the earth even harder to till. Cain became a fugitive in the earth, a scavenger rather than a true husbandman. Here, Winstanley made his argument in mystical and biblical terms, but Cain's sense of estrangement not only from the earth but also from his own labour keeps resurfacing in his writings and in the anti-property literature more generally. The idea of exile is also resonant: Cain was expelled from the imagined community, excluded from belonging. The curse rested within man and around him, alienating him from the earth and undermining his right to cultivate the land for his own subsistence. The final stage of the Fall was when mankind began to buy and sell the enclosures of land so that the younger or weaker brother was 'more forcibly shut out of the earth'.[33] Buying and selling private property was the outward expression of the sense of separation, claiming a monopoly, a right to exclude. This process of the Fall was intensified in England by the commercialisation of agriculture and by the changing pattern of landholding based on a market in land and labour.

Winstanley's argument was that private property, the result of the Fall, suppressed universal liberty. The 'first Adam', the cause of the Fall, was the rule of one part of mankind over another, Cain over Abel, a rule sustained through private property and intensified by the buying and selling of the earth. Landowners and the system of wage labour created tyranny and misery. As long as private property was upheld, 'the common people shall never have their liberty'.[34] The division between the poor and the gentry, the labourers and their landlords, meant that subjects were denied their birth-right freedoms. Inferior tenants and labourers bore all the burdens, especially of war, and Winstanley made a connection between their exploitation and their need. The poor laboured the earth and paid their taxes while the gentry landlords lived idly: 'then he does take my right from me, which I have purchased by my money in Taxes, free quarter and blood.'[35] Rich men lived at ease, off the labour of others, and so the connection between labour and selfhood was damaged. This leisured way of life was a badge of shame, not of nobility: for Winstanley, and for all the reformers of the seventeenth century and beyond, there was no such thing as honourable unemployment, either for the poor or for the rich.

For Winstanley, it was the poor who had the potential and the power to change things. They were the agents of change, but also fellow creatures, uncorrupted by the tyranny of self-love, and so somehow more 'human' than the rich.[36] This sense of the poor as fellow creatures, as 'elementary humans' uncorrupted by mercenariness, runs from Winstanley through the ideas of William Godwin and Karl Marx. In Winstanley's theory, the poor would defeat the 'first Adam' and receive the gospel first. Through working and living together and reasserting their right to cultivate the commons, they would recapture humankind's original 'evenness' and order. They would preserve one another through love and tenderness against the covetous rich. Winstanley envisaged the rise of the righteous law, under which no one would desire to have more than another, private property would be abolished and 'they shall all live as brethren'.[37] He advocated a universal law of equity, an end to the distinction between mine and yours, the abolition of buying and selling. England could not be a free commonwealth while the poor had no land and no 'free allowance to dig and labour the commons'.[38] The earth was made to preserve all her children. In theory and in practice, 'access to the soil became the essential condition of freedom and liberty.'[39] For Winstanley, belonging to the earth was inseparable from freedom. Being denied access to the soil meant being a fugitive and an exile.

– A Common Treasury? –

It was this strong version of the claim that the earth was a common treasury that defenders of appropriation and private property needed to counter. Winstanley argued that once mankind began to buy and sell the enclosures of land, the younger or weaker brother was forcibly shut out of the earth. The earth itself was no longer available to him, and so he had lost his natural right to dominion and to subsistence. Property was a relationship ultimately based on force, and the younger brother (the poor) could still rightfully claim the land, since 'we give no consent to be shut out'.[40] The elder brother had no authority to buy or sell the earth, or to cheat his brother and cast the poor out of the earth. When the stronger brother enclosed the land by force and turned the poor off the land, he made war against his weaker brother and acted unreasonably. God's intended principle of usufruct had to be understood as universally applicable: it could not entail the exclusion of the poor, who were fellow creatures with an equal privilege, from the right to cultivate the land with their own labour. For Winstanley, private property usurped usufruct. By changing the character of the land and by buying and selling the earth, private landowners were not fulfilling their obligation to conserve the substance of God's property.

John Locke, writing forty years later than Winstanley, after the economic crises of the 1650s had passed, shared very similar concerns. The background economic conditions remained the same, and the earth was still widely regarded as a gift from God, and a common treasury. For Locke, God as the creator was also the first proprietor and retained a right to everything he had made. God gave men dominion over the earth and the other animals; he 'gave the World to Mankind in common'.[41] Locke's problem was to explain how individuals came to use and enjoy a world that had been given to them in common, without relying on the idea that original collective ownership had been abolished and divided by universal consent. He was not directly answering Winstanley, but he wanted to deny that the poor had been shut out without their consent, and to argue that it was impossible for humankind to abolish property and return to an original evenness. For Locke, the property given to humans by God was private. He argued: 'God gave the World to Men in Common; but since he gave it them for their benefit, and the greatest Conveniencies of Life they were capable to draw from it, it cannot be supposed he meant that it should always remain common and uncultivated.'[42]

In Locke's theory, individuals used their reason to understand that unless they laboured they would starve, and so fail in their first duty, which was self-preservation. Men had to turn the common world into property through their labour. Consent was not necessary, since each person was acting to ensure their own survival and God had given them the right to make use of food and other necessities rather than 'make them depend upon the Will of a Man for their Subsistence'.[43] Humans, according to Locke, were by nature independent and rational. Locke recognised the problem of subsistence, but he did not see property as estranging and alienating. His vision of God's purposes for humankind meant that all men were equally members of the human species, shaped by God and 'sent into the World by his order and about his business'.[44] Everyone was bound to preserve himself and ought, as much as he could, to preserve the rest of humankind: 'The duty to preserve oneself as God's workmanship cannot be divorced from a duty to preserve the rest of those of God's creation which are in all essentials similar to oneself.'[45] This sense of being a part of God's workmanship knitted all of humanity into a whole, and turned private property into a thread which held people together rather than tore them apart.

Since humans were knitted together, no one had such a property that he could deny his needy brother a right to the surplus of his goods when his needs called for it. It was always a sin to let your brother perish because you did not offer him relief out of your plenty. Justice and charity had to co-exist:

> As *Justice* gives every Man a Title to the products of his honest Industry, and the fair Acquisition of his Ancestors descended to him; so *Charity* gives every Man a Title to so much out of another's Plenty, as will keep him from extream want, where he has no means to subsist otherwise.[46]

Property, in Locke's scheme, was not meant to leave one man at the mercy of another, but the obligation to protect others did not require that one's own life be put seriously at risk.[47] This was because, for Locke, the right that each individual had in common was the right to the means of preservation, a claim-right not to be excluded from the use of the common materials needed to subsist. Everyone in the state of nature 'had both a privilege to make use of the earth's resources and a right not to be prevented from exercising that privilege'.[48] This was different from a right to access to the soil. The connection between property and self-preservation was, for Locke, about self-defence.

Winstanley drew the connections between self-preservation and common preservation in different ways, and sought not to rely on charity to guarantee subsistence. He began with a proposition close to Locke's idea that individuals ought 'to *preserve the rest of Mankind*'.[49] For Winstanley, magistracy was based on common preservation and 'the principle in everyone to seek the good of others as himself, without respecting persons'.[50] This original law was written in the heart of every individual, to be his guide, and it formed the basis of the law of necessity, that the earth should be planted for common preservation and peace. Tyranny, by contrast, was built on the laws of self-preservation 'when particular officers seek their own preservation, ease, honour, riches and freedom in the earth ... and regard not the peace, freedom and preservation of the weak and foolish among their brethren.'[51] This was where Winstanley and Locke parted company. For Winstanley, the two were incompatible: common preservation and self-preservation (in the sense of self-interest) could not be reconciled. The buyers and sellers of the land and its fruits always encroached on the rights of others: 'these are they that take away another man's right from him; and that overthrows righteous property, to uphold particular property'.[52] Private property could never be righteous or just, in Winstanley's terms, and it always pushed people apart.

It was central to Locke's theory, and to the workmanship ideal, that justice was connected to industry, making it righteous. The links between the self, labour and material goods made property a moral space. Gold and silver were concealed in the earth, but human beings had the means in their labour and their reason to dig it out. The earth was not simply a womb that brought forth plenty. Men had to equip themselves, 'and it is with great labour that those resources which lie hidden in darkness are to be brought to the light of day. They do not present themselves to idle and listless people'.[53] Common lands were incompatible with God's purposes for the earth: 'it cannot be supposed he meant it should always remain common and uncultivated. He gave it to the use of the Industrious and Rational'.[54] It was only the rational and industrious who were entitled to the products of their industry, and who were able to labour so that paradise emerged from the wastes. The contrast between the industrious and the idle was clearly drawn and constantly reiterated. In Locke's theory, we were born free and rational, but we had to exercise our reason and our freedom in order to fulfil our duties to God and to ourselves. This, as Geraint Parry points out, was 'a strenuous and unremitting task' and it was not surprising that there were many who did not recognise their duties or found them too demanding.[55] Part of this strenuous task was to appropriate the earth by labouring on it. Humans were obliged to labour: 'And hence subduing the Earth, and having Dominion, we see are joyned together. The one gave Title to the other.'[56]

Humans had a fundamental, natural right to preserve themselves, and the conditions of human life required labour and materials to work on. For

Locke, this necessarily introduced private possessions. Mere availability was not enough. The general entitlement to the earth entailed a general duty to appropriate. Against Winstanley, Locke argued that this could be done without harming others or excluding the poor: 'No Mans Labour could subdue, or appropriate all: nor could his Enjoyment consume more than a small part; so that it was impossible for any Man, this way, to intrench upon the right of another.'[57] Locke disconnected labour from access to the soil and denied the idea of a necessary conflict between the rich proprietors and the poor. Moderate possession was possible without injury to anybody. For him, Cain could take the land he needed, and still leave enough for Abel's sheep to graze on. Property emerged gradually and naturally as families increased and industry spread.[58] Private property did not have to involve exploitation or exile. For Locke, nature's resources were inexhaustible and endlessly available. Under these conditions, individual appropriation did not violate anyone's right to property in common.

In Locke's scheme, these laws of nature and of God established the right of each individual to remove from the common stock enough to satisfy the needs of himself and his family. He had a right to subsistence. The legitimacy of this property was subject to two central provisos, limitations imposed by the law of nature.[59] First, property was given to humankind by God for them to enjoy, and this enjoyment limited the right to property:

> As much as any one can make use of to any advantage of life before it spoils; so much he may by his labour fix a Property in. Whatever is beyond this, is more than his share, and belongs to others. Nothing was made by God for Man to spoil and destroy.[60]

This spoilage limitation could not be overridden, even by consent. The second proviso – the sufficiency limitation – stated that the appropriation of land 'by improving it' did not damage the interests of anybody else 'since there was still enough and as good left' that others could use: 'For he that leaves as much as another can make use of, does as good as take nothing at all.'[61]

Property under these conditions was moderate, but not necessarily equal. Individuals had different needs and capacities; they made use of different things in different ways. In addition, the contrast between the industrious and the idle already existed. The rational and the industrious could legitimately appropriate more effectively and accumulate more property than those who could not rouse themselves from listlessness.

Locke argued that money was introduced in an attempt to overcome the spoilage and sufficiency limitations imposed by nature on property. Having gathered a hundred bushels of acorns or apples, the individual in the state of nature had a property in them – they had become his goods, but he needed to make sure that he used them before they spoiled 'else he took more then [sic] his share, and robb'd others'.[62] Hoarding was foolish and dishonest, until the people invented money: 'some lasting thing that Men might keep without spoiling, and that by mutual consent Men would take in exchange for the truly useful, but perishable Supports of Life'.[63] The invention of money gave industrious and rational people the opportunity to enlarge their possessions beyond their families, and made it worth their while to improve and enclose the land because they could trade its products with others elsewhere in the world. Without it, 'we should see him give up again to the wild Common of Nature, whatever was more than would supply the Conveniencies of Life'.[64]

As Parry argues, the invention of money accelerated the movement towards unequal holdings, whittling away at the limitations on the accumulation of property by changing the circumstances of the state of nature.[65] Gold and silver, once they had been dug out of the earth, had value only by men's consent, and Locke made clear that by consenting to money, men had agreed 'to the disproportionate and unequal Possession of the Earth'.[66] Winstanley understood the same process differently. As we have seen, he argued that 'buying and selling' was the final stage of the Fall and inextricably linked to 'kingly power'. Once the digging communities and the true commonwealth had been established, 'money must not any longer … be the great god that hedges in some, and hedges out others'. The introduction of money had solidified the inequalities between men, breaking down the 'evenness' between men as brethren. Surely, Winstanley argued, 'this was the project of tyrant-flesh'.[67] No one would consent to the unequal possession of the earth, and so to their own exile.

IMPROVEMENT AND LABOUR

The unequal possession of the earth was underpinned by the contrast between the industrious and the rational on one side and the listless and the idle on the other. For Locke, this was a moral distinction. The use an individual made of his property, his life, liberty and possessions, was always the outcome of a choice and connected to the process of developing an individual character.[68] This involved individuals choosing whether to improve their property and themselves, becoming active proprietors of their persons and their property. The alternative was constructed as taking a much more passive, 'listless' attitude to the world, expecting the earth to act as a womb, able to nourish and maintain everybody from her spontaneous gifts. The language of Chapter 5 of the Second Treatise echoed that of the agricultural improvers. Locke emphasised the capacity of labour and cultivation to achieve transformation, and condemned the sin of idleness. The language of enclosure, in particular, was central to his theory of property. Like the other improvers, he recognised the process as involving the possibility of releasing the potential of the fruits of the earth for private use and ownership. Enclosure, labour and the subjection of the earth were all part of the same process. This provided the basis of his justification of property in the earth itself. In his resonant phrase: 'As much Land as a Man Tills, Plants, Improves, Cultivates, and can use the Product of, so much is his Property. He by his Labour does, as it were, inclose it from the Common.'[69]

Locke's opposition to common land was based on the same objections as the improvers'. The earth was given to men by God to provide conveniences and benefits. This involved a duty on mankind's part to recognise the potential of the earth, and harness it. In the same way as Winstanley objected to the rich who attempted to live on the spoils of other men, Locke encouraged men not to meddle with what had already been improved, but to labour directly on 'the Ground which God had given him'.[70] Indeed, the Second Treatise can be read as a defence of the industrious and trading part of the nation against the idle, court-dominated aristocracy, and this links Locke to an important strand of liberalism, critical of the stultifying effects of living off wealth that was fundamentally unearned.[71] Mere enclosure was not enough. The fruits of the earth could still be left to spoil and waste in unimproved enclosed land.

It was labour that made the difference. Value and productivity were created by improvement and enclosure, not by the natural abundance of common lands. Land left in common was left to nature and so was effectively waste land. Bread was worth more than acorns, water or leaves because of the labour and industry that had been added to it. Locke's argument was that value came from labour; land was worth very little without it. The common stock of mankind was increased by appropriation and improvement. Enclosing the land and employing labour on it increased its productivity, so that improving the land helped to sustain a growing population and to provide for subsistence:

for I aske whether in the wild woods and uncultivated wast of America left to Nature, without any improvement, tillage or husbandry, a thousand acres will yield the needy and wretched inhabitants as many conveniencies of life as ten acres of equally fertile land doe in Devonshire where they are well cultivated?[72]

Locke's argument was that labourers in Devonshire being paid a wage by their employers were better off than they would have been trying to make a living from unimproved, unenclosed land. They were less likely to rely on charity, and although they were not left with as good and 'as much they were left with "enough"'.[73] For Locke, unlike for Winstanley, even where there was not enough and as good actual land left for others 'there is enough and as good (indeed a better) living left for others'.[74] Unequal appropriation (and not access to the soil) was the only way of satisfying the equal right to subsistence.[75]

For Winstanley, inequality could not be compatible with subsistence and preservation. True freedom lay in the free enjoyment of the earth: it was inseparable from belonging. Those who had been shut out of the earth could not be free. In his *Law of Freedom in a Platform*, a manifesto for the digging movement and a vision of a true commonwealth, Winstanley argued that the earth needed to be set free from kingly bondage, so that individuals could dig and labour the commons, and live together in orderly communities within which they could reclaim their original and equal right to cultivate the earth for subsistence. They would carry the harvest into storehouses to be distributed according to need and to provide a common stock for every family. It was part of the digging experiment that 'our Maker may be glorified in the work of his own hands'.[76] Winstanley insisted on the universal obligation to labour. Each individual was to be obliged, and if necessary forced, to work, but he was also guaranteed 'the just deserts of his labours'.[77] Winstanley insisted on the equitable distribution of the products of the land, and so disrupted the distinction Locke made between the industrious improvers and the listless poor.

This did not mean that Winstanley did not see a moral dimension to labour. Both he and Locke appealed to 'labour's abundance': they both required that everyone laboured for subsistence.[78] In his *Law of Freedom*, Winstanley made clear that idleness would be punished in his ideal society. Anyone who refused to work, to learn a trade or to work in the storehouses would find themselves admonished by the overseer, first in private and then in public. If they continued idle, they would be whipped, and finally set to work for twelve months 'or till he submit to right order'.[79] In a close parallel, Locke's proposals to reform the existing English Poor Law in 1697 suggested that beggars should be sentenced to houses of correction and hard labour, where punishments should include whipping, ear loss and transportation to the plantations. He proposed that subsistence and education should be guaranteed to young children, and apprenticeships guaranteed to fourteen-year-olds. For them both, the 'right order' rested on labour, and the productivity of the commonwealth: 'Every man shall be brought up in trades and labours, and all trades shall be maintained with more improvement, to the enriching of the commonwealth.'[80]

The difference between Winstanley and Locke lay in how they connected this labour to property and to the land. Winstanley argued that true freedom came from the use of the earth, being able to live as a free commoner in a free commonwealth. People laboured in order to enjoy the free use of the earth, and it was oppressive for landlords 'to say their brethren shall not work upon the earth, nor eat the fruits thereof, unless they will hire that liberty of them'.[81] Selling labour for subsistence, for Winstanley, always curtailed original liberty and true freedom. Labour, or at least righteous labour, was not alienable: people should not be put in a position where they had to put their freedom up for hire. Once the true commonwealth had been established, there would be 'a provision for livelihood in the earth both for the elder and younger brother; and not the one enslaving the other, but both living in plenty and freedom'.[82] The system of waged labour was one of the ways in which the rich cheated the poor, part of the elder brother's claim that the earth and its fruits belonged to him and had to be either rented or bought from him. The rich substantiated their claim by appealing to a false version of religion, and by denying that the earth was a common treasury. The younger brother, weak in spirit and crushed by the power of the 'subtle clergy', was terrified 'and lets go his hold in the earth, and submits himself to be a slave to his brother for fear of damnation in hell after death'.[83] For Winstanley, working for a wage on another's land was a sign that you had let the earth, and so true freedom, slip away from you.

For Locke, on the other hand, labouring on another's land was a legitimate means of preservation and subsistence. Labour, in Locke's sense, could be detached from the land and from access to the soil. It was, in itself, the foundation of property, and it lay not in the earth but in the individual and their property in the person. His argument, unlike Winstanley's, was not about peasant proprietorship or the right to cultivate an allotment of the earth, but about a right to subsistence from labour. For them both, labour was a uniquely human act, and one which brought humankind closer to God, but they disagreed about how that connection was made. For Locke, as we have seen, men were 'the Workmanship of one Omnipotent and infinitely wise Maker … they are his Property, whose workmanship they are, made to last during his, not one anothers pleasure'.[84] Human property could not be founded on the same right of creation, but humans were capable of dominion on the workmanship model as makers, labouring directly on the earth or working on preexisting materials to produce something new. As Matthew Kramer argues, it was plausible for Locke to see a cultivated field 'as something which the labourer has brought into existence'.[85] For Winstanley, cultivating the land glorified the Maker 'in the work of his own hands', but a buyer could not claim a parcel of land as his own on the grounds that he had laboured on it. He challenged the conflation of labour and creation: 'If any man can say he makes Corn or Cattle, he may say, That is mine.'[86] Corn and cattle were made by God for the use of his creation, and they were inseparable from the principle of usufruct, and so undetachable from the earth.

For Locke, such detachment was both possible and inevitable, and the process of separating labour from the land and attaching it to the person was central to his theory of property. He made clear that it was property in the person and in labour that could ground a natural right to private property in goods and land: 'Though the things of Nature are given in common, yet Man (by being Master of himself, and *Proprietor of his own Person*, and the Actions or *Labour* of it) had still in himself *the great Foundation of Property*.'[87] He was envisaging property rights as rooted in the individual, severed from the whole and separate from the right to cultivate the earth. He accepted the separation of land and labour, based entitlement to property in labour alone, and extended this property to alienated waged labour. Each individual had a right within himself to alienate his labour, and 'the more emphatically labour is asserted to be a property, the more it is understood to be alienable'.[88] Once labour was understood to be alienable, the poor could sell their labour to the rich proprietor, the listless could be reformed by the industrious, and paradise could emerge from the wastes.

– IMPROVING THE WORLD –

In the Lockean world, then, appropriation could take place without violating anyone's rights. Once money has been invented and the land enclosed, the right to appropriate was modified. It no longer only involved labouring directly on the earth, since that was no longer practically possible for everyone. Instead, the industrious and the rational were in a position to consolidate their wealth and pass it on to other 'enterprising proprietors' by inheritance or purchase. The effect, as Parry points out, was 'to create a category of landless persons'.[89] Each person had a right to the means of self-preservation, and so it made sense for them to sell their labour for subsistence, mixing their labour with land and raw materials owned by others, letting go of their own hold on the earth, turning themselves into exiles and fugitives. In Locke's theory, the free man made himself a servant to another 'by selling him for a certain time, the Service he undertakes to do, in exchange for Wages, he is to receive'.[90] The contractual nature of the exchange meant that he remained free (and never became a slave to his elder brother), because the master's power was only ever temporary, and limited by the terms of the contract. The servant did not give up his property in the person: his property remained that which could not be taken from him without his own consent.

Under the terms of the contract, the employer had the right to direct the employee's labour, and so it became 'his' labour. In a famous passage from the *Second Treatise*, Locke made clear that this exchange was possible, even in the state of nature, before the introduction of money. Taking any part of what was common and removing it from the state of nature began a property: 'Thus the Grass my Horse has bit; the Turfs my Servant has cut; and the Ore I have digg'd in any place where I have a right to them in common with others, become my Property, without the assignation or consent of any body.'[91] To the enclosers in England and to the colonists of the New World, this did not count as living off the spoils of other men: this was their own labour. Winstanley pointed out that no man could be rich, except by his own labours or the labour of other men helping him. When rich men lived at ease off the labours of other men, they 'receive all they have from the labourer's hand, and what they give, they give away other men's labours, not their own'.[92]

In the Lockean scheme, then, the industrious and the rational, the active proprietors, improvers and enterprisers, were able to extend what counted as their labour beyond direct labouring on the earth without becoming plunderers and pirates, dishonourably living off the spoils of other men. As long as their efforts resulted in increased productivity, enough and as good was left for others, and no one's rights had been encroached upon. The labour of the improvers could remain righteous and their possession moderate. Disproportionate possession of the earth was initially decided by 'different degrees of Industry', and then the invention of money gave the industrious 'the opportunity to continue and enlarge them'.[93] Locke made his point in relation to America, where men 'are rich in Land, and poor in all the Comforts of Life'.[94] Nature had furnished them with fruitful soil, capable of producing food and other resources in abundance, but Americans had failed to improve it with their labour, and as a result 'a King of a large and fruitful Territory there feeds, lodges, and is clad worse than a day labourer in *England*'.[95] Unimproved America was understood to be outside the market society; men living there had no hope of commerce with the rest of the world, and so for Locke it functioned as a kind of state of nature: 'Thus in the beginning all the World was *America*, and more so than it is now; for no such thing as *Money* was any where known.'[96]

The English colonialists carefully contrasted themselves to the Spanish by insisting that the Spaniards wished to devastate, not to cultivate. The aim of the Spanish, the English claimed, was to occupy the land and benefit from the labour of others by living in idleness.[97] Their own ownership, on the other hand, was based on agricultural plantation and cultivation, growing sugar in Barbados and tobacco in New England, crops identified by Locke as epitomising the value that labour can create.[98] The English presented their wealth as productive, not created by plundering the riches of others, but by establishing dependent colonies and expropriating the labour of servants and slaves. Barbara Arneil argues that the *Second Treatise* should be read not just as a defence of the industrious against the aristocracy, but beyond that as a defence of England's colonial policy in the New World against the sceptics in England. Against the violence of Spanish conquest, English colonists stressed that their versions of colonialism and property were to be 'based on industry and rationality rather than violence'.[99]

The Earl of Shaftesbury, Locke's patron, was a leading defender of the gains to be had from trade and settlement. He advocated the establishment of the Council of Trade and Plantations as an overarching body 'to ensure a settlement of agrarian labourers, rather than one of adventurers, miners, or manufacturers'.[100] Carolina, in particular, was held up as an alternative to the Spanish method. The land was cultivated, towns were established to trade with England, and the industrious were encouraged to leave England and settle there. Carolina was a clear example of a colony where agrarian cultivation of the land was the only legitimate basis for claiming property, following Locke's maxim: 'Whatsoever he tilled and reaped, laid up and made use of, before it spoiled, that was his peculiar Right; whatsoever he enclosed, and could feed, and make use of, the Cattle and Product was also his.'[101] The possession of too much land was seen as a prime cause of decline in many of the New England colonies. In Carolina, the civil laws and the Fundamental Constitutions regulated property to ensure that settlers did not take more land than they could make use of. Unregulated acquisition was understood to undermine the social order.

Having separated labour and freedom from belonging and access to the soil in England, the colonisers felt that they had God's authority to appropriate and enclose the 'vacant lands' of America. Making use of the land, following the principle of usufruct, was not enough to ground a right to property once it was clear that the earth was no longer to be regarded as a common treasury, and that true property was in the person. The Native Americans were commanded by the English courts to fence their land. Where they did not do so, America was regarded as lying waste. Its inhabitants were seen as 'actively neglecting' the land. Without the outward signs of private ownership, they had left the land to nature. Native Americans were understood to have failed to subdue the earth. Mere occupation, even mere enclosure, was not enough to ground their ownership:

> If either the Grass of his Inclosure rotted on the Ground, or the Fruit of his planting perished without gathering, and laying up, this part of the Earth, not withstanding his Inclosure, was still to be looked on as Waste, and might be the Possession of any other.[102]

Only the colonists could properly transcend the spoilage limitation. They had the resources to appropriate and cultivate the land in America and to sell the goods to the rest of the world, converting the wealth of the land into hard currency. Without hope of commerce with other parts of the world, Native Americans were understood to be unable to go beyond subsistence and so to have given themselves up to nature, and to passivity.

The English in America wanted to present themselves as living in a state of nature, surrounded by Native Americans who were wild and primitive, lacking self-control and the inclination to labour. Rather than working the land, they 'depended instead on the spontaneous productions of nature to supply almost all their wants', and this reliance on unimproved nature came to define what it meant to be 'savage'.[103] They were not labourers or improvers, but mere occupants of vacant lands. As Anthony Pagden argues, the Native Americans failed to fulfil the obligations that had been placed on them by nature. It was not just that they had chosen one inferior means of subsistence over another, but that they had violated the law of nature, failed in their duty to themselves as men and so made themselves less than human.[104] Civilising the Native American 'savages' meant turning them into farmers who would build fences, cultivate the land, raise a surplus and understand the value of property in land and of trading in the market. They had to learn how a little well cultivated and properly enclosed land was more valuable than a great deal of unimproved land. It was expected that they could be 'converted into Lockean people' by inculcating in them a sense of the value of private property, and written law, and persuading them to give up their identity, their culture and their land.[105] Their land was acquired for white settlement and expansion; they were forced to let go of their hold on the earth, and became fugitives and exiles in their own land.

Only property in the white person was enough to ground a property in righteous labour, in the drudgery of others and so in the land itself. Native American forms of possession did not fit the structure of Locke's argument, and so were deemed to be too ambiguous and unclear.[106] The attitudes to property rooted in ideas about improvement and ownership of a property in the person underpinned and reinforced the central idea that blacks and Indians were not masters of themselves, proprietors of their own persons, with the foundation of property in themselves. The distinction between the industrious and the idle resurfaced in a racialised form, mapped onto the distinction between civilisation and savagery. In the Native Americans (and, as we shall see later, in Africans and slaves as well), idleness was understood to have triumphed over accumulation, listlessness over industry. The moral space of property was racialised: 'savages', as well as the poor in England, were forcibly shut out. They were excluded from industriousness and rationality, and so were understood to live as scavengers and exiles, and so as the negative embodiment of the rights of exclusive private property and land ownership in England.

– CONCLUSION –

The twin processes of improvement and colonialism were underpinned by the construction of the doctrine of vacant lands, hedging the weak out of the earth and forcibly shutting out the poor. The sense of separation and dissociation and the distinction between labour and drudgery were covered over by the myth of honourable labour that belonged to the enterprising proprietors. The labour of their landless employees and the property rights of the original owners in America had to be hidden from view in order to sustain the idea that labour was the foundation of property. If industry and rationality were to be claimed as a legitimate basis for colonialism and government, then any other labour had to be rendered invisible, and so did the possibility that anything other than improving labour could justify possession of the earth. The rights of the poor to the commons, claimed on the basis of need, were eclipsed by the 'peculiar right' of the lord of the manor, 'shutting us out'.[107] Access to the soil was removed from those who could not prove themselves to be rational and industrious, and it became a freedom that was attached to self-preservation and not to common preservation. The force behind its removal, the underlying violence, was hidden from view at the same time.

The discourse of conquest was underpinned by a particular conception of property that was able to construct the land as vacant in both England and America. It was a discourse rooted in attitudes to labour and to the land, and so it spreads out in two directions, and this book traces its path through both freedom and belonging. The possibility of owning private property in land was consolidated and contested throughout the eighteenth and nineteenth centuries as the customary rights of the poor to the commons were blotted out, and their alternatives to wage labour stripped down. The woodmongers did not disown all private merchandise, and they reappear in Godwin and in Marx as robbers of the poor, still whittling away at property rights that were not private and exclusive. The same process was at work in the colonial project in Ireland and in Zimbabwe, defining colonial settlement as legitimate and excluding the more ambiguous indigenous modes of ownership. Property in labour underwent a similar transformation to become a resource, alienated from its original owners and attached to those who lived off the labour of others. Slavery runs like an almost invisible thread through all of the property literature, and we shall return to it in more detail in Chapter 8. Its near invisibility is part of the story, one of the ways in which the sense of separation and dissociation described by Winstanley as central to private property is repressed, and replaced by the notion that appropriation and accumulation do not encroach on the rights of others.

– NOTES –

1. Robert A. Williams, *The American Indian in Western Legal Thought: the Discourses of Conquest* (New York and Oxford: Oxford University Press, 1990), p. 6.
2. Liz Sperling, *Women, Political Philosophy and Politics* (Edinburgh: Edinburgh University Press, 2001), p. 112.
3. John Locke, *Two Treatises of Government* (Cambridge: Cambridge University Press, [1698] 1991). Second Treatise, §4, p. 269.
4. Ibid. §27, pp. 287–8.
5. Jeremy Waldron, *The Right to Private Property* (Oxford: Clarendon Press, 1988), p. 140.
6. Locke, 'Second Treatise', §193, p. 395.
7. Waldron, *Right to Private Property*, p. 19.
8. Ibid. p. 179.
9. Christopher Hill, *Reformation to Industrial Revolution* (London: Weidenfeld and Nicolson, 1967), p. 93.
10. Joan Thirsk, *The Rural Economy of England* (London: Hambledon Press, 1984), p. 193.
11. Walter Blith, *The English Improver: or, A New Survey of Husbandry* (London, 1649), p. 4.
12. *The Waste Land's Improvement* (London, 1653), p. 2.
13. Blith, *English Improver*, p. 6.
14. Graham Parry, 'John Evelyn as Hortulan Saint', in Michael Leslie and Timothy Raylor (eds), *Culture and Cultivation in Early Modern England: Writing and the Land*. (Leicester: Leicester University Press, 1992), p. 144.
15. Adam Moore's *Bread for the Poor* was written in 1623 but published thirty years later, during 'a more improving season'.
16. Moore, *Bread for the Poor*, p. 13.
17. Alan Macfarlane contests this model, emphasising that in the thirteenth century in almost every village some villagers worked for others as hired labour. This section is concerned with *perceptions* of the role of the commons and the effects of enclosure and their implications for ideas about property. See Alan Macfarlane, *The Origins of English Individualism: the Family, Property and Social Transition* (Oxford: Blackwell, 1978).
18. Gerrard Winstanley, 'A Declaration from the Poor Oppressed People of England', in Christopher Hill, *Winstanley: The Law of Freedom* (Harmondsworth: Penguin, 1973), p. 104.
19. Ibid. p. 105.
20. Gerrard Winstanley, 'Fire in the Bush', in Hill, *Winstanley*, p. 267.
21. Gerrard Winstanley, 'The Law of Freedom in a Platform', in Hill, *Winstanley*, p. 287.
22. T. W. Hayes, *Winstanley the Digger* (Cambridge, MA: Harvard University Press, 1979), p. 127.
23. Gerrard Winstanley, 'True Levellers' Standard', in Hill, *Winstanley*, p. 84.
24. For more detail, see Donald R. Sutherland, 'The Religion of Gerrard Winstanley and Digger Communism', *Essays in History* 33, 1990–1991, http://etext.lib.virginia.edu/journals/EH/EH33/suther33.html
25. Winthrop S. Hudson, 'Economic and Social Thought of Gerrard Winstanley', *Journal of Modern History* 18, 1946, p. 11.
26. Timothy Kenyon, 'Labour–Natural, Property–Artificial: the Radical Insights of Gerrard Winstanley', *History of European Ideas* 6:2, 1985, p. 116.
27. Winstanley, 'A Letter to Lord Fairfax', in Hill, *Winstanley*, p. 289.
28. Ibid., p. 290.

29. Winstanley, 'Fire in the Bush', in Hill, *Winstanley*, p. 264.

30. Winstanley, 'The New Law of Righteousness', in Hill, *Winstanley*, p. 158.

31. Winstanley, 'Fire in the Bush', in Hill, *Winstanley*, p. 264. This is worth comparing with Rousseau's description of the origins of property in the 'Discourse on the Origins of Inequality' in *Social Contract and Discourses* (London: Dent, 1973), p. 84.

32. Winstanley, 'True Levellers' Standard', in Hill, *Winstanley*, p. 254.

33. Winstanley, 'Fire in the Bush', in Hill, *Winstanley*, p. 264.

34. Winstanley, 'New Law of Righteousness', in Hill, *Winstanley*, p. 159.

35. Gerrard Winstanley, 'Law of Freedom in a Platform or True Magistracy Restored', in Hill, *Winstanley*, p. 508. On the significance of connecting exploitation and need for the socialist tradition, see Chapter 6.

36. Marx, too, talked about the particular humanity of the poor. See below.

37. Winstanley, 'New Law of Righteousness', in Hill, *Winstanley*, p. 183.

38. Winstanley, 'True Levellers Standard', in Hill, *Winstanley*, p. 260.

39. David W. Petergorsky, *Left-wing Democracy in the English Civil War*. (New York: Gollancz, [1940] 1972), p. 184.

40. Winstanley, 'Fire in the Bush', in Hill, *Winstanley*, p. 265.

41. John Locke, *Two Treatises of Government* (Cambridge: Cambridge University Press, [1698] 1991). First Treatise, §30, p. 161.

42. Locke, Second Treatise, §32, p. 290.

43. Locke, First Treatise, §41, pp. 169–70.

44. Locke, Second Treatise, §6, p. 271.

45. Geraint Parry, *John Locke* (London: Allen and Unwin, 1978), p. 41.

46. Locke, First Treatise, §42, p. 170.

47. Parry, *John Locke*, p. 41.

48. Matthew H. Kramer, *John Locke and the Origins of Private Property: Philosophical Explorations of Individualism, Community and Equality* (Cambridge: Cambridge University Press, 1997), p. 108.

49. Locke, Second Treatise, §6, p. 271.

50. Winstanley, 'Law of Freedom in a Platform', in Hill, *Winstanley*, p. 315.

51. Ibid. p. 316.

52. Gerrard Winstanley, 'An Appeal to the House of Commons', in Hill, *Winstanley*, p. 121.

53. Parry, *John Locke*, p. 43. The quotation comes from Locke's *Essays on the Law of Nature* II.

54. Locke, Second Treatise, §34, p. 291.

55. Parry, *John Locke*, p. 43.

56. Locke, Second Treatise, §35, p. 292.

57. Ibid. §36, p. 292.

58. Ibid. §38, p. 295.

59. Gopal Sreenivisan, *The Limits of Lockean Rights in Property* (New York and Oxford: Oxford University Press, 1995), p. 39.

60. Locke, Second Treatise, §31, p. 290.

61. Ibid. §33, p. 291.

62. Ibid. §46, p. 300.

63. Ibid. §47, pp. 300–1.

64. Ibid. §48, p. 301.

65. Parry, *John Locke*, p. 54.

66. Locke, Second Treatise, §50, p. 302.

67. Winstanley, 'A Declaration', in Hill, *Winstanley*, p. 100.
68. Parry, *John Locke*, p. 50.
69. Locke, Second Treatise, §32, p. 290.
70. Ibid. §34, p. 291.
71. See Sreenivisan, *Limits of Lockean Rights*, and Neal Wood, *John Locke and Agrarian Capitalism* (Berkeley: University of California Press, 1984).
72. Locke, Second Treatise, §37, p. 294.
73. Parry, *John Locke*, p. 53.
74. C. B. Macpherson, *The Political Theory of Possessive Individualism* (Oxford: Oxford University Press, 1962), p. 212.
75. Parry, *John Locke*, p. 56.
76. Winstanley, 'True Levellers' Standard', in Hill, *Winstanley*, p. 84.
77. Timothy Kenyon, *Utopian Communism and Political Thought in Early Modern England* (London: Pinter, 1989), p. 199.
78. Sreenivisan, *Limits of Lockean Rights*, p. 143.
79. Winstanley, 'Law of Freedom in a Platform', in Hill, *Winstanley*, p. 381.
80. Ibid. p. 303.
81. Ibid. p. 295.
82. Ibid. p. 312.
83. Ibid. p. 353.
84. Locke, Second Treatise, §6, p. 271.
85. Kramer, *John Locke*, p. 86.
86. Winstanley, 'New Law of Righteousness', in Hill, *Winstanley*, p. 197.
87. Locke, Second Treatise, §44, p. 298.
88. Macpherson, *Political Theory of Possessive Individualism*, pp. 214–15.
89. Parry, *John Locke*, p. 54.
90. Locke, Second Treatise, §85, p. 322.
91. Ibid. §28, p. 289.
92. Winstanley, 'Law of Freedom in a Platform', in Hill, *Winstanley*, p. 287.
93. Locke, Second Treatise, §48, p. 301.
94. Ibid. §41, p. 296.
95. Ibid. §41, p. 297.
96. Ibid. §49, p. 301.
97. Anthony Pagden, *Lords of All the World: Ideologies of Empire in Spain, Britain and France c.1500–c.1800* (New Haven and London: Yale University Press, 1995), p. 93.
98. See Locke, Second Treatise, §40, p. 296. Locke invested in Barbados in 1673, where sugar was the staple crop.
99. Barbara Arneil, *John Locke and America: the Defence of English Colonialism* (Oxford: Clarendon Press, 1996), p. 165.
100. Ibid. pp. 94–5.
101. Locke, Second Treatise, §38, p. 295.
102. Ibid. §38, p. 295.
103. Ronald T. Takaki, *Iron Cages: Race and Culture in Nineteenth-Century America* (New York: Knopf, 1979), p. 13.
104. Pagden, *Lords of All the World*, p. 79.
105. Takaki, *Iron Cages*, p. 60.
106. Cheryl I. Harris, 'Whiteness as Property'. *Harvard Law Review* 106, 1993, p. 1724.
107. Winstanley, 'A Declaration', in Hill, *Winstanley*, p. 105.

CHAPTER 3

Godwin and Bentham:
The Shadow of Slavery and Sweat

This chapter takes up the themes of how to fit self-preservation together with preservation of the whole, and how to fit the despotic dominion of the individual into a collective context. It is about how property holds people together and apart in the thought of Jeremy Bentham and William Godwin; the role of law and government; and their background assumptions about human nature and individuality. Is it possible to reconcile individual autonomy with community or with government? Godwin and Bentham were not engaged in a direct debate with one another, but they are both central figures in the development of the principle of utility. Behind the structure of their arguments and the appeal to the greatest happiness of the greatest number, we can see the conflict between security and equality which is crucial to the development of ideas about property. They take forward the arguments we have already encountered in Locke and Winstanley about the tensions between self-preservation and common preservation into utilitarianism. They continue to explore the problems of estrangement and encroachment, and the particular difficulty of how to maintain an individual sphere of discretion against the common good, balancing self-regard and sympathy. This brings out the tension between freedom and belonging, and how that tension is connected to ideas about civilisation, progress and poverty.

The eighteenth century saw property moving away from being primarily based in land ownership and towards more mobile forms. These new, more commercial forms of property were linked to the rise of reputation and credit, and a culture based on consumption and display. Society was commercialised, but not yet fully industrialised. In this climate, security of property and expectation became a particular concern. At the same time, private property rights were being consolidated and the separation of land and labour continued, leaving the landless to be treated as resource, a cheap and exploited labour force. As questions of consumption and class came to the fore, property crystallised into spectacle and reinforced class difference. In the process, class difference was entangled with moral difference through the mechanisms of property and self-ownership, and class and morality operated together to define the boundaries of the imagined community. This, in turn, raised the pressing problem of equality and how it could be reconciled with security and with liberty.

During the eighteenth century, the scientific revolution was unfolding out of its improvement context. The concerns of the Council of Trade to stimulate manufacturing and release the wealth-creating potential of the New World were still current, and so was the confidence in the capacity of the human intellect to solve economic and social problems. The knowledge that grew out of the new science and the Enlightenment could not be disentangled from the progress of empire. New forms of knowledge in astronomy, cartography and measurement all mapped the American wilderness, and commerce was understood to be the key to improvement in natural knowledge. The empire of reason was expanding, and a new vision of nature as ordered by laws was emerging.[1] Nature was understood to be subject to rational laws that could be discovered and then applied to human purposes. The tools used for understanding, mapping and improving the natural world were being applied not only to the universe, but also to human society. Such knowledge was then expected to form the basis of more efficient and informed government and legislation. The Enlightenment of the eighteenth century expressed a new confidence in harmony of the universe, and also in the efficiency of human reason. The problem was how to bring this individual reason into harmony with the whole.

The processes at work in the seventeenth century to narrow the definition of property rights, and to render labour invisible, were intensified during the eighteenth century. The consolidation of property in its new commercial forms brought the connections between property, liberty and equality to the heart of conceptions of government and the law. Godwin declared property to be 'the keystone that completes the fabric of political justice'[2] and the discussion of the development of utilitarian thinking in this chapter is framed by the Black Act of 1723 and the Anatomy Act of 1832. There was a sense in which property was identified with justice 'until justice itself was seen as no more than the outworks and defences of property and of its attendant status'.[3] This was bound to have implications for the poor, and for the ideas of reformers like Godwin and Bentham. Their contrasting arguments demonstrate the complexity of the Enlightenment and its legacy as they were passed down and modified by the crises of the 1790s and the reform era of the early nineteenth century. Where they shaded into Romanticism and anarchism, the strands of thought that emphasised nature and the individual came to the fore, connected to (and in tension with) schemes for equality and utopia. In Bentham's more technological and scientific utilitarianism, a different legacy reached its logical conclusion within which security took precedence over equality and anarchism.

Bentham argued that property needed protecting so that individuals could feel secure in their expectations of life and able to plan for their own happiness, and so as to encourage the spirit of industry and innovation. Law and government could then have a positive role in imposing sanctions and restraints to maintain security. For Bentham, the demands of equality strained the achievement of prosperity, and prosperity and security were essential for progress towards equality. Godwin's critique of private property involved the belief that government was incapable of effecting improvement. Progress towards justice was only possible through reason and the truth. Property was bound to corrupt the process by undermining independence and private judgement, bringing individuals into dangerous material and psychological dependence on one another. This complicates the model of property as estranging and dissociating, emphasising the dangers of connection and taking seriously the problems of encroachment and engulfment.

– GODWIN: SPECTACLE AND SWEAT –

Godwin's enlightenment credentials meant that he argued for the supremacy of reason and believed in its power to direct human conduct and to secure justice. The radical leap that Godwin made was to argue that reason demanded the welfare of each person to be looked on as equivalent in importance to that of any other.[4] Godwin argued that egoism, the pursuit of pure self-preservation without any concern for the common, had not proved to be a valid theory of human motivation. Instead, he suggested the possibility of motives other than selfishness: he insisted that 'human beings can be motivated by the apprehension of truth, even when this truth leads them to act contrary to self-interest'.[5] Godwin assumed that we have a deep obligation and attachment to the immutable and timeless truth with the strength to motivate our actions.[6] There were objective standards of good and evil, and people were capable of grasping these truths through public discussion and the exercise of private judgement. Knowledge of human nature, of political institutions and of individual motivation were indispensable for virtuous action. The natural good within people, and their potential to seek the truth, made the causes of inequality social and artificial rather than natural. This meant that, according to Godwin, the causes of inequality could be combated, and people could be refashioned to bring them into line with the truth. For Godwin, the source of inequality was class difference based on arbitrary distinctions, stifling the unique potential of each individual and undermining their 'perpetual progress towards truth'.[7] This kind of inequality destroyed independence and self-reliance. When the majority was forced to depend on those with economic power, the result was submissiveness and servility.

Godwin insisted that all human beings shared a common nature, and since this was the case, the needs of each person should be accorded equal value. There was no valid basis for preferential treatment and our obligation was to produce the greatest good. Godwin's *Enquiry Concerning Political Justice* set out to find the form of public or political society that would 'be found most to conduce to the general benefit'.[8] He presented a scheme for making individuals contribute most substantially to general improvement and happiness. From the start, he made clear that this was an attempt to alter the morals of mankind, a work of ethics as well as politics. Property was a contested moral space as well as an economic question. The inequality of property that was prevalent in most of the refined states of Europe was a moral evil. Property was transferred by violence and fraud, and vast numbers of people were deprived of almost every possibility of making life tolerable and secure. Godwin rejected the Lockean notion that the wages paid to a labourer would enable him to maintain a higher standard of living than he could manage by living on common, unenclosed land. Instead, Godwin argued that the separation of land and labour meant that the poor could work to the limits of their industry and still scarcely secure enough to support themselves. The poor lived in poverty and wretchedness, their lives a perpetual struggle. For Godwin this meant that their rights had been encroached upon. It was not surprising that they had been

> induced to regard the state of society as a state of war, an unjust combination, not for protecting every man in his rights and securing to him the means of existence,

but for engrossing all its advantages to a few favoured individuals, and reserving for the portion of the rest want, dependence and misery.[9]

Godwin emphasised morality as well as economics, and, for him, the calamity of the poor's objective situation was aggravated by the insolence of the rich and their determined efforts to instil envy in the poor. In the eighteenth century, enormous wealth was accompanied by luxury and pageantry, and Godwin was particularly concerned by what he termed the insult of 'the spectacle of indolence and ease in others"[10] This concern connects back to John Locke and Gerrard Winstanley's opposition to idleness and unemployment in the rich as well as the poor. Like Winstanley, Godwin argued that the desire to possess the substance of another made men vehement, restless and violent, and that property needed to be understood as a conflictual relationship between individuals. In Godwin's view, this individual relationship was then reflected in the system of manners in society that emphasised opulence over integrity, virtue, understanding and industry. Property pulled people apart, and the division between the working class and the 'leisure class' created and reinforced an 'invidious comparison of persons' that translated class difference into moral difference.[11] These new divisions involved particular conceptions of honour and degradation, and the denigration of labour. At the root of the motivation for ownership was the wish to emulate others, to consume conspicuously and to satisfy the rage to distinguish ourselves from others. Wealth was pursued for the love of distinction and out of fear of contempt: 'If admiration were not generally deemed the exclusive property of the rich, and contempt the constant lackey of poverty, the love of gain would cease to be an universal passion.'[12]

Godwin was condemning the particularly 'spectacular' economy of the eighteenth century, within which social relations crystallised around the display of wealth. The idea of luxury fed into prolonged debates over morals, manners and national survival, in particular over the growth of commerce, poverty, social inequality and moral and political corruption. Warnings against the dangers of luxury, for example, were central to republican theories of good government based on independence, and to the connections between property and conduct. Republicans and the country party were united in their opposition to mercantile greed and political corruption. Gentlemen needed to civilise themselves by civilising society, resisting the corruption and decadence that made leaving the state of nature and entering society such an inherently risky business.

Utopian writers and their critics were 'centrally concerned with how far civic and personal virtue could be institutionalized or sheltered against the ravages of time and the moral frailty of humanity'.[13] This was a pivotal problem for Godwin's theory, at the heart of his distrust of government, his defence of private judgement and his dilemma over how to abolish property without damaging individual freedom.

The inevitability and necessity of luxury became the subject of intense debate in the eighteenth century, and polarised ideas about progress. The excesses of property came under particular scrutiny from those who regarded the inherited wealth of the aristocracy as undeserved, unearned and stultifying. In response, defenders of luxury argued that its excesses were an acceptable consequence of the material improvement of societies. The desire for luxuries helped to instil a love of property which in turn guaranteed the preservation of wealth and stimulated industry, helping to bring an end to idleness. This view was underpinned by the equation of savagery with subsistence; moving beyond simply meeting needs was understood to be inherently civilised, and so honourable. For opponents of luxury, art and nature were being ransacked, corrupted and tortured to create new appetites and manners and to feed the opulent and idle habits of the rich. Luxury exhausted art and nature and depraved the manners of society, making luxury fundamentally dishonouring.[14] In the magazine debates of the 1780s, a consensus was reached that accepted the necessity of luxury for civilisation but demanded measures to prevent its excess and corruption. Its excess was clearest in the display of wealth and so the luxury debate focused on consumption, and on how consumption was represented to others. It became a debate about propriety, manners and taste, and property was entangled with 'the proper': critics saw the eighteenth century's obsession with politeness and civility as disguising underlying luxury, vice and slavery. The imagined community of property expressed through these debates was not so much about land ownership, but about ideas of politeness and civility, and whether they were values that were shared across class boundaries or that acted to disguise fraud and force and so to bolster class divisions. Critics of luxury called for a genuine reformation of manners encompassing women's rights, religious toleration, the abolition of slavery and reform of the laws of property. As Gregory Claeys argues, these concerns reflected a growing awareness of the threat of poverty and social dislocation, and the tensions underpinning the 'new commercial humanism.'[15]

Godwin was concerned with these underlying shifts in property and power. He argued that by engrossing the wealth of nations, the rich had also concentrated power in their own hands, and become directly or indirectly the legislators of the state, 'perpetually reducing oppression into a system, and depriving the poor of that little commonage of nature, which might otherwise have remained to them'.[16] The poor had lost their access to the soil, and the rich had converted their wealth into kingly power. He argued that once in positions of power, they passed legislation that favoured the rich against the poor by, for example, reducing the taxes on land and shifting the burden to indirect taxes which fell on the poor as well as the rich. This was part of the process of consolidating private property rights, and of entrenching the division between civil and human society. Godwin drew particular attention to the game laws, and to the death penalties imposed for robbery. These were both enshrined in the Waltham Black Acts, passed in 1723 and made perpetual in 1758. They added at least fifty new capital offences to the penal code, so that people could be sentenced to death for theft and poaching. The death penalty was extended to rebellious acts such as stealing deer and cutting and burning trees. The Black Acts epitomised the kind of legislation on behalf of the rich that Godwin had in mind.

Traditional rights to hunt and forage on common lands had been curtailed by the enclosure laws, and in the process the law took away common-use rights and gave them to the propertied. In Winstanley's terms, the woodmongers were continuing to rob the poor. The law in the eighteenth century was a forum for contesting right and power, as Winstanley had argued it was in the seventeenth century. Kingly power had shifted its focus since then and the law was less about dispossession and more about consumption and display. The Black Acts were enforced to meet the demands of the rich for deer parks as a means for displaying their wealth. In true forest areas the villagers had a duty to support the king's deer and allow them to stray into their corn and crops in return for grazing rights on the waste. Farmers and forest officers were prevented from building fences and hedges by the king, and the deer became symbols of royal authority for the poor, 'an authority which threatened their economy, their crops, and their customary agrarian rights'.[17] The central issue was the question of who had the right to use the available land. This was not so much a pure conflict between use rights and ownership claims as a contest between differing perceptions of property rights and whose version would prevail.[18]

E. P. Thompson argues that the Black Acts allowed 'forest officialdom' to enlarge and revive what were essentially feudal claims to forest land use, 'using the deer as a screen behind which to advance their own interests'.[19] Thompson sees the Black Acts as an expression of shifting attitudes towards property and poverty. They 'could only have been drawn up and enacted by men who had formed habits of mental distance and moral levity towards human life'.[20] This is very close to Godwin's point. He argued that the existing inequality of conditions, exacerbated by legislation such as the Black Acts, was calculated to excite deference and to try and return to the principle of the feudal system, where 'the vassal, who was regarded as a sort of live stock upon the earth, and knew no appeal from the arbitrary fiat of his lord, would scarcely venture to suspect that he was of the same species'.[21] Property had achieved separation and estrangement between individuals, and men had hardened their hearts against one another. Property had been elevated above all other values, and it was this prior consensus about the value of property and the pursuit of wealth that allowed legislation such as the Black Acts to be passed. As Caroline Norton argued later, it was property and not morality that was held sacred.

For Godwin, as for Winstanley, private property corrupted human nature, killing the power of love and freedom within each individual. For them both, the climbing power of self-love created tyranny and damaged the social instinct, so that eventually rich and poor felt like members of different species. For Godwin, however, it was impossible to find a way behind the Fall, and foolish to seek to recover an original 'evenness'. Instead of seeking to recapture such fictional innocence, humankind should be striving for virtue, and virtue required the active employment of the mind in the promotion of the general good. Government was not a bequest from distant progenitors and it was dangerous and misguided to look back to our ancestors 'rather than forward to the benefits derivable from the improvements of human knowledge'.[22] Human beings had undergone great changes as intellectual beings, and Godwin insisted on the probability of improvements in the future. Moral improvements would keep pace with intellectual progress. The excellencies and defects of the human character could be modified and corrected. For Godwin, the only way out was through reason. He saluted the power of the modern Enlightenment and its liberating force.[23]

– MORALITY, UTILITY AND PROPERTY –

For Godwin, morality and happiness were not personal, individual matters, but intimately connected to the general good. He believed in the possibility of gaining access to a view that was in some sense beyond human experience, a truth that was not just one among many. This meant that he had to get beyond a notion of individuals as partial selves, inextricable from their families, for example. He began from the premise that we 'are not connected with one or two percipient beings, but with a society, a nation, and in some sense with the whole family of mankind'.[24] While this holds out the promise of wholeness and harmony, it is important to recognise that he started from the idea of being 'not connected': the individuals he was talking about were radically abstracted from one another. From this starting point, Godwin formulated a rigorous principle of impartiality. This meant that there was no basis on which to give one person preferential treatment over another and the needs of each person had to be accorded equal value. The soundest criterion of virtue was to put ourselves in the place of an impartial spectator. Godwin challenges us to consider: 'What magic is there in the pronoun "my", that should justify us in overturning the decisions of impartial truth?'[25] Rationality, for Godwin, had to entail impartiality.

The magic of the pronoun 'my' immediately raised the problem of property. It suggested the possibility of an individual holding himself apart, enclosing himself and saying 'this is mine'.[26] By doing so, he shut himself off from the common nature of mankind and concerned himself instead with just 'one or two percipient beings'. This enclosure of the self, using property to protect self-interest, meant that the individual failed in his duty to pursue the greatest good of society and to regard his property as a trust, at the disposal of society.[27] For Godwin, this was a trust which could be used to increase liberty, virtue and knowledge and could not be disposed of at the suggestion of individual caprice. Even our property in the person was held as a trust on behalf of mankind. Our talents, understanding, strength and time should all be disposed in producing the general good, orientated towards common preservation rather than a narrow version of self-preservation and self-interest. In Godwin's view, society had a right to require a contribution to the welfare of society from each individual. Utility created an obligation and imposed a duty.

Since human beings shared a common nature, it followed that the good things of the world were a common stock. Each individual had as valid title as another to draw what she wanted from it. One individual did not need to encroach on another. Godwin was arguing that individuals did not need to use property as a means of protection against others. Reasonable humans, in his view, could live together without encroaching on one another. Self-ownership did not need to be defensive, primarily concerned with excluding others and insulating the self. Each person had a sphere marked out by the equal sphere of his neighbour: 'I have a right to the means of subsistence; he has an equal right. I have a right to every pleasure I can participate without injury to myself or others; his title, in this respect is of similar extent.'[28]

Property owning involved particular duties, where duty was defined as 'that mode of action on the part of the individual, which constitutes the best possible application of his capacity to the general benefit'.[29] People failed in their duty when they claimed property and rights as their own: 'Few things have contributed more to undermine the energy and virtue of the human species, than the superstition that we have a right, as it has been phrased, to do what we will with our own.'[30] Godwin insisted that we have nothing that is strictly speaking our own; he aimed to strip the pronoun 'my' of its magic. Godwin's was a teleological thesis. Everything had a destination already prescribed to it by reason and justice: people associated with each other in order to secure the good of others, and pursued the common good because it was just to do so.[31] Having done away with the superstition attached to property, Godwin was left with the problem of finding a way to secure individual independence. There was a danger that the individual would dissolve into the general benefit, unable to identify and pursue every pleasure or to recognise her unique capacities. Godwin needed to find some way of protecting the sphere marked out by the equal sphere of her neighbour.

He argued that each person's right to subsistence and pleasure, and their right not to be encroached upon by others, required a certain 'sphere of discretion', which they had a right to expect would not be infringed by their neighbours.[32] Once this sphere of discretion was operating properly, Godwin was convinced that utility would be paramount and individual reason respected. Under these conditions, individuals would not necessarily use their property to encroach on others or to defend themselves, but as a trust. In a world where Godwin's moral rules applied, property became 'precisely that over which an individual exercises his private judgment'.[33] The destination of property was prescribed by the common good, but how to reach that destination had to be left to fallible, individual reason and understanding. Godwin was advocating property held as a trust, but not common ownership: 'Property is sacred: there is but one way in which duty requires the possessor to dispose of it, but I may not forcibly interfere, and dispose of it in the best way in his stead.'[34] One man could advise another, censure him and judge him, but he was not to resort to force or violence or forcibly extort his property from him. Individuals had to be left to themselves, to exercise their private judgements over their own property in order to function as dignified and rational beings. Their shared dignity and honour came from exercising their reason and judgement, and so freedom was linked to self-determination rather than exclusion.[35]

Having stressed the centrality of the common good and the benefits of the public state, but also the importance of individual reason and understanding, Godwin found himself caught in the dilemmas that are there in Locke and Winstanley, clustered around how to balance justice and charity, self-preservation and common preservation. And behind those lurks the problem of violence and force – the possibility that men might really invade one another. Mark Philp argues that Godwin reintroduced the notion of rights into his theory in response to the crisis for intellectual culture posed by the turn of events in France between 1793 and 1795. British radicals and enthusiasts who believed that the only true means of progress was through the cultivation and improvement of knowledge and understanding found themselves confronted by 'the spectre of restive, unenlightened and unsocialised mobs'.[36] By 1796 and the second edition of *Enquiry Concerning Political Justice*, Godwin felt the need to stress the importance of avoiding violence and trespass on the sphere of discretion and private judgement. He moved towards a more 'territorial' vision of the individual, concerned with self-defence and the exclusion of others. However, he still wanted to limit the sacredness of property by subordinating it to justice, and so the dominion he suggested was not entirely despotic.

Ownership was not a right in itself, unconnected to the common good or exempt from the judgement of others: 'Every man has a right to that, the exclusive possession of which being awarded to him, a greater sum of benefit or pleasure will result, than could have arisen from its being otherwise appropriated.'[37] The principle of non-interference was suspended when this was not the case, and the right to subsistence and the principle of usufruct reasserted themselves. Godwin asked: 'What shall prevent me from taking by force from my neighbour's store, if the alternative be that I must otherwise perish with hunger?'[38] Exclusive possession, in Godwin's terms, was not about shutting off from one another, but about mutual respect. Shared rationality and dignity meant that the abstract individuals of Godwin's theory *were* in fact connected to one another, by reason and the common good rather than by more familiar bonds. Human society could not exist without frequent encroachments of one man on his neighbour: 'We sufficiently discharge our duty, if we habitually recollect that each man has his province, and endeavour to regulate our conduct accordingly.'[39] Godwin's argument was that property broke the connections of reason and dignity, and encouraged individuals to forget that each man had his province.

– GODWIN'S THEORY OF PROPERTY –

The starting point for Godwin's theory of property was the injustice of accumulated property, which encouraged the pride of the rich and the servility of the poor. Pride and servility undermined the dignity of rational beings. Godwin distinguished between what he called three degrees of property. The first degree was things of use. Someone's entitlement to such things as a place to live, a toothbrush, furniture, clothes and food was legitimate and recognised by the members of their community. Godwin's second degree of property was based on the principle that every man is entitled to the produce of his own industry. Individuals who laboured were entitled to the produce, but in Godwin's account they became stewards rather than absolute owners: 'He is only the steward. But still he is the steward.' As a steward, the individual labourer could exercise some reasonable independent judgement over his property, but he was not entitled to encroach on the province of anyone else. Making judgements about the destination of his property involved a 'sort of usurpation', since the distribution of that property was already determined by considerations of justice and the public good, but Godwin conceded that this sort of usurpation was not inherently damaging. [40]

The third degree of property was where Godwin's objections to accumulated property took effect. This was the system by which one man disposed of the produce of another man's industry. Superfluities and insignificant luxuries were procured by the rich by depriving the poor of essentials. Wealth, expenditure and splendour were produced by a labour force condemned to 'slavery and sweat', drudgery, unwholesome food, hardship and ignorance in order to supply the idle rich with luxuries. This drudgery, as distinct from the righteous labour of the second degree of property, did not form the basis of entitlement to the produce. The insistence of the rich on their right to their accumulated and inherited property was, for Godwin, 'a gross imposition, that men are accustomed to put upon themselves, when they talk of the property bequeathed to them by their ancestors. The property is produced by the daily labour of men who are now in existence'.[41] Their labour and its product had been monopolised by the rich 'by fraud or force'.[42] Godwin's argument closely echoed Winstanley's condemnation of wage labour, and he was equally committed to making labour visible, uncovering the slavery and sweat, and exposing the fraud behind the idea of owning the 'turfs my servant has cut'.

The centrality of private judgement and an individual sphere of discretion to Godwin's theory meant that he could not countenance compulsion, either in forcing people to be more productive or in imposing a redistribution of wealth to fit a predetermined pattern. The distribution of wealth in every community had to be left to the discretion of the individual members of that community. Godwin was confident that once reason and justice had prevailed, wealth would be estimated at its true value, accumulation and monopoly would be recognised as injustices and so inequality of conditions would be destroyed. For Godwin what was required to effect change was a 'revolution of opinions.'[43] Reason would be enough. Force would not be necessary. People should never attempt to correct inequality by violent means. For Godwin, if property were equalised today, without a change in dispositions and sentiments, it would simply revert to inequality tomorrow. He regarded government control and agrarian laws as pernicious remedies to the problem of inequality. They were bound to threaten the primacy of private judgement, and like the unsocialised mob, they raised the spectre of forcible interference and trespass. When the state resorted to extortion, restraint and penalties, it undermined the dignity of rational beings. This meant that, for Godwin, the state was incapable of effecting improvement: 'The stark alternative for him was to rely upon the progress of truth through human reason.'[44]

This left Godwin in a difficult position. He was concerned to stress the moral and psychological evils that arose out of the established administration of property. For him, the worst effect was a sense of dependence, in direct contrast to the sense of independence which the sphere of discretion was supposed to foster. The danger was that the will to own would undermine the basis of rational ownership. Everybody desired to go beyond subsistence, and as soon as they did so they found themselves caught up in the rage of distinction, living in the opinion of others. Accumulation 'brings home a servile and truckling spirit, by no circuitous method, to every house in the nation'.[45] The home was part of the moral and economic space of property, and in their homes the rich put their pride and the servility of their servants on display. The injustice of accumulated property was based on the rich's attempt to purchase the submission of the poor. Servants, for example, not only performed certain tasks and showed a servile disposition, but were also, as Thorsten Veblen argued, trained in the 'tactics of subservience', knowing how to make their servility conspicuous.[46] The development of the servant class was a means of showing superfluity, displaying the ability to consume a large amount of service, and so live off the labour of others. As well as encouraging this dependence and servility, existing inequalities in property maintained the continuous spectacle of injustice and bolstered the pernicious love of opulence. Established property relations accustomed people to the sight of injustice, oppression and inequity until their feelings were made callous, and this callousness 'treads the powers of thought in the dust'.[47] The established system of property was responsible for oppression, servility and fraud.

Godwin's difficulty was how to respond to the injustice of accumulated property without resorting to violent methods of change. People needed to feel safe from the threat of restive mobs and unenlightened governments in order to be able to exercise their rational judgement and recognise the public good. They needed to feel secure, and that security needed to be protected even when it involved defending property in the short term. For Godwin, it was a necessary expedient, 'protecting one injustice, the accumulation of property, for the sake of keeping out another evil, still more formidable and destructive'.[48] The risks to individual independence involved in attempting to abolish property were too great. Property was founded in the sacred and indefeasible right of private judgement: 'Without permitting to every man, to a considerable degree, the exercise of his own discretion, there can be no independence, no virtue and no happiness.'[49] Security and property were buffers to the irregularity and caprice of others, necessary defences against invasion and forcible interference. In the end, Godwin's version of self-ownership had to involve a degree of self-defence and the exclusion of others.

Godwin's solution was not revolution, but moral improvement and in particular an end to the love of distinction, the 'false glare which wealth, through the present puerility of the human mind, reflects on its possessor'.[50] Godwin had to trust to reason and to the inherent tendency of the human intellect to improvement. In his scheme, equality could not be introduced by force or maintained by laws. It could not be the result of accident or authority. Instead, it 'is produced by the serious and deliberate conviction of the public at large'.[51] He had to trust that the truth would be strong enough to prevent a return to vices, and that equality of conditions would be fixed by a shared sense of justice and rational dignity. Rational people would come to recognise the justice of distributing property according to need, and they would no longer be tempted to monopolise, but would content themselves with a healthy existence and inexpensive pleasures, contemplating the general happiness and no longer relying on the economy of opulence based on complacence, servility and terror. Godwin relied on a degree of co-operation between rational individuals to overcome the irrationality of the rage to own. He looked forward to a society where the genuine needs of an individual would constitute the only legitimate claim to appropriation and consumption. He insisted that conflicts over property arose from people trying to use property to insulate themselves from one another because they could not rely on a shared rational dignity under the prevailing conditions of inequality. He argued that we 'are deceived by the apparent mercenariness of mankind, and imagine that the accumulation of wealth is their great object'.[52] Property was, for Godwin as it was for Winstanley, part of imagination, deception and superstition, part of the fraud, but it was also part of justice, independence and freedom. It expressed the moral frailty of humanity, and at the same time offered the possibility of shelter for civic and personal virtue by making space for the exercise of rational, private judgement. Godwin's theory relied on the notion that individuals would seek out and subject themselves to the truth, and in the process shed their mercenariness and become 'elementary humans' again.[53]

– BENTHAM: THE ANATOMY OF REASON –

Bentham's starting point, like Godwin's, was that mercenariness was not necessarily part of the 'hard core' of human nature. For them both, the individual was not defined entirely by self-interest or by insulation from others. Bentham argued that ideas about human nature were simply used to legitimise custom and to ground inequalities, making them appear fixed and immutable, rather than social and modifiable. The eighteenth-century discovery of happiness informed a new system of morals within which morality consisted in the pursuit of happiness for all and the welfare of others rather than an individual, internal struggle against evil or original sin. Self-love was not the source of all our passions: disinterested benevolence was part of human nature too.[54] Bentham's explicit assumptions about human nature were that people were basically self-interested and self-aggrandising, and those with power were bound to pursue their narrow self-interest at the expense of the common good. However, for Bentham, each individual had the capacity both for self-regard and for sympathy. Their concern for self-preservation and physical survival was more fundamental, but everyone had the potential for sympathetic action. In Bentham's theory, the role of the legislator was to increase the influence of sympathy by creating institutions that would prevent self-interested individuals from harming one another. Through legislation, each person would identify some of their private interests with the public interest of society, and through this process of identification they would find their own interests advanced and their capacity for sympathetic action enhanced.

Bentham dealt with the fraught moral space of property by trying to make politics and morality into an experimental and objective science, so that they reflected the human capacity to transform and improve the world and to satisfy human needs. Morals and legislation could have the same principle and method as long as they were grounded in a science of behaviour. Bentham's utilitarianism offered the possibility of 'gathering *all* the phenomena of the moral world under a single principle'.[55] The study of man had the potential to become a new kind of natural science based on empirical experiment and observation: 'Nature has placed mankind under the government of two sovereign masters, *pain* and *pleasure*. It is for them alone to point out what we ought to do, as well as to determine what we shall do.'[56] This offered the possibility of measurement, quantification and improvement by making pleasure and pain the fundamental units of morality. People's ends were pleasure and the absence of pain, and so the value of an act consisted in the pleasures and pains that resulted from it. The perniciousness of an act was determined by its consequences. This was a necessary and normal law of human action, and it was this that set the standard of right and wrong. It also underpinned moral reformation: 'the principle of utility allowed ethics, law and politics to be founded on earthly happiness'.[57] Ethics and politics were interdependent, and property was central to them both.

For Bentham, all the state could do was provide the general conditions within which the individual would be secure in the pursuit of happiness. The principle of sociality – relations based on virtues such as forbearance, politeness and kindness – could be left to the good will of individuals. Government should constantly explore how to maximise the happiness of its subjects by guaranteeing economic security, a better distribution of wealth and a social climate of service. Human happiness 'depends on countless small services that men render to one another'.[58] Government had a duty to cultivate the spirit of benevolence by doing things like fighting religious and sectarian prejudices, prohibiting cruel sports, encouraging charitable organisations and upholding a code of political morality. Through such measures, it had the capacity to foster a civil and civilised society, within which individuals could safely activate their potential for sympathetic action and benevolence. Bentham was 'thus able to assign the government a positive and creative role in the life of the community'.[59] This had particular consequences for Bentham's theory of property, and for his solution to the problem of balancing a sphere of discretion with political reform, conflict with co-operation, self-regard with sympathy.

In Bentham's discussion of property, the key was to balance security and equality. Happiness consisted of subsistence, abundance, equality and security. Bentham took it for granted that the commercial society of the eighteenth century had moved beyond subsistence. The wealth of society was made up of the sum of all individual wealth. The usefulness of different forms of property could be measured in terms of how far they encouraged labour, increased social wealth and so opened up greater chances of happiness to a greater number. For Bentham, each portion of wealth was connected with a corresponding portion of happiness, but the excess of happiness on the part of the wealthiest would not keep pace with the excess of his wealth. The greater the disproportion between the two masses of wealth, the greater the inequality of happiness. In his view, where the actual proportion approached equality, the total mass of happiness would be greater.[60] Equality was therefore desirable in promoting happiness, but Bentham argued that permanent equality in property was impossible. It would require 'perpetual meddling', which was bound to prove despotic and neglect individual judgement, as well as prove damaging to economic development.[61] Like Godwin, he was prepared to countenance one injustice in order to rule out what he regarded as a greater evil.

However, Bentham was not a straightforward advocate of unalloyed free trade, opposed to all 'meddling'. He was prepared to sanction limited government intervention in the economic sphere: he argued, for example, that the state had a positive responsibility towards the poor during temporary slumps in trade. In 1776, he suggested that the unemployed should be put to work for the public, digging canals, deepening harbours and making roads. His theory held that it was necessary for government to provide for subsistence, and in the 1790s he proposed a system of agricultural communes and Industry Houses to care for the indigent by providing work under supervision and compulsion. Industry Houses were expected to take care of orphans, foundlings and abandoned children by providing education, medical dispensaries and a bank for the poor. Bentham also advocated various legislative measures to curb the concentration of wealth in the hands of the few. He proposed limiting the freedom to bequeath, instituting the equal division of property between children, and redistributing the estates of those without descendants among all their relations via the public exchequer. He proposed to tax estates not left to immediate relatives at levels up to 50 per cent, and to use this form of tax to replace inequitable taxes on medicines, windows, soap and salt. Bentham agreed with Godwin that society was fundamentally divided into the few and the many, the rich and the poor. The aristocracy and elements of the middle class formed themselves into a wealthy ruling class that was indigent, opulent, corrupt, wasteful and irresponsible. They engaged in 'the power-seeking exploitation of the poor for the satisfaction of their own narrow interests'.[62] Through measures such as Industry Houses and death duties, Bentham attempted to devise a system where self-interested men 'bent on corruption and tyranny, will none the less be induced to follow the constitutional rules by the apprehension of the advantages of doing so'.[63]

While Bentham advocated such measures to maintain equality, his real focus was on security and expectation. His proposals to limit the freedom to bequeath, for example, were structured so as take effect at the moment of death, when the expectations of the original proprietor could not be damaged, and the heirs and legatees were not yet proprietors themselves. For Bentham, there could be security without equality, but equality without security was bound to prove unsustainable. Overturning property to establish equality would be counter-productive: 'The evil would be irreparable. No more security, no more industry, no more abundance!'[64] Security 'justifies that feeling of safety which makes it possible for man to make a general scheme of conduct, to bind together the various successive moments of his existence, so as to make of them a single life'.[65] Bentham emphasised this psychological aspect of security, and its moral force. Property played a pivotal role in this binding process, overcoming the pain of frustrated expectation and disappointment and replacing it with the certainty of advantage to the individual. Property became a 'justified expectation', and this was crucial in connecting the individual to his labour and to the future.[66] It could not be overturned without severe damage to the self.

Laws establishing property allowed people to activate their labour, their courage and their foresight, as well as giving them the right to exclude others, and so protect themselves from invasion: 'If industry creates, it is law which preserves.'[67] For Bentham, in contrast to Godwin, the state offered the only way to protect the individual's sphere of discretion. It could protect rather than threaten the primacy of private judgement, and it was safer to rely on legislation than on the possibility of a revolution of opinions and the progress of truth through reason. For Bentham, with the protection of law, individuals would be able to enclose a field and cultivate it in the hope of a future harvest. Where individuals had a clear view of their own interest, an article of property, such as an estate in land, enabled them to produce pleasures and avert pains. Its value was linked to the length of time the individual had it, and to the degree of certainty he could feel in its possession. Everything which an individual possessed, Bentham argued, he considered in his own mind as destined always to belong to him. This formed the basis of his own expectations and of the hopes of those dependent on him. Property connected individuals to the future.

Bentham argued that expectation was crucial in forming a general plan of conduct and making a life into a continuous whole, and so overcoming the disorientation of individualism. Without property, individuals risked remaining fractured and free-floating. With property established, the binding process could hold over generations: 'Expectation is a chain which unites our present existence to our future existence, and which passes beyond us to the generation which is to follow.'[68] This sense of the incompleteness of property links Bentham's theory to conservative ideas. In these terms, property is not about separation and estrangement, but about overcoming these, and regarding it as an expression of humanness and continued existence. For Bentham, property and law were born together and die together: 'That which, in the natural state, was an almost invisible thread, in the social state becomes a cable.'[69] Property had an intrinsic value and a 'value of affection' that came from inheritance from ancestors, the reward of the individual's own labour and the part of himself that he had put into it: 'Thus our property becomes a part of our being, and cannot be torn from us without rending us to the quick.'[70] The psychological aspects of property, for Bentham, were not just to do with consumption, display and corruption, but about constituting the self as a whole individual and as a member of a community.

Security, for Bentham, was required for imagining the community, civil society and its boundaries. It was 'the distinctive index of civilization'.[71] In his view, it was property that set civilised men apart from the savages: 'To form a just idea of the benefits of law', Bentham argued, 'it is only necessary to consider the condition of savages.'[72] Savages were locked in a constant battle against famine and for survival, and their struggle for subsistence was equated with their savagery. As Locke had argued, 'savages' by definition attempted to live off the spontaneous products of nature. Rivalry for subsistence created cruel wars and men pursued men as a means of sustenance. This was the nightmare vision of Thomas Hobbes's version of the state of nature as a state of war, where men had a right to all things, even to one another's bodies. In the savage state, all the boundaries between individuals had broken down, and there could be no vision of the future. In Bentham's thought, cannibalism, and the fear of cannibalism, created the ultimate insecurity and the distortion of benevolence: 'The fear of this terrible calamity silences the softer sentiments of nature; pity unites with insensibility in putting to death the old men who can hunt no longer.'[73] Civil men as property owners were surrounded by a threatening and dangerous state of nature made up of other people. For Bentham, unlike for Godwin, people did need to use property to insulate themselves from one another and to maintain their spheres of discretion. The threat did not come only from the state or from restive, unenlightened mobs, but from lack of security and civilisation. This made invasion a real possibility.

According to Bentham, men's health was more precarious in hot climates, and this meant that men living in such places lacked strength, vigour and steadiness of mind. Their sensibilities were more intense, and their habitual occupations were more of sloth than activity.[74] Ownership could help them to emerge from the state of nature, but it could prove fragile and needed to be carefully fostered by the system of law. If industry was to create, then the law had to preserve; the invisible thread had to be carefully spun into a cable. Bentham argued that the spirit of industry needed development and encouragement. It would be smothered by tyrannical government, bad legislation, intolerant religion and super-stition. Bentham gave the example of 'the absurd despotism' of the Turkish government that meant that one of the finest countries of the earth was left 'wasted, barren, and almost abandoned' with no respect for property.[75] On the other hand, it was the right of property, bringing with it pleasure, abundance and security, that vanquished the natural aversion to labour and 'has given to man the empire of the earth'.[76] As we saw in the discussion of Locke, the boundaries of belonging to this empire of the earth were not simply geographical, but were connected to the division between the industrious and the idle, the civilised and the savage. It was not only those who lived in hot climates who might find themselves savages. Poverty, for Bentham, was 'the primitive condition of the human race' and the individual who subsisted from day to day 'is precisely the man of nature – the savage'.[77]

In Bentham's view, North America provided a striking contrast to this sorry picture of absurd despotism in Turkey and savage poverty in Britain. There, savage nature existed side by side with civilised nature. Bentham figured the interior as a region of frightful solitude, impenetrable forests and sterile plains, populated by fierce tribes without fixed habitation living by hunting game and divided by implacable rivalries. Elsewhere, the forests had given way to cultivated fields, meadows, pastures and domestic animals. The earth had been covered by cities, roads, harbours and an increasing population living on their labour: 'Who has renewed the surface of the earth? Who has given to man this domain over nature – over nature embellished, fertilized, and perfected? That beneficent genius is *Security*.'[78] According to Bentham, a prosperous nation with flourishing agriculture, manufacture and commerce and without any shackles on industry and trade would make continuous progress towards equality. Reformers from the 1790s onwards had been interested in 'replicating America in Europe' and Bentham was convinced it could only be achieved by protecting the principle of security.[79] Security could eventually guaran-tee equality, economic prosperity and social peace.

This meant that property was more than a necessary evil for Bentham. Poverty was the primitive condition of the human race, and the savage was made savage by being forced to live a life of day-to-day subsistence, without foresight, expectations or security. Not having property was enough to risk breaking down the boundaries between individuals, even-tually breaching them entirely so that people would end up eating one another. The scientific revolution and the possibility of efficiency in government and legislation had implications for Enlightenment and empire, and for the poor at home. Many of his contemporaries associated Bentham with his Panopticon plan for a model prison, developed as an alternative to transportation to Australia. Coupled with his scheme for Industry Houses, it gave the impression that his approach to society was authoritarian and manipulative. Bentham's critics were concerned that his theory of sovereignty placed the power to create all laws and rights in the hands of the supreme legislative authority. The danger was that without natural rights or a sphere of discretion, individuals would be left with no defences against the state. Under such conditions, poor people, already reduced to the status of savages, seemed to be available for social experimentation. His critics argued that Bentham had a 'tendency to treat individuals as human materials to be conditioned and manipulated by the managers of society'.[80]

This tendency surfaced particularly clearly in Bentham's support for the Anatomy Act of 1832. The study of anatomy by dissection emphasised that the spread of scientific knowledge sometimes required what William Hunter termed 'a kind of necessary Inhumanity', a sense of detachment that was also present in the calculations of utilitarianism.[81] In the later eighteenth and early nineteenth centuries, hanging was popularly regarded as preferable to dissection. For a dissected corpse, rescue and revival was impossible. The dead person was denied any hope of survival, and control over the body passed from their relatives to the medical profession. In popular opinion, body snatching was wrong because it demonstrated a lack of respect for the dead, and failed to accord them dignity and justice. The body snatchers were subjected to violence by people seeking to defend customary funeral arrangements and the bodily integrity of the dead. Those opposed to dissection saw body snatching as a pitiless example of free trade, and the grave robbers as the 'living exemplars of innovative market logic'.[82] The human corpse did not constitute property, but the anatomists, medics and the judiciary were treating it as though it were property, by investing it with monetary value and trading in bodies.

This disjunction between treating the body as sacred and treating the body as property was particularly clear in the case of grave robbery. Alan Hyde, in his book about how legal discourse configures the body, begins by pointing out that the use of the word 'body' implies a separation of the body from something else, its 'dangerous supplement', the mind, spirit or soul. The separation '*dematerializes* "something else" as it *materializes* the body'.[83] The body which materialises is commodified, a thing to be owned and traded, dug up and dissected. At the same time, the body is understood to carry its owner with it – an autonomous being with free will, sacred and not for sale: 'the commodity body is accompanied by its spirit shadow', and so has the capacity to resist commodification.[84] The idea of a 'spirit shadow' had important class dimensions in the nineteenth-century debates about body snatching. Grave robbing crystallised some of the ways in which class difference was understood as moral difference, and in which class was used to draw the boundaries around the imagined community. It was the poor who were dissected. Dissection was often part of a criminal's punishment, and, as we have seen in both Winstanley and Godwin, the use of the death penalty for crimes against property increased during the eighteenth century. The wealthy sought to defend their bodily integrity and their spirit shadows, and to protect themselves from the market in bodies by spending money on strong vaults and stronger patent coffins. They employed funeral guards and insisted on deep graves. The poor were the most vulnerable to grave robbery, but there was a general sense that no one was immune. The precautions taken by the rich demonstrated a shared conception of respect for the dead, recognition of the spirit shadow that accompanied the commodity body, a shared vulnerability and the 'social breadth of revulsion from grave-robbery and dissection'.[85]

Ruth Richardson argues that the anatomists and the resurrectionists had different social aspirations, reflected in their different attitudes to the limits of property. The anatomists wanted to emphasise the medical benefits of dissection, and hence their own professional prestige and skill. They took care to assert their gentility against the taint of 'trade' associated with body snatching. The resurrectionists were more concerned with their respectability as men of property engaged in a legitimate business enterprise.[86] Both the anatomists and the resurrectionists objected to the idea of defining grave robbery as a criminal act, and to indulgent official attitudes to cases of riots against body snatchers and surgeons. In direct contrast to the harsh treatment of poachers and rioters under the Black Acts, those who violently objected to body snatching were often leniently treated. The shared vulnerability and revulsion felt by those at risk of dissection meant that supplying bodies to the anatomists was a risky, dangerous and stigmatised enterprise, and that anatomy itself was tainted and reviled. In Bentham's view, the whole messy system had lost sight of the ultimate medical benefits of dissection, and so of the public good. The situation failed to promote the greatest happiness of the greatest number, or to contribute to the efficiency of the scientific revolution and the spread of knowledge.

The terms of the Anatomy Act of 1832 emerged from a Select Committee enquiry and reports packed and manipulated by Benthamites. The committee heard evidence of the overwhelming need for anatomical knowledge and enquiry, and of the enormous difficulties involved in obtaining a regular supply of bodies. In response, the Act established the first centrally financed and administered national inspectorate for corpses. The Anatomy Act's key recommendation was that by applying for treatment, all hospital patients should automatically be deemed to have given consent to their dissection. In return for their charitable treatment during their lives, they had tacitly agreed to be dissected after death. This meant that 'Bentham's chosen constituency for dissection material would be all those who died in poverty with no relatives to bury them, and those whose relatives were too poor to do so'.[87] The Act gave legal recognition to an unspoken contract between the patient and the charity or hospital, and so formally brought the spirit shadow and the commodity body back together. At the same time, the proposals codified the commodification of the corpses of the poor, and undercut the shared vulnerability between the classes. In its place, the Act created the possibility for the same kind of moral levity and distance as informed the Black Acts. It redefined the boundaries of belonging to the imagined community, and suggested that the poor, as shadow members of society, did not carry their spirit shadows with them, or have the right to exercise private judgements over their own spheres of discretion.

The committee recommended that the bodies of those who died in workhouses, hospitals and other charitable houses should, if not claimed by next of kin, be given to the anatomists. Workhouses were a major source of unclaimed bodies, since claiming the body would mean assuming responsibility for funeral costs. The idea was to dissect the bodies of those with no relations who could be outraged or distressed. It was assumed by the Select Committee members, Richardson argues, that unclaimed bodies either had no relations, or were to be left unburied because their relatives were indifferent to their fate. Being poor was in itself enough to undermine sympathy, and to remove the possibility of benevolent motives. Their unclaimed dead were commodified and 'sacrificed to save the rest of society from liability to exhumation'.[88] Under the terms of the Act, the bodies of the poor were worth more dead than alive. Their vulnerability to dissection after death meant that the poor could not be secure in their expectations, or confident of their membership of a civilised society. The invisible thread was broken, and the poor were reduced to the status of savages, without even the capacity to exclude others. The rich would scarcely venture to suspect that they were of the same species. The effects of the Anatomy Act closely paralleled those of the Black Acts, cementing the sense of separation and estrangement created by property and sharpening class difference. As Don Herzog argues, the 1832 Act was part of a process of dehumanising paupers and legislating on the basis of their disgrace and the disgust felt by the legislators. The Anatomy Act codified the distinction between a human being and a person that underpinned much of the treatment of the poor. He gives the example of the food given to the poor in workhouses and hospitals: potatoes were regarded as animal feed, and stewed ox heads were defined as waste, but given to the poor. Herzog concludes: 'We can see the poor law as grudgingly nourishing human beings but moving decisively to undercut persons.'[89]

Godwin and Bentham were both raising the problem of the conflicts generated by private property, and in particular the problem of poverty. Bentham's emphasis on security at the expense of equality, and even Godwin's overriding concern to protect an individual sphere of discretion from invasion, were crucial to the development of ideas about property as the ability to exclude others and guard against encroachment. Throughout the eighteenth and nineteenth centuries, it became increasingly clear that it was most important to be able to exclude the poor. Marx argued that the poor lost their place as fellow members of human society, and the beginnings of this process were visible in the provisions of the Black Acts, the Anatomy Act and the New Poor Law. These are themes that are taken up in the next chapter on Hegel and Marx, as pauperism became a pressing social problem and the poor were increasingly understood as outsiders to the social system and shadow members of civil society.

– NOTES –

1. Richard Drayton, 'Knowledge and Empire', in P. J. Marshall (ed.), *The Oxford History of the British Empire: the Eighteenth Century* (Oxford: Oxford University Press, 1998), p. 234.
2. William Godwin, *Enquiry Concerning Political Justice*, ed. K. Cordell Carter (Oxford: Clarendon Press, [1798] 1971), p. 278.
3. E. P. Thompson, *Whigs and Hunters* (London: Penguin, [1975] 1990), p. 197.
4. John P. Clark, *The Philosophical Anarchism of William Godwin* (Princeton: Princeton University Press, 1977), passim.

5. Ibid. p. 62.
6. Mark Philp, *Godwin's Political Justice* (London: Duckworth, 1986), pp. 32–3.
7. Clark, *Philosophical Anarchism*, p. 79.
8. Godwin, *Enquiry Concerning Political Justice*, p. 17.
9. Ibid. p. 24.
10. Ibid. p. 24.
11. Thorsten Veblen, *The Theory of the Leisure Class* (New York: Dover Publications, [1899] 1994), p. 10.
12. Godwin, *Enquiry Concerning Political Justice*, p. 25.
13. Gregory Claeys (ed.), *Utopias of the British Enlightenment* (Cambridge: Cambridge University Press, 1994), p. x.
14. See James Raven, 'Defending Conduct and Property: the London Press and the Luxury Debate', in John Brewer and Susan Staves (eds), *Early Modern Conceptions of Property*. (London and New York: Routledge, 1996).
15. Claeys, *Utopias of the British Enlightenment*, p. xxi.
16. Godwin, *Enquiry Concerning Political Justice*, p. 25.
17. Thompson, *Whigs and Hunters*, p. 64.
18. Daniel H. Cole, '"An Unqualified Human Good": E. P. Thompson and the Rule of Law' (1999), http://www.iulaw.indy.indiana.edu/instructors/cole/thompson.pdf
19. Thompson, *Whigs and Hunters*, p. 99.
20. Ibid. p. 197.
21. Godwin, *Enquiry Concerning Political Justice*, p. 26.
22. Ibid. p. 68.
23. Bernard Williams, 'Necessary Identities', in Tommy L. Lott (ed.), *Subjugation and Bondage: Critical Essays on Slavery and Social Philosophy* (Boulder, CO and Oxford: Rowman and Littlefield, 1998), p. 21.
24. Godwin, *Enquiry Concerning Political Justice*, p. 70.
25. Ibid. p. 71.
26. On this 'territorial' vision of the self, see my 'Imagining the Boundaries of a Sovereign Self', in Laura Brace and John Hoffman (eds), *Reclaiming Sovereignty* (London: Pinter, 1997).
27. Godwin, *Enquiry Concerning Political Justice* , p. 74.
28. Ibid. p. 279.
29. Ibid. p. 83.
30. Ibid. p. 86.
31. Philp, *Godwin's Political Justice*, p. 51.
32. Godwin, *Enquiry Concerning Political Justice*, p. 89.
33. Philp, *Godwin's Political Justice*, p. 140.
34. Godwin, *Enquiry Concerning Political Justice*, p. 108.
35. For further discussion of this important distinction in liberal theory, see Chapter 5.
36. Philp, *Godwin's Political Justice*, p. 139.
37. Godwin, *Enquiry Concerning Political Justice*, p. 279.
38. Ibid. p. 109.
39. Ibid. p. 110.
40. Ibid. p. 283.
41. Ibid. p. 283.
42. Ibid. p. 284.
43. Ibid. p. 286.

44. Martin Fitzpatrick, 'William Godwin and the Rational Dissenters', *Price-Priestley Newsletter* 3, 1979, p. 15.
45. Godwin, *Enquiry Concerning Political Justice*, p. 292.
46. Veblen, *Theory of the Leisure Class*, pp. 38–9.
47. Godwin, *Enquiry Concerning Political Justice*, p. 293.
48. Ibid. p. 288.
49. Ibid. p. 291.
50. Ibid. p. 296.
51. Ibid. p. 297.
52. Ibid. p. 299.
53. Heinz Lubasz, 'Marx's Initial Problematic: the Problem of Poverty', *Political Studies* XXIV:1, 1977, p. 31.
54. Don Locke, *A Fantasy of Reason: the Life and Thought of William Godwin.* (London: Routledge and Kegan Paul, 1980), p. 174.
55. Lea Campos Boralevi, 'Utilitarianism and Feminism', in Ellen Kennedy and Susan Mendus (eds), *Women in Western Political Philosophy* (Brighton: Wheatsheaf, 1987), p. 160.
56. Jeremy Bentham, *An Introduction to the Principles of Morals and Legislation* (Oxford: Clarendon Press, 1907), p. 1.
57. Boralevi, 'Utilitarianism and Feminism', p. 161.
58. Bentham, *Introduction*, p. 42.
59. Ibid. p. 43.
60. C. B. Macpherson (ed.), *Property: Mainstream and Critical Positions* (Oxford: Blackwell, 1978), pp. 47–8.
61. James Steintrager, *Bentham* (London: Allen and Unwin, 1977), p. 62.
62. Frederick Rosen, *Jeremy Bentham and Representative Democracy* (Oxford: Clarendon Press, 1983), p. 21.
63. Ibid. p. 232.
64. Macpherson, *Property*, p. 57.
65. Elie Halevy, *The Growth of Philosophical Radicalism* (London: Faber & Faber, 1972), p. 46.
66. Ibid. p. 46.
67. Bentham, *Introduction*, p. 50.
68. Ibid. p. 51.
69. Ibid. p. 52.
70. Ibid. p. 54.
71. Ibid. p. 49.
72. Ibid. p. 50.
73. Ibid. p. 50.
74. Ibid. p. 62.
75. Ibid. p. 55.
76. Ibid. p. 53.
77. Macpherson, *Property*, pp. 52–3, quoting Jeremy Bentham, *Principles of the Civil Code* (London: Trubner & Co., [1802] 1864).
78. Bentham, *Introduction*, p. 56.
79. Claeys, *Utopias of the British Enlightenment*, p. xxvi.
80. J. R. Dinwiddy, *Radicalism and Reform in Britain, 1780–1850* (London: Hambledon Press, 1992), p. 357.

81. Ruth Richardson, *Death, Dissection and the Destitute* (London: Routledge and Kegan Paul, 1987), p. 31.
82. Ibid. p. 90.
83. Alan Hyde, *Bodies of Law* (Princeton: Princeton University Press, 1997), p. 9.
84. Marina Warner, 'Is there a place from which the dickhead's self can speak?', *London Review of Books*, 20:19, 1 October 1998, p. 8.
85. Richardson, *Death, Dissection and the Destitute*, p. 99.
86. Ibid. p. 103.
87. Ibid. p. 110.
88. Ibid. p. 126.
89. Don Herzog, *Poisoning the Minds of the Lower Orders* (Princeton: Princeton University Press, 1998), p. 200.

CHAPTER 4

Hegel and Marx:
Civil and Human Society

The nineteenth century consolidated the shift away from traditional agrarian relations of dependence and witnessed the rise of the bourgeoisie, and so of new forms of property in capital and labour. Trade and industry flourished in the towns and cities, and nature was treated as a resource, a raw material that needed to be exploited and transformed by labour. Labour became increasingly specialised, divided and mechanised. The rising bourgeoisie, having triumphed over the aristocracy, became increasingly reflective, and saw its aim as profit. The age of commerce and industry was an age of expanding artificial and abstract needs that could be satisfied only by commercial exchanges and increased production. These processes were bound to separate individuals from one another and their communities, but they also had an explicitly social character.[1] It was clear that there was no going back to the immediate unity of the individual with the political community, no return to a golden age of 'evenness' between people. Modernity, industrialisation and political economy all meant that human beings had been estranged from their grounding in nature, forcibly pulled apart and divided from one another. For G. W. F. Hegel, being torn from the land and from nature was a spiritual as well as a social and economic process and he looked for an all-encompassing system of philosophy to overcome his 'anguish in the face of the social and political fragmentation around him'.[2] For both Hegel and Karl Marx, this fragmentation was part of the necessarily progressive character of human history, at the heart of a new view of the relationship between humanity and nature expressed through their different narratives of emancipation and their theories of property.

Property was central to this new relationship between humans and the natural world because it required individuals to act in determinate ways in the external world. Through property 'men dominate nature and distinguish themselves from nature'.[3] Through this process of domination and distinction, property also formed the basis for intersubjectivity, sociability and patterns of belonging and exclusion. Property took individuals beyond the material and the economic and into issues of individuality and freedom. For Hegel, property was a philosophical and political necessity for men to lead an ethical life of reason, to allow them to act in the world and to determine themselves. For Marx, private property was always a distortion of humanity, a fetter on individual development and freedom.

Both Hegel and Marx saw private property as separating individuals from one another and bringing them into conflict. For Hegel, this conflict could be managed. By owning property, men acted in the external world by dominating nature and creating social institutions such as public authorities, corporations, the state and the family, which all mediated the conflict between individuals and brought men together into universality. For Marx, the conflicts generated by private property could not be mediated, and private property itself narrowed, limited and stunted individuals rather than developing them. Work was developing and liberating, helping men to overcome obstacles and master nature. An individual objectified himself through work, not through private property and civil society: 'Where Hegel saw private property as the means by which the will of the individual became determinate, embodied itself, Marx saw it as the means by which man dehumanized himself.'[4]

This chapter explores property as a social, moral and political question as it emerged in the mid-nineteenth century, and in particular its relation to subjectivity, labour and poverty. It is in part about the ways that property came to be seen as central to personality and self-consciousness, and about the connections between property and civil society. This means looking at what it meant to be a member of civil society, ethically incorporated into the whole, and what it meant to be dispossessed, left outside and excluded. Hegel and Marx both explored the connections between property and the self, property and civil society, the problem of poverty, and the role of the state in dealing with conflicting property rights. Property emerged clearly as a social and political relationship, and the domination of nature as a central issue for modernity. As Peter Stillman argues, and as this chapter hopes to make clear: 'Behind the apparent immobility of property as a thing is hidden, for Hegel, the historical activities of work and interaction that have domesticated nature.'[5] These activities and interactions included the banishment of the poor from civil society and the system of private property rights.

The processes of industrialisation and the development of commercial and market society involved a huge increase in urbanisation. This, along with the intensified commercialisation of agriculture, left very little space for small landholders, working for subsistence on their own plots. Land and labour were pulled apart, so that people needed to find new ways of imagining their communities and their sense of place and self. Conceptions of property had to adapt to the new commercial society and to the conflicts it brought with it. Under these new circumstances, the division between the industrious and the idle was not always clear cut, but was often conflictual. Conflicts and inequalities were generated within the commercial and market system. Notions of freedom, belonging and labour were caught up with each other and attached to ideas about civil society and the state. The separation of labour from the land was seen as creating a new class of landless labourers, without capital and dependent on selling their wages. The separation was a struggle. Exclusion from the land, Herbert Spencer and Henry George argued, made you a serf or a slave. The landless became trespassers and fugitives who only existed by sufferance and whose lives were sustained only by permission of the landowners: 'To be debarred from access to the natural means of production', they declared, 'is to be deprived of liberty.'[6]

The problem with the new pressures of modernity was that it was impossible to return all the people to the land. The idea of 'the land' could no longer form the basis of a stable and permanent community of the imagination. It had become a site of struggle, inseparable from the market and the state. David Ricardo had argued that society was 'an internally divided camp' with rising industrialists opposing the aristocratic landowners who benefited from the protection given to them by the Corn Laws.[7] It was in the interests of the aristocrats to keep low-priced wheat out, while the industrialists insisted that food prices were too high, driving up their labour costs. In 1813, for example, bad crops and the war with Napoleon pushed wheat prices to fourteen shillings a bushel (eight gallons), nearly twice the male labourer's weekly wage. Ricardo saw the interest of the landlord as opposed to the interest of every other class in the community and in this opposition he saw 'the crucial political struggle of a growing market system'.[8] Economic expansion meant that capitalists had to pay higher wages and workers were condemned to subsistence. Property rights operated at different levels: profits gained from absolute ownership of the land came into conflict with the customary rights of those who tried to scrape a living from the land, and the moral principles of improvement were undermined by the separation of land and labour. The same separation intensified class conflict and the bifurcation of society and nature.[9]

– HEGEL AND INDIVIDUALITY –

To explore what it meant to be dispossessed, to be counted as a trespasser or a mercenary rather than as a property-owning individual, it is important to explore the connections between property and selfhood. For Hegel, these were dynamic concepts: ownership could never be a static fact, and property could never be about immobile things. As an individual subject, a person was related to the world of nature through his will. His will gave him a personality which he could use to confront the world of nature and become a subject, separate from that world. The will struggled to give itself reality, 'to claim that external world as its own'.[10] Property was central to this struggle, and it was through property that individuals could translate their freedom into an external sphere. By being able to determine objects as immediately different and separable from the self, as part of the external world, people exercised their will. Property was 'the necessary form that will must take in order, as it were, to emerge from our heads and exist in interpersonal space'.[11]

In Hegel's theory, the minimum characterisation of a person was being able to distinguish what was him from what was not. An individual could not occupy, or own, another person, but he or she was capable of owning things. As subjects, people were capable of controlling objects which, by definition, had no will of their own. This 'relationship of *possessing*' was central to Hegel's theory of property.[12] Ownership, for Hegel, was not about appropriating objects in isolation from each other. In his theory, we need other people to acknowledge and recognise our possession of things and so 'we express our status as free subjects by occupying mere objects'.[13] By being taken into possession, the thing becomes 'mine', but behind the immobility of the thing is the relationship of possessing. Something cannot be 'mine' unless others recognise that it is not theirs. For Hegel, then, property existed as an embodiment of the will. Property was not just physical possession. It was about the ways in which we make use of things by changing, destroying and consuming them. This made clear that the object was an object – it did not have a will, or a self, and existed only to satisfy the need of a person.

Hegel's starting point for his theory of property was not an isolated individual, but the behaviour of individuals in a social context.[14] This starting point created a complicated theory of freedom, individuality and self-ownership. Hegel's conception of the person involved elements of possession, but not the idea that we own our own persons and capacities, owing nothing to society for them, or the idea of despotic dominion. Unlike John Locke, he did not emphasise the right to exclude others as the basis of individuality. As Alan Ryan argues, Locke's account of property rights in the self was 'essentially defensive', based on the idea that my property is that which I cannot be deprived of without my consent.[15] In contrast, for Hegel, property had an irreducibly social and expressive (rather than defensive) dimension.

The relationship of possessing extended to an individual's ownership of herself. As a person, I 'possess my life and body, like other things, only in so far as my will is in them'.[16] This meant that in Hegel's theory, the body had to be taken into possession by the mind. The inward idea that something was mine would not be enough to make it my property. It had to be embodied and recognised by others. As Donna Dickenson argues, 'our individuality has to be created', and property was the first arena of interaction with the world outside the self.[17] In Hegel's version of self-ownership, an individual's property in their person was not given to them by God as a natural right, as it was in Locke's scheme. Instead, a person had to take possession of his own self, becoming his own property and no one else's. His self-consciousness was established as his own, and as owned by him. This meant that 'property in one's own person is to be achieved not assumed'.[18] In this process of achieving possession of myself, 'I take possession of my personality, of my substantive essence, and make myself a responsible being', capable of possessing rights and of leading a moral and religious life.[19] The relationship of possessing was expressed through interaction, recognition and responsibility, and 'the abstract identity of persons is replaced by the concrete identity of mutually recognizing selves'.[20]

Hegel moved from this social version of self-ownership to analyse the individual's interaction with the world. Other persons were always present. Once the individual had taken possession of himself, he was able to alienate his property and yield it to the will of another. By making himself exist as a person with rights and moral principles, the individual began to create the conditions for social recognition and a social world. For Hegel, it was through property that individuals created their imagined community. Social existence presupposed proprietorship: 'We create a social world by imposing our wills onto things which have themselves no purposes, and possessing them.'[21] The projection of our will required 'an objective destination beyond ourselves'.[22] That destination could only be another person. Property was not only about the relationship between subject and object, but also about this 'relation of will to will'.[23] This relation took property beyond the immobility of things, and into the arena of interaction with other selves. The relationship of possessing started with the self, but for Hegel could not end there. The relation of will to will created the sphere of contract. Contract presupposed that the parties entering into it 'recognize each other as persons and property owners'.[24]

This relationship of recognition complicated the idea of property and made it both a force for fragmentation and for overcoming that fragmentation. Freedom, for Hegel, was about separation and individuality, but it immediately had a social aspect. In Hegel's account, property was not based on our physical natures, or our material needs, but was part of our consciousness. This meant that property was 'a chief source of individuality'[25] and a powerful differentiating force in human society. The idea of self-ownership in Hegel's account made clear that the individual could only own herself, and not anyone else. In this sense, the personality of the will stood out against the world as a single subjectivity, and fragmented the self away from the world of nature. There was a degree of radical separation, but at the same time, property became a bond, 'an extension of the notion of *relationship* rather than *appropriation*'.[26] Possession may have been a differentiating force, but property, expressed through alienation and contract, bound individuals together. It gave individuals a concrete identity and mutual recognition, expressed through social sanctions. Hegel justified property in terms of self-development and experience of the external world. The sole route to individual autonomy and self-sufficiency was through the recognition of others who also possessed self-consciousness. Property as a right had to be recognised and incorporated into the normative order. Seyla Benhabib quotes from Claude Levi-Strauss to make the point that goods were not only economic commodities, 'but vehicles and instruments of an other order of reality: strength, power, sympathy, status and emotions'.[27] Property created special bonds of obligation and reciprocity.

These special bonds meant that, for Hegel, property had a humanising effect, connecting individuals to one another. This 'other order of reality', though, was not created without a struggle. It was central to Hegel's theory that individuals acted in and through the world. Through their productivity, individuals 'confront, transform and learn from external reality'.[28]

In the new commercial and industrialised world, the self aimed to control what it experienced as the external world, and sought a sense of self that was not embedded in nature or tied to the land, but was defined in terms of social and historical purposes. Under these new conditions, 'the self must prove its freedom not in a world of nature but in a world inhabited by other persons'.[29] Like the individual in conservative ideology, each person was set up against nature, himself and others, and so lived in the web of three kinds of opposition. There was a great deal at stake here. Hegel's social conception of self-ownership meant that self-consciousness existed only in being acknowledged by another self-consciousness. This required the complex process of recognition. Recognition was rooted in the desire for self-certainty, to achieve despotic dominion by overcoming the other. Because people did not live in radical isolation from one another, each of them wished to see their selfhood reflected back to them in another person. For Hegel, this led immediately to a confrontation because 'each of us wants recognition from the other, but sees no reason to recognize the other'.[30] The danger was that if he attested to the independent existence of the other, he threatened his own self-certainty, his own independent existence. Each self operated on the presumption that they were absolute, and it was a shock for the self to find itself 'othered', to discover that it was not universal, but particular.[31] Each was certain of its own self 'but not of the other, and therefore its own self-certainty still has no truth.'[32] Individuality proved to be disorientating.

In Hegel's argument, the desire for recognition inevitably generated the *battle* for recognition. If it were the case that individuals lived in radical separation and isolation, and then they found themselves confronted by another person, the result would be a duel that was bound to end in death. The recognition they required from one another would be unsustainable because it would have to be absolute. However, since Hegel's theory was expressive rather than defensive, and his version of self-ownership had a social element, he argued that the life-and-death struggle for recognition could be made social. He presented the institution of slavery as a way of socialising the fear of death. In his account, the master–slave dialectic was an advance over 'the sheer slaughter that would take place if the desire for recognition had remained absolute and unqualified'.[33] Coercion and violence were restrained and institutionalised and the inequality of recognition was transformed into lordship and bondage. The master's independence was the basis of the slave's dependence because the slave preferred survival to death, and 'sinks to the level of a mere commodity, not only for the master but also for himself'.[34] Having sunk to this level, the slave no longer existed, and by negating the slave's existence the master seemed to have solved the problem of recognition. The slave could not negate the master, and the master's existence was enhanced by the slave because another person lives through him and by him.[35] The fear of the master imposed discipline on the slave, who lost his individual will in serving the master. The master could then interpose the slave between himself and the world, and win the recognition of the slave. The slave was fixed in his dependence on the master, and this became the first form of human dependence that could be understood as social.[36]

In Hegel's account of the master–slave relationship, however, the slave's abject dependence created an impasse. The problem was that the lord now achieved his recognition through another consciousness, but that other consciousness was dependent and uncertain of the truth of himself. The slave, sunk to being a commodity, offered only a worthless, coerced and inauthentic recognition to the master. In the experience of slavery, the self-consciousness of the bondsman 'has been quite un-manned, has trembled in every fibre of its being, and everything solid and stable has been shaken to its foundations'.[37] The slave was not genuinely an other; he had become merely an extension of the master and so he could not offer the truth of self-certainty to the master. His recognition did not count because 'the recognition that stems from domination is a fraud'.[38] The master depended on the slave and struggled with him for a sense of self. The battle for recognition was not won by either of them.

In Hegel's account, this impasse was overcome because the master–slave relationship was transformed by work. The master did not labour himself, but remained idle. This takes us back to Gerrard Winstanley's point about hired labour. It was damaging not only because the slave sank to the level of a commodity, but also because the master was left without labour to forge a sense of self. When masters lived at ease off the labours of their slaves, they 'receive all they have from the labourer's hand, and what they give, they give away other men's labours, not their own'.[39] The slave transformed the world through his own labour, and the possibility of liberation lay in this transformation. Unlike the master, who lived at ease off the labour of others, the slave worked on someone else's behalf, and gave away his own labour. At the same time, the slave achieved mastery over nature by objectifying himself in the products of his work. The bondsman struggled with the world, rather than living at ease off it. In Hegel's account, this labour and struggle with the external world and with the self was central to subjectivity: 'The propertyless gain greater agency and self-development from their labour in the external world than do men who rely on property to protect them *from* the external world of work.'[40] In his productivity, the slave rediscovered himself and 'the bondsman realizes that it is precisely in his work wherein he seemed to have only an alienated existence that he acquires a mind of his own', a kind of freedom in his servitude.[41]

This idea of 'freedom in servitude' was a very different conclusion from Winstanley's, and was central to Hegel's theory of property. For Hegel, freedom was located in intersubjectivity, and while this was distorted in the relationship between master and slave, this intersubjectivity was central to property relations. This reflected the social dimension of Hegel's idea of self-ownership, and his insistence that 'there is no self apart from the dynamics of recognition'.[42] Freedom was not about the capacity to exclude others, but was located in relationships and recognition. Property had to be socially recognised and sanctioned: it could only exist in the context of social relations that made taking possession legitimate. Recognition 'implies the existence of other persons actively involved in the constitution of my property relationships'.[43] It created a responsibility in others to acknowledge and respect my property. Owning property involved a claim to entitlement, and that claim brought with it a claim for integration into a normative order of rights and duties. In Hegel's argument, through the institutional recognition of property, contract and exchange 'I am seen and see myself to be an agent', capable of owning, contracting and being accountable to others.[44] Freedom required this accountability; liberty needed restrictions, freedom and duty relied on civil society for their fullest expression. Property and civil society unfolded together.

Hegel's social view of self-ownership and property meant that his theory did not have isolated, abstract individuals as its starting point. Such abstraction would disconnect individuals from one another, from history and from nature. Instead, Hegel argued that individuals lived within a web of attachments, as interacting, mutually recognising selves. Freedom and belonging were inextricable, and individuals were part of an ethical community structured by the family, civil society and the state. Ethical life in Hegel's theory was structured by the unity of the family, the division of civil society and the relation of the state. In each phase, intersubjectivity and the relation between freedom and servitude were expressed in different ways. The family, based on love, was an intimate intersubjective unity. Marriage, for Hegel, was an essentially ethical relationship, where both the husband and the wife were conscious of the union as an indissoluble end in itself. Each consented to constitute a single person, to give up their natural and individual personalities to this union. They found themselves in another person, through reciprocal recognition and spiritual union.[45] Hegel insisted that not all relationships between individuals were contractual relationships. Some relationships required the cancellation and transcendence of the standpoint of contract and the sacrifice of personality. They emphasised instead feeling and community. The family was a natural ethical community, based on an inner notion of the ethical order.[46] In the relationship between husband and wife, one consciousness immediately recognised itself in the other, and this mutual recognition was natural and not contractual. It did not move them away from nature and towards society. The self and its personality was not negated or alienated, ' it gains itself back in union with another person'.[47]

The law of the family was an implicit, inner essence, and so was exempt from existence in the real world because it did not involve a struggle. The ethical life of the wife, her substantive destiny, lay in the family. Her vocation, her individuality and her pleasure all centred on the family and the household.[48] For her husband, however, this natural, passive, inner notion of the ethical order was not enough. Women engaged in 'a more peaceful process of unfolding whose principle is the more indeterminate unity of feeling'.[49] Men's substantive destinies lay elsewhere and could only be achieved through a less peaceful process of fighting their way to self-subsistent unity through labour and struggle with the external world, 'because it is only as a citizen that he is actual and substantial, the individual, so far as he is not a citizen but belongs to the Family, is only an unreal impotent shadow'.[50] The family as a legal entity in relation to others was represented by the husband as its head. In Hegel's theory, it was his prerogative to go out and work for its living, attend to its needs, and control its capital. His wife remained in the shadowy 'nether world' of the family.[51] Her mind had nothing to struggle against and so maintained itself in unity. Her knowledge took the form of concrete individuality and feeling, and 'once she enters the marital bond for which her whole life is destined, she never leaves the family'.[52] She never entered civil society, the sphere of property and struggle with the external world.[53]

Civil society was 'the phase of division', a battlefield: it 'tears an individual from his family ties, estranges the members of the family from one another, and recognizes them as self-subsistent persons'.[54] The individual man was 'a son of civil society', made up of private persons whose end was their own interest.[55] Robert Williams argues that this means that it was based on 'universal egoism and reciprocal exploitation'.[56] Individuals interacted with others, but only out of necessity. They satisfied their needs in relation to others, but these other people remained impenetrable to them. Civil society was not a genuine, cohesive society. It was particularity indulging itself, encouraging self-sufficient individualism and private interests: 'Thus it spawns and legitimates an atomistic principle that abandons all individuals to contingency.'[57] Conservatives saw in this the disorientation of individualism, the ways in which individuals were 'unroofed' and robbed of a harmony between themselves and the world.

Civil society was thus a risky venture, and the particularity and contingency it spawned needed to be overcome. The state welded these separate sons of civil society together into a universal order orientated towards public life and unity. The system of private property was therefore part of individuality and separation, but also a necessary stage on the way to universality. In civil society, individuals became concrete persons with particular aims, wants and needs, but they were never entirely separate, in the sense that they escaped each other; 'the particular person is essentially so related to other particular persons that each establishes himself and finds satisfaction by means of others'.[58] Individuals were selfish and self-seeking, but their selfish ends formed a system of complete interdependence 'wherein the livelihood, happiness and legal status of one man is interwoven with the livelihood, happiness and rights of all'.[59] This interdependence, however, was an intermediate stage – universality remained the final end.

This society of self-interested, private persons engaged in civil and economic life, and so '[made] themselves links in this chain of social connexions' by choosing a vocation, becoming a corporation member, joining a class. It was through this process of engagement and connection that their particularity was transformed into a new kind of subjectivity that was not empty or self-enclosed, or based on their immediate desires and inclinations.[60] Particular interests were developed and recognised and then passed over into the interest of the universal. In Hegel's theory, the mechanism for this transformation was work. Men were dependent on and reciprocally related to one another in their work and the satisfaction of their needs; 'subjective self-seeking turns into a contribution to the satisfaction of the needs of everyone else'.[61] Civil society thus involved a complex interdependence of each on all, with everyone involved in 'infinitely complex, criss-cross, movements of reciprocal production and exchange'.[62] Their integration into this criss-crossed system of inter-dependencies meant that individuals gained recognition in their own eyes and in the eyes of others. They found that they held ethical dispositions, values and interests in common with others in their estate, and these were institutionalised in corporation membership. As members of a particular trade or profession individuals expressed their concern for the welfare of others and for the common good of society. It was this system of pro-duction and exchange that crystallised into estates and classes, and eventually created the universal state.

The emphasis on the welfare of the co-operative created a sense of belonging to a corporate whole with a shared identity. Their activities were specifically recognised as part of society's ethical life, and public recognition required corporations. Corporations brought with them collec-tive responsibility, a sense of identity and honour and the assurance of economic security. Without such integration, an individual engaged in trade was isolated, selfish, unstable and lacking in 'the honour of his estate'. The individual by himself was 'empty, formal, indeterminate, lacking substance or purpose'.[63] He became a 'freelance hustler of what-ever resources, skills or other commodities I may have for sale. My destiny is simply to sell myself'.[64] Such 'freelance hustlers' found that their self-worth was determined by their market price. They had no determinate self-identity and no self-satisfaction. They found themselves with 'no proper bounds or measures for my life'. Instead, 'my participation in civil society is reduced to boundless individual self-seeking, which is self-defeating by its very nature because it can never lead to happiness or self-actualization'.[65]

Existence in civil society required individuals who were conscious of themselves as engaged in activities whose objective worth was recognised by others. As members of civil society, individuals possessed civil rights. These rights gave individuals the feeling of counting as a person. Diffi-culties arose and social conflicts were created where such objective worth was not recognised, and those without civil rights were not granted the feeling of counting as a person. The poor were not incorporated into guilds, their work was casual and intermittent and so they were denied social standing, membership and salvation from particularity. They were abandoned to contingency and self-seeking as hustlers and scavengers on the face of the earth, hedged out of civil society and denied the humanising possibilities of property ownership.

– THE PROBLEM OF POVERTY –

By the 1830s and 1840s, the problem of pauperism had become a pressing social question. Early nineteenth-century Germany included two kinds of poor. The traditional, incorporated poor belonged to a guild or a landlord and so to civil society. They were entitled to support from guild, master and charitable institutions. The 'unincorporated poor', the scavengers and hustlers who were 'outsiders to the social order', were coming to constitute the majority of the population: in Prussia in 1846, they made up two-thirds of the population.[66] The development of a modern economy meant the spread of property rights and the dispossession of the poor as their access to land was denied. They were not only economically deprived, but were also 'cut adrift from the culture in which they live', to become a 'rabble of paupers'.[67] For Hegel, the misery of the poor man was a result of 'his exclusion from the physical and ethical benefits of society'.[68] Without corporation membership, they were isolated from one another. Their failure to belong, their status as trespassers and fugitives, meant that they had no grounds from which to establish their self-respect and no means to inspire the respect of others. The poor were bound to remain trespassers. Poverty, for Hegel, was about relative deprivation. The poor were cut off from the advantages of society such as skills, education and access to justice – all the mediating activities and institutions that linked people to the social order. 'Bereft of these mediating links, men become estranged' from themselves and from one another.[69] The result of this estrangement was alienation and social hostility, generated by the structures of modern society.

This was exacerbated by the pressures of industrial society. For Hegel, the workings of the system of needs with private property and wage labour led to capital, and the development of capital brought with it the creation of new social groups – the very rich and the very poor. In Hegel's conception of property, individuality and civil society, everyone had to own property. The successful separation of man and nature required everyone to participate in recognising each other as agents. Property, however, had to be distributed unequally 'because humans are different and because ethical life requires variety and differentiation'.[70] Poverty posed problems for Hegel, bringing with it misery, suffering, anxiety and ethical degeneration. It needed to be mitigated by social institutions and its effects mediated by civil society and the state. For those living in civil society, there was room for modern individuality and the means to limit it. The individuality and particularity of civil society was 'constantly on the verge of going too far' and destroying itself. The division of labour, for example, alienated an entire portion of the population, 'pushing it outside the reach of ethical life and making it susceptible to coordination only through force and coercion'.[71] The dislocations that civil society created for itself made the comprehensive state necessary.

Hegel argued that in the state, duty and right were identical in form but different in content. The individual fulfilled his duties by performing tasks and services for the state, and in doing so reached a new level of self-consciousness, 'the consciousness that my interest, both substantive and particular, is contained and preserved in another's (in the state's) interest and end.'[72] Habitual recognition of the community became the substantive end of the individual who had fought his way to unity with himself. The role of the state was to lift men's consciousness above the level of competing interests in civil society to this recognition of shared community that transcended particular interests.[73] This idea of the universal, transcendent state informs one strand of conservatism with its focus on freedom in servitude, and the inextricability of freedom and belonging.

For Marx, in direct contrast to Hegel, the state was bound to reflect the conflicts and the particular interests of civil society rather than mediate or transcend them. The estates were intrinsically at odds with the supposed universality of the state. It served the interests of the bourgeois modern society to turn the state into an abstraction, to promote the illusion of a shared community, so that it could then make the abstract claim that its citizens were free. For Marx, there was no transcendental moment of transformation. The state arose from civil society. Man as he was in civil society determined the nature of the state, and man in civil society was 'man determined by property rights'.[74] This obsession with exclusive private property filtered through to legislation: the Diet legislated in its own interest, the interest of private property, and then proposed its legislation to the state. In Marx's view, the Prussian state then legislated in the interests of the estates, descending to the level of private interests, in contrast to Hegel's vision of the state welding individuals to a universal order.

The Marxian project was 'an attempt from the first to found an empirically grounded and practical science of society, rather than a speculative inversion of a ready-made philosophical world-view'.[75] This meant that Marx had to take account of the social and political dimensions of property and propertylessness, poverty and penury. The poor were not naturally without property, but were being made propertyless through the historical process of transforming feudal into modern property. As civil society created property, it also made the poor poor. The relation of the poor to civil society was one of differentiation and exclusion: 'The poor are identified as the negative embodiment of precisely that of which civil society is the positive embodiment: rights of exclusive private (modern) property.'[76] The poor and the propertied, in Marx's view, were related to each other through the consolidation of exclusive property and the accompanying process of dispossession. They were involved in '*an active process of existential and thus reciprocal self-differentiation*: the propertied have made the expropriated what they are'.[77]

The Sixth Rhenish Diet of 1842 demonstrated how the problem of pauperism had become a social and political question. The Diet proposed a new law on thefts of wood, depriving the poor of their customary right to gather windfallen wood for fuel. The new legislation echoed the Black Acts and Winstanley's claim that 'woodmongers' and rich freeholders were robbing the poor. Gathering dead wood was alleged to damage live trees and to facilitate poaching. It was proposed to revise the law to make the taking of windfallen wood a criminal offence. Marx presented the issue as one of conflicting property rights, where the customary rights of the poor to certain products of the earth were opposed to the exclusive property rights of the owners of the woods and forests, the rich free-holders. Marx argued that the poor were being dispossessed by civil society and its laws. The unity suggested by Hegel was an impossibility; it was bound to be pulled apart by the social realities of class and poverty. Capitalist private property was the basis of 'a class-based intersubjectivity characterised by struggle'.[78] It was a struggle based on 'conquest, enslavement, robbery, murder, in short, force'.[79] In the process, the place of the poor as 'fellow members of *human* society' (fellow creatures in Winstanley's terms) was being lost from sight.[80]

The process of dispossession encouraged the estates to act out of self-seeking, private and particular material interests. Exclusive private property, Marx argued, had made them inhuman and inhumane, prepared to sacrifice human beings for trees, in the same way as the Black Acts sacrificed human livelihoods for deer, requiring the same mental distance and moral levity. Marx contrasted 'the inherent humanity of simple natives with the property-fetishism of the members of the Diet'.[81] Property was dehumanising, disconnecting individuals from one another and their common humanity. In Marx's view, the unincorporated poor represented 'humanity in its elementary form, untainted by the distorting, dehumanizing effect which exclusive private property has on human beings.'[82] He argued that the state ought to see the poor's right as universal and make room for their global, social right as members of the universal human society and their human nature as productive. The propertied members of civil society made property rights sacrosanct and by doing so they became incapable of humanity and a sense of universal right. The capitalist 'is sunk into his external existence and unable to extract himself from his property'.[83] Private property polarised society into civil society and proletarian outsiders. Marx argued that this was the result of the process of primitive accumulation, the expropriation of the peasant from the soil, the moment 'when great masses of men are suddenly and forcibly torn from their means of subsistence, and hurled onto the labour-market as free, unprotected and rightless proletarians'.[84] They were all destined to be hustlers and scavengers and to sell themselves. The proletarian outsiders were elementary humans who acted from an instinctive sense of right, like 'the untutored natives of distant lands'.[85] Through property, elementary humans were being transformed into mercenaries.

– Marx and Alienation –

In Marx's account, private property could never be sacrosanct. It was always a distortion, always dehumanising. Unlike Hegel's theory of connection and recognition brought about through property, Marx saw property as fundamentally *disconnecting* individuals from one another and from themselves, and so as essentially alienating. Hegel and Marx shared an emphasis on the importance of labour for notions of honour, freedom and belonging, but Marx denied the possibility of 'freedom in servitude'. His conclusion was much closer to Winstanley's, that wage labour was inherently corrupting and needed to be abolished. Labour itself was productive and creative. It was through labour that people transformed the natural world and it was this transformation of environment that 'inaugurates human history'.[86] This meant that, for Marx, modern bourgeois society 'contained within itself the seeds of its own redemption'[87] – not through improvement and the spread of proprietorship but through the reclamation of labour as a genuinely human and productive activity. Through their honourable labour, elementary humans could overcome the polarisation and the disconnection of property and civil society and build a genuinely human society.

Hegel's view that property was an external projection of our will into an interpersonal space meant that he saw property as entailing consciousness rather than material being.[88] In contrast, for Marx alienation was a material process. Humans created things out of nature, and eventually came to be dominated by things: 'The more the worker externalizes himself in his work, the more powerful becomes the alien, objective world that he creates opposite himself, the poorer he becomes himself in his inner life and the less he can call his own.'[89] The worker was externalised in his product, and his labour came to exist outside him as an independent, hostile and alien power. Under capitalist relations, there was no reciprocal web of recognition, no institutional setting for property which could help us towards self-certainty. Alienation 'was thus the externalization of human creativity into forms which not only obscured but denied their human, creative origins'.[90]

The more the worker produced, the less he had to consume: 'the more values he creates the more valueless and worthless he becomes'.[91] Both he and his products became unrecognisable. As work became more powerful, the worker became more powerless and, for Marx, more barbaric. Rather as Winstanley argued, labour was forced and external, and so no longer belonged to the worker: 'He does not belong to himself in his labour but to someone else.'[92] Work was no longer his own spontaneous, creative activity, but instead was independent of him and directed against him. For Marx, it was work as a vital activity and a central part of productive life that made man a species-being. Alienated labour 'reverses the relationship so that, just because he is a conscious being, man makes his vital activity and essence a mere means to his existence'.[93] In this dehumanising version of Hegel's process, the individual was alienated from his own body, from nature and from his human essence.

The objectification of labour, its estrangement from the labourer and its independent existence implied that if it had ceased to belong to the worker it could belong to someone else. It had become an object, and the same process created a new class of owners. It was not that the property-less gained greater agency and self-control, but that they turned their productivity into a loss by giving greater agency to the propertied: 'Just as he turns his production into his own loss of reality and punishment and his own product into a loss, a product that does not belong to him, so he creates the domination of the man who does not produce over the production and the product.'[94] There was no freedom in this servitude. Labour was extracted as profit from the wage of employees by the capitalist. Those profits were then used to create more capital through investment. Capital was command over labour. The labourer working for a capitalist increased the total amount of capital available, and so found that his labour and his life escaped his control, and independent existence was impossible. This was the structure of alienation, a 'distortion of human productive activity'.[95]

In Marxist theory, private property was the necessary consequence of externalised labour, and the whole of human slavery involved the relationship of the worker to his product. All slave relationships were modifications of this central relationship. Private property was exterior to man, not a condition of humanness nor an expression of the social instinct. It was an expression of the fact that man had lost himself and become 'a hostile and inhuman object to himself'.[96] Private property 'dissociates our creations from their social and human context' so that they came to have value only in terms of money.[97] It was a force for tearing people apart, not an element in the dynamics of recognition. Under a money system everything, including labour, lost human value and came to represent the amount of money it could fetch in the market. Sociability and creativity were obscured from view by the immobility of property.

For Marx, this was a distortion that had to be overcome. Communism was the positive expression of overcoming private property, a genuine solution for the antagonism between individuals and nature and between individuals, 'the real reappropriation of the human essence by and for man'.[98] In a genuinely communist society, work would be a free expression of life, a way of affirming the uniqueness of individuality: 'Work would thus be genuine, active property.'[99] Private property meant that activity was so far externalised from the individual that it had become a torment to her, imposed on her by an exterior, arbitrary need. The abolition of private property would mean the abolition of alienation. Private property made us stupid and narrowminded: 'all the physical and intellectual senses have been replaced by the simple alienation of all these senses, the sense of having.'[100] Acquisitiveness was not part of the hard core of human nature, but a distortion. As William Godwin argued, the powers of thought were trodden in the dust, and established property rights accustomed people to the sight of injustice and oppression. It became an unspoken and unquestionable assumption that private property was the optimum system for satisfying need. Elementary humans were pulled into the market, and the power relations between them were concealed by the mechanisms of private property and contractual exchange. People are deceived by the 'apparent mercenariness' of mankind into regarding accumulation as their final end, and the younger brother lets go of his hold on the earth. The question of whether this 'mercenariness' and the 'sense of having' are apparent or real resurfaces everywhere in ideological accounts of the relationship between private property and human nature.

– CONCLUSION –

For Hegel, property was a source of creativity and individuality, an expression of an individual's relationship to himself, to others and to the world. The apparent immobility of property was shadowed by activity, by work and by interaction. Property relationships appeared as dynamic – individualising and isolating and at the same time binding, carrying the promise of overcoming fragmentation, bringing men and nature back together, achieving a kind of alchemy: 'the magic of property turns sand into gold'.[101] Understanding property as action, as attached to the will, immediately raises the question of who counts as a creative and self-conscious individual, who has achieved property in their own person?

For Hegel, the answer was connected to individual agency, recognition and ethical incorporation into civil society. The individual was a member of a corporation, an agent who was part of a complex web of recognition. Hegel required the institutions of civil society, and a vision of inter-dependence, to provide the institutional setting for the achievement of individuality and identity. For Hegel, property was developmental, educative and identity-creating. Some were left outside its sphere: the poor presented a problem, freelance hustlers remained boundlessly self-seeking. Women remained in the shadowy world of the family. Property involved membership of civil society, and so its opposite implied non-membership and barbarity. Hegel's theory was about relationship, development, experience and agency and at the same time about the primacy of separation and conflict.

For Marx, private property was never an expression of individuality and creativity; it had to be a distortion of the productivity of human nature. Capitalism demanded that individuals become hirelings, 'a degraded and almost servile condition of the mass of the people, their transformation into mercenaries, and the transformation of their means of labour into capital'.[102] Capital was dehumanising, and part of the process was that it led people to mistake civil society for human society, not recognising the distorting effects of private property, the narrowing effects of alienation, the futility of their struggles with the external world. The solution to such distortion, for Marx, could never be more private property. Property had to be socialised to allow individuals to overcome obstacles, master nature and realise their manifold capacities. Work was developing and liberating, labour offered the possibility of self-realisation. Without private property, people would cease to be mercenaries, connected only to civil society, and become individuals, members of a fully human society.

In the nineteenth century, and specifically in the colonial context, the connections between property and humanity came to the fore. The conflict between civil society and human society, the problem of poverty and propertylessness, and the role of the state in resolving or reflecting the conflicts of civil society and the interests of the propertied were all crucial political questions. The understanding of property as central to individuality and subjectivity gave the same questions an ethical and moral dimension, and the structures of imperial thought meant that debates about property as civilising or dehumanising were anything but abstract. They underpinned ideas not only about class and capital, but also about slavery, empire, gender and race. The poor and the 'untutored natives of distant lands' were drawn into the complex web of recognition, an intersubjectivity based on struggle and a nexus of work and interaction hidden behind the immobility of property as a thing. The next three chapters looks at how the complex relations between individuality, freedom and property were filtered through the ideologies of liberalism, socialism and conservatism. The final chapters return to questions about slavery, empire, gender and race.

– NOTES –

1. Iain Hampsher-Monk, A History of Modern Political Thought (Oxford: Blackwell, 1992), passim.
2. Bernard Cullen, 'Hegel's Historical Phenomenology and Social Analysis', in David Lamb (ed.), Hegel and Modern Philosophy (London: Croom Helm, 1987), p. 2.
3. Peter G. Stillman, 'Property, Freedom and Individuality in Hegel's and Marx's Political Thought', in J. Roland Pennock and John W. Chapman (eds), Nomos XXII: Property (New York: New York University Press, 1980), p. 130.
4. Heinz Lubasz, 'Marx's Initial Problematic: the Problem of Poverty', Political Studies XXIV:1, 1977, p. 34.
5. Stillman, 'Property, Freedom and Individuality', p. 138.

6. Ursula Vogel, 'The Land Question: A Liberal Theory of Communal Property', *History Workshop* 27, Spring 1989, p. 126.
7. Robert Heilbroner, *The Worldly Philosophers* (Harmondsworth: Penguin, 1988), p. 61.
8. Ibid. p. 63.
9. Cullen, 'Hegel's Historical Phenomenology', p. 2.
10. G. W. F. Hegel, *The Philosophy of Right*, tr. T. M. Cox (Oxford: Oxford University Press, [1821] 1967), § 39.
11. Hampsher-Monk, *A History of Modern Political Thought*, p. 432.
12. Alan Ryan, 'Hegel on Work, Ownership and Citizenship', in Z. A. Pelczynski (ed.), *The State and Civil Society* (Cambridge: Cambridge University Press, 1984), p. 185.
13. Ibid. p. 190.
14. Seyla Benhabib, 'Obligation, Contract and Exchange: on the Significance of Hegel's Abstract Right', in Pelczynski (ed.), *The State and Civil Society*, p. 172.
15. Ryan, 'Hegel on Work', p. 187.
16. Hegel, *Philosophy of Right*, § 47, p. 43.
17. Donna Dickenson, *Property, Women and Politics* (Cambridge: Polity Press, 1997), p. 97.
18. Joan B. Landes, 'Hegel's Conception of the Family', *Polity* 14, 1981, p. 9.
19. Hegel, *Philosophy of Right*, § 66, p. 53.
20. Benhabib, 'Obligation, Contract and Exchange', p. 170.
21. Hampsher-Monk, *History of Political Thought*, p. 432.
22. Ibid. p. 431.
23. Hegel, *Philosophy of Right*, § 71, p. 57.
24. Ibid. § 71, p. 57.
25. Raymond Plant, 'Hegel and Political Economy', *New Left Review*, 103–4, 1977, p. 87.
26. Dickenson, *Property, Women and Politics*, p. 92.
27. Benhabib, 'Obligation, Contract and Exchange', p. 162.
28. Dickenson, *Property, Women and Politics*, p. 135.
29. Cynthia Willett, *Maternal Ethics and Other Slave Moralities* (New York and London: Routledge, 1995), p. 111.
30. Allen W. Wood, *Hegel's Ethical Thought* (Cambridge: Cambridge University Press, 1990), p. 86.
31. Robert R. Williams, *Hegel's Ethics of Recognition* (Berkeley: University of California Press, 1997), passim.
32. G. W. F. Hegel, *Phenomenology of Spirit*, tr. A. V. Miller (Oxford: Clarendon Press, [1807] 1977), p. 113.
33. Williams, *Hegel's Ethics of Recognition*, p. 61.
34. Ibid. p. 62.
35. Orlando Patterson, *Slavery and Social Death: a Comparative Study* (Cambridge, MA and London: Harvard University Press, 1982), p. 98.
36. J. M. Bernstein, 'From Self-Consciousness to Community: Act and Recognition in the Master–Slave Relationship', in Pelczynski, *State and Civil Society*, p. 23.
37. Hegel, *Phenomenology of Spirit*, §194, p. 117.
38. Willett, *Maternal Ethics*, p. 116.
39. Gerrard Winstanley, 'The Law of Freedom in a Platform', in Christopher Hill, *Winstanley: The Law of Freedom* (Harmondsworth: Penguin, [1651] 1973), p. 287.
40. Dickenson, *Property, Women and Politics*, p. 99.
41. Hegel, *Phenomenology of Spirit*, §196, p. 119.
42. Willett, *Maternal Ethics*, p. 120.

43. F. R. Christi, 'Hegel on Possession and Property', *Canadian Journal of Social and Political Theory* 2, 1978, p. 115.
44. William E. Connolly, *Political Theory and Modernity* (Oxford: Blackwell, 1988), p. 117.
45. Williams, *Hegel's Ethics of Recognition*, pp. 211–12.
46. Hegel, *Phenomenology of Spirit*, § 450, p. 270.
47. Williams, *Hegel's Ethics of Recognition*, p. 213.
48. Hegel, *Phenomenology of Spirit*, § 457, p. 274.
49. Williams, *Hegel's Ethics of Recognition*, p. 221. Williams is quoting from what Hegel is reported to have said in a student note.
50. Hegel, *Phenomenology of Spirit*, § 451, p. 270.
51. Ibid. § 460, p. 276.
52. Landes, 'Hegel's Conception of the Family', p. 21.
53. Dickenson, *Property, Women and Politics,* p. 110.
54. Hegel, *Philosophy of Right*, § 256, p. 155.
55. Ibid. § 238, p. 148.
56. Williams, *Hegel's Ethics of Recognition*, p. 233.
57. Ibid. p. 242.
58. Hegel, *Philosophy of Right*, § 182, pp. 122–3.
59. Ibid. §183, p. 123.
60. Ibid. §187, p. 124.
61. Ibid. §199, p. 129.
62. Ibid. §210, p. 130.
63. Williams, *Hegel's Ethics of Recognition*, p. 255.
64. Wood, *Hegel's Ethical Thought*, p. 241.
65. Ibid. p. 242.
66. Lubasz, 'Marx's Initial Problematic', p. 27.
67. Hampsher-Monk, *History of Modern Political Thought*, p. 457.
68. Stillman, 'Property, Freedom and Individuality', p. 147.
69. Raymond Plant, 'Hegel and Political Economy II', *New Left Review*, 104, 1977, p. 112.
70. Stillman, 'Property, Freedom and Individuality', p. 144.
71. Connolly, *Political Theory and Modernity*, p. 119.
72. Hegel, *Philosophy of Right*, § 268, p. 164.
73. Hampsher-Monk, *History of Modern Political Thought*, p. 469.
74. Ibid. p. 493.
75. Lubasz, 'Marx's Initial Problematic', p. 25.
76. Ibid. p. 41.
77. Ibid. p. 41.
78. Stillman, 'Property, Freedom and Individuality', p. 154.
79. Karl Marx, *Capital*, Vol. I (Harmondsworth: Penguin, [1890–4] 1976), p. 874.
80. Lubasz, 'Marx's initial problematic', p. 30.
81. Ibid. p. 31.
82. Ibid. p. 31.
83. Stillman, 'Property, Freedom and Individuality', p. 151.
84. Marx, *Capital*, Vol. I, p. 876.
85. Lubasz, 'Marx's Initial Problematic', p. 31.
86. Plant, 'Hegel and Political Economy', p. 84.
87. Ibid. p. 85.
88. Hampsher-Monk, *History of Modern Political Thought*, pp. 432–3.

89. Karl Marx, 'Economic and Philosophical Manuscripts', in David McLellan (ed.), *Karl Marx: Selected Writings* (Oxford: Oxford University Press, 2000), p. 87.
90. Hampsher-Monk, *History of Modern Political Thought*, p. 499.
91. Marx, 'Economic and Philosophical Manuscripts', p. 88.
92. Ibid. p. 89.
93. Ibid. p. 90.
94. Ibid. p. 92.
95. Hampsher-Monk, *History of Modern Political Thought*, p. 503.
96. Marx, 'Private Property and Communism', in McLellan, *Selected Writings*, p. 99.
97. Hampsher-Monk, *History of Modern Political Thought*, p. 501.
98. Marx, 'Private Property and Communism', p. 97.
99. Marx, 'On James Mill', in McLellan, *Selected Writings*, p. 132.
100. Marx, 'Private Property and Communism', p. 100.
101. John Robson, 'Civilization and Culture as Moral Concepts', in John Skorupski (ed.), *The Cambridge Companion to Mill* (Cambridge: Cambridge University Press, 1998), p. 358. Mill, in his *Principles of Political Economy*, quoting from Arthur Young's *Travels in France*.
102. Marx, *Capital*, Vol. I, p. 881.

CHAPTER 5

Liberalism

Envisaging and understanding relationships based on property and ownership is central to individuality, and to individuals' relationships with each other, civil society and the state. This means that property relations inform the structure of ideologies, and also make clear how contested and fractured those traditions are. The tensions encountered in the debates between John Locke and Gerrard Winstanley, William Godwin and Jeremy Bentham, and G. W. F. Hegel and Karl Marx all resurface in the different strands of thought woven into liberalism, socialism and conservatism. The struggle to deal with the morality of *Recht* (justice), the disorientation of individualism and the mercenariness of humankind (apparent or otherwise) is in part an ideological struggle to come to terms with the appearances and illusions of property, and with the dangers inherent in individualising it. Liberalism, socialism and conservatism all try to work out the implications of understanding property as 'despotic dominion', and to balance the mixture of endowment and anchorage, separation and connection, self-preservation and the common good that underpins any system of property ownership. They return to the question raised by Hegel and Marx, of whether civil society and the state mediate or express the conflicts between individuals. Can property be used to enable individuals to find a footing with others and ground a sense of belonging, or is private property bound to prove dehumanising and disorientating? Is it possible to escape from the contingency and instability of property into the authentic and the essential by abolishing private property, or by anchoring it to natural hierarchies?

Since liberalism does not advocate either abolition or entrenchment of private property, it has to work harder than either socialism or conservatism to find a way of managing the conflicts of private property and negotiating property as a moral space that can protect individuals as self-determining subjects. Liberalism works with the individual as its basic unit, and liberalism has been characterised as '*the* theory of the modern individual'.[1] In response to the rise of capitalism, industrialisation and democracy, and the ways in which they reinforced each other, liberals developed a theory of the individual who would not be lost in the crowd, suffocated by the claustrophobia of society or tyrannised by the majority.[2] Liberalism insisted that individuals need room to expand and flourish, to develop multiple, creative selves in different contexts so that each individual is free to pursue their own good in their own way, to find their own path and to follow it. Individuals are sovereign, over themselves and their own bodies and minds. They are, as John Stuart Mill argued, guardians of their own spiritual, bodily and mental health, the best judges of their own interests and the most concerned in their own actions. The individualism at the heart of liberalism entails a strong version of anti-paternalism, the sense that the individual is sovereign except where her conduct threatens harm to others. Indeed, Mill's 'simple principle' is that the 'only purpose for which power can be rightfully exercised over any member of a civilised community, against his will, is to prevent harm to others'.[3] Unless one individual is likely to harm another, she remains sovereign over herself. This is an important metaphor for liberals. As John Day points out, it means that 'the individual should have ultimate authority over his own life'.[4]

This 'ultimate authority' is bound to have implications for the relationship between liberalism and property, and for the connections between the individual, civil society and the state. The idea of being sovereign over the self brings us to the heart of individualism, and helps us to understand that liberalism has more than one theory of the modern individual. These different theories of how sovereignty over the self operates underpin and inform the different strands of liberalism, and in particular their different interpretations of property, freedom and belonging. One version of individual self-sovereignty, most clearly associated with classical liberalism and libertarianism, equates the individual's ultimate authority over him or herself with self-ownership. The significance of sovereignty, for them, lies in the right to exclude others. In order to own himself, the individual has to have the right not to be invaded by others, and to defend himself, his liberty and his property against those who seek to invade him. On this account of sovereignty over the self, conflict and competition are presupposed as the characteristic mode of interaction between individuals.

The sovereignty metaphor draws attention to the sense of separation between individuals, the ways in which they are cut off from one another. It fosters the importance of protection, insulation, a sense of the danger of invasion and intrusion by others. It works on the assumption of the individual as a bounded space, and invokes the idea of the 'territories of the self'.[5] Respect then becomes acknowledging the territory of a person and implicitly conceding to the concepts of jurisdiction, exclusion and legitimate force loaded into the notion of a territory. This notion of a 'territorial self' reflects a preoccupation with fear, risk and insecurity that feeds into particular constructions of property, the market and the state.[6]

This territorial notion of the individual interprets the idea of sovereignty as despotic dominion. For other liberals, sovereignty is less about the exclusion of others and more about the individual's own agency and subjectivity. Dan Avnon and Avner de-Shalit focus on the creative dimension of the liberal individual, and the promise held out by liberalism that persons create their own lives and enjoy a rich and creative inner life. In this account, each person is a unique human being, 'gifted with innumerable potentialities'.[7] These include the potential to develop in more than one way, to create diverse forms of life, and to react to and reject the authority of external power. This, as Michael Sandel argues, is a liberating vision: 'Freed from the dictates of nature and the sanction of social roles, the human subject is installed as sovereign, cast as the author of the only moral meanings there are.'[8] Individuals are then free to choose their own purposes and ends, and their own principles of justice. In this situation, our conceptions of the good carry weight by virtue of our having chosen them: what is important about our own plan of life is not the plan itself, but that it is our own. The essence of sovereignty involved in this account lies in self-determination, in being a fully self-determining subject. Self-determining subjects, with their innumerable potentialities, will not necessarily regard others as potential invaders and enemies. Their preoccupations are likely to be less concerned with fear, risk and security and more with fostering 'internal pluralism', or the multiple self. The outside is no longer necessarily a threat to the inside, and the particular constructions of property, market and the state that flow from the self-determining subject 'enable external pluralism to enhance, and thereby respect, the internal pluralism of the multiple self'.[9]

The distinction between the territorial and the self-determining notions of the individual brings out some of the tensions within liberalism, and between freedom and belonging. The notions carry with them distinctive ideas of self-respect, honour and degradation and from there different conceptions of conflict, competition and co-operation. One of the important points of difference is in their view of association and co-operation, of how individuals are understood to become members of groups and of civil society. Those who hold a territorial vision of the self value the capacity of individuals to dissociate as well as associate, to avoid fusion and engulfment by insisting on a radical separateness. This brings with it a strong presumption of conflict and competition as the 'human condition'.[10] Those who focus on self-determination tend instead to stress the values of co-operation, trust and inclusion, and to expect cohesion and some form of dependency on the collectivity to win out over outright conflict and competition. Individuals, in this account, have the ultimate authority of sovereignty vested in themselves, but they are also members of the 'civilised community' mentioned by Mill, and are perhaps less despotic in their dominion.

There is, of course, some common ground between these different strands of individualism. Alan Ryan sees a common cluster of liberal values in its opposition to absolutism. The central anti-absolutist liberal claim is that 'absolute rule violates the personality or the rights of those over whom it is exercised.'[11] Liberals are concerned with the limits of authority, especially since for them it cannot be conferred by God or history, but can only come from the individual members of society, and so has to rest on notions of consent and legitimacy. Those within the fortress have to be able to resist invaders, and to invite others in. Self-determining individuals have to have authority over themselves. Absolutism militates against civil society and concentrates power in the hands of the state, and so has to be resisted by all liberals. Private property is an important buttress: monarchs who respect private ownership are bound to govern through consent and taxation rather than by eminent domain and seizing the goods of their subjects. In this sense, property limits power and counters absolutism. This maps onto the division between civil society and the state, and between the private and the public. Liberals will usually want to expand civil society, the market and voluntary associations and protect the private realm from incursions by the state, although this is complicated by twentieth-century liberal concerns to promote the welfare state.

The anti-absolutism of individualism has its origins in the French Revolution, which ended in 1799, with the political influence and power of the aristocracy decisively weakened. The aristocracy lost their privileges based on birth and status, and the French state throughout the nineteenth century consolidated bourgeois values of liberal individualism. Before the mid-nineteenth century, liberal thought in Britain as well as France tended to regard capitalism as emancipatory and anti-aristocratic. It was seen as helping to release individuals from the crushing weight of tradition by insisting on natural rights, individual responsibility and an end to feudal, naturalised hierarchies. For nineteenth-century liberals, the aberrations of private property were associated with the inherited landed wealth of the aristocracy, the 'products of the lawless feudal era'.[12] Landlords were corrupted by the hereditary principle, and by having acquired their lands through conquest rather than labour. Liberal thinkers continued the themes developed in different ways in the thought of Locke, Winstanley and Godwin. The chief abuses of the economic system were identified in the 1860s by liberals as rooted in conquest, the violence with which rights over land had been acquired and exercised, and the continued influence of landlordism, luxury and recklessness, forces that militated against improvement, efficiency and reform. Aristocratic property was characterised as unearned, undeserved and stultifying: it fixed wealth and property in one section of society, so that the ownership of property became 'the badge of a class' rather than an attribute of society.[13] This raised questions about both freedom and belonging. For liberals, aristocratic property and attitudes were fundamentally dishonourable, so that they undermined the possibility of self-respect. Landlords were figured as parasites, who did not rely on their own righteous labour or their active proprietorship of themselves, but lived entirely off the drudgery of others. Aristocratic power rested on a naturalised, fixed hierarchy and on membership of a group. It fixed the criteria of belonging and exclusion, and ignored any questions of desert or fairness. Membership did not rely on co-operation, civility or trust but on privilege. For both territorial and self-determining individualists, capitalism and the market offered a dynamic and progressive alternative. For liberals, market attitudes represented progress, an emancipation from tradition and a move towards a new meaning of liberty based not on privilege and hierarchy, but on the liberty to buy and sell, free from violence, theft and trespass.

– TERRITORIES OF THE SELF –

This construction of the individual as free to buy and sell, as long as she is not trespassed upon or invaded by others, brings us back to the territorial account of the individual and how it connects to the market, to capitalism and so to property. In this account, the sovereignty of the individual over himself, his talents and his property 'is at once the basis of limited government, the rule of law, individual liberty and a capitalist economy'.[14] It is founded in the individual's capacity to be a rational market actor, to buy and sell freely, to co-operate and compete with other separate, but equally self-interested, market actors through the mechanism of contract. The contract is constructed as the opposite of invasion, limited in scope and resting on consent and exchange. Fundamentally competitive people do not seek society for its own sake, but they meet to trade with one another and 'a certain Market-friendship is begotten.'[15] They are dissociated from one another, but through the mechanism of the free market they can create a network of exchange. Contractual relations, enforced by a minimal state, guarantee enough security to allow individuals to buy and sell without fear of invasion.

One outgrowth of the territorial conception of the self was the development of libertarianism, related to liberalism through the concept of liberty. Its two core principles are identified by Michael Freeden as liberty and the restriction of power, and he argues that libertarianism is a 'liberal pretender' and 'not a serious contender for the current mantle of liberalism'.[16] For Ryan, on the other hand, libertarianism is a development of the 'classical variation' of liberalism associated with Locke, Adam Smith and Friedrich von Hayek. I agree with Freeden that libertarianism over-emphasises liberty and breaks significantly from the Millite core of liberalism, and in particular its focus on self-determination within a 'civilised community'. I would not want to argue that liberalism has now become libertarianism. However, we do need to maintain a sense of continuity from Locke, and his focus on owning a property in the person. We need, with C. B. Macpherson, to recognise and understand the varying 'possessiveness' of the different strands of individualism and liberalism. This chapter presents libertarianism as a form of pro-capitalist liberalism, a development of the focus on the territorial self, but it is important to recognise that the tension between paternalism and libertarianism emerges just as clearly within conservative thinking and ideology. Libertarianism is just as much a 'conservative pretender' as it is a liberal one. Its anti-statism and its focus on laissez-faire individualism and free-market economics means that elements of this 'old-fashioned liberalism' have been absorbed into Tory philosophy.[17]

In this libertarian and pro-capitalist variation of liberalism (and of conservatism), liberty is emphasised at the expense of other liberal concepts, and the sovereign individual emerges 'as the centre of the social world and the repository of the qualities needed for progress and economic flourishing.'[18] The libertarian individual is self-seeking, competitive, and initiative-taking, driven by maximising his or her own interests. The private pursuit of individual benefits is expected to be mutually advantageous, and so the general interest and the concept of the civilised community are downgraded in importance. Free contracts provide 'the model for the just institutionalization of voluntary human intercourse'.[19] This voluntary model of human relationships involves surrounding liberty with private property, bringing it to the 'brink of core status'.[20] Property is connected to the individual through the construction of freedom as the right to exclude others. Libertarians stress the notion of liberty as non-restraint, not being infringed on by others. Liberty is being left alone and secure in your possessions, able to satisfy your own wants out of the proceeds. Property connects an individual to his or her goods, and to other individuals through the mechanism of contract. It helps strangers to remain strangers and to be members of a civil society.[21] The focus on property and exclusion creates a particular version of civil society, one that associates human identity with the market.

For libertarians, the accumulation of property underpins liberty and provides a clear mechanism of rewarding merit and desert. Liberty is about freedom of enterprise and the security of property. Virtue and ethics inhabit a realm outside the political, and libertarians assert 'the sovereignty of the private'.[22] It is a sovereignty that is maintained and protected by private property. Property and liberty are both about exclusive control and the absence of coercion by others. To be free is to be in control of your own environment and circumstances, not to be forced to act to serve the ends of someone else. In Hayek, for example, freedom involves non-constraint and being able to form and act upon coherent life plans. Once these are brought together, 'freedom of contract resurfaces ... as the vital link between liberty, security and the obtaining of property, all of which combine to allow individuals to realize their plans'.[23] It is then up to individuals to determine the contents of contracts, and the rules of the market will allocate rewards and punishments on the basis of skill and chance.

For Robert Nozick, the central core of a property right in X is the right to determine what shall be done with X by choosing between a constrained set of options. As they were for Locke, property rights are natural rights, 'they are the very same rights which individuals possess and can claim against one another in a state of nature'.[24] Absolute and exclusive property rights are protected, but not created, by the minimal state. Like Locke, Nozick links this notion of property as a natural right to the idea of owning a property in the self and one's own labour. This set of property rights entails each person's title to his or her own body, and an entitlement to the exclusive use of that body and to the labour of that body. Not having such a right is what makes a slave a slave.[25] For Nozick, the crucial, self-defining freedom is self-ownership and the right to exclude; what makes a slave a slave is their inability to defend their territory of the self. Each person must be regarded 'as having a right to decide what would become of himself and what he would do, and as having a right to reap the benefits of what he did'.[26] Freedom, for Nozick, is the ability to exclude others: 'One's person [is] property not metaphorically but essentially: the property one [has] in it [is] the right to exclude others from its use and enjoyment.'[27]

Nozick's libertarian theory revolves around the notion of justice in holdings, tying together property and the territorial vision of the individual through the notion of self-ownership. It is a historical theory that focuses on how unheld things came to be held and exchanged justly. In opposition to 'current time-slice theory' (epitomised by John Rawls), Nozick insists that it is relevant to consider how particular entitlements and distributions of property came about. Like the anti-aristocratic liberals of the nineteenth century, he argues that how holdings are produced and come to exist has an effect on who should own what. The idea, for example, that workers are entitled to the product and full fruits of their labour is based on some past history, and on notions of earning, producing, entitlement and desert. Nozick's argument is that past circumstances or actions create differential entitlements.[28] No one else deserves the fruit of another person's labour. Only the proprietor of his own labour is entitled to his '*self*-generated holdings'.[29] Nozick's focus is on the inside of the territorial self, on what goes on inside the fortress, without reference to the civilised community on the outside. Nozick's is a theory of separateness, and it is in this separation that he locates freedom. He assumes that individuals are the sole generators of their productions.[30] This emphasis on the individual as an active proprietor of themselves, their labour and their property takes Nozick into a theory of justice based on an individual's entitlements to his or her own private property.

Nozick's 'entitlement theory' rests on the primacy of individual rights and on his defence of a minimal state. According to him, any distribution of goods is just so long as it is brought about through free, voluntary exchanges between rational actors. Holdings – by which he means goods, money and property of all kinds – have to be justly acquired or transferred. Just acquisition occurs 'if you take something that belongs to nobody, without thereby making worse the position of others no longer able to use the thing'.[31] Nozick interprets Locke's 'enough and as good' proviso as being meant to ensure that the situation of others is not worsened. The individual cannot transfer his or her holding so as to make the situation of others 'worse than their baseline situation' in the state of nature.[32] S/he may not, for example, appropriate the only water hole in the desert and then charge those without water whatever s/he likes for access to it. Just transfers are legitimate means of exchanging things you own. As long as the acquisitions and transfers are just, and do not involve fraud or force, violence or trespass, then the resulting distribution is just. According to entitlement theory, people make individual choices about investments, gambling or giving gifts, and as long as their original holdings were justly acquired, then so is the outcome. As Peter Singer puts it: 'The entitlement theory of justice makes the justice of a given set of holdings depend on the history of those holdings, and not on the conformity of the outcome to a given pattern.'[33]

This means that individuals are entitled to their inherited assets and their natural talents, whether or not they deserve them. This echoes Macpherson's characterisation of self-ownership, that each individual owns their own person and capacities and owes nothing to society for them. Ownership implies the right to use, control and exclude, to choose what you do with what you own, providing you violate no one else's rights in the process. As long as you do not invade anyone else's territory, you are sovereign over yours. Each person remains separate, and so do their holdings. In contrast, Nozick argues, theories of redistribution in the direction of equality undermine the logic of individual entitlement, and assume that the social product, the wealth of the nation, somehow belongs to everybody and should be distributed as fairly as possible. Redistributive theories discover that the richest fifth of the world has 90 per cent of the world's income and assume that something is wrong, and some action needs to be taken. Nozick argues that 'the facts do not in themselves suggest that we ought to do anything'. It all depends on how the present distribution came about: if it turns out to have been based on a series of legitimate acquisitions and transfers, then the compulsory redistribution of wealth (through taxation, for example), would be a serious violation of individual rights.[34] If it turns out to have been based on fraud and force, then some rectification is necessary and those who are now worse off are entitled to some form of reparation.

In Nozick's view, theories of distribution put sovereignty over the self at risk. Through mechanisms such as taxation on wages and seizure of profits, some persons are 'appropriating the actions of other persons' and seizing the results of someone's labour. This takes away your right to decide what should become of you, and taking away that decision 'makes them a *part-owner* of you; it gives them a property right in you'. The boundaries of the territory of the self are breached, and despotic dominion undermined. For Nozick, this involves a shift from a classical notion of self-ownership to 'a notion of (partial) property rights in *other* people'.[35] For libertarians, the problem of partial ownership by others of people, their actions and their labour creates property rights in other people and raises the possibility of the permissibility of slavery. Against this, the equal-liberty principle 'imposes on all rights holders the duty to deprive no one of his original entitlement'.[36] The territorial notion of the self behind the principle of entitlement involves respecting the sovereignty of others. Honour, self-esteem and freedom, in Nozick's account, are 'based on criteria that differentiate'[37] and not on what is shared or held in common. As Jennifer Nedelsky argues, the metaphor of the territorial self means that owning always comes before sharing.[38] The notion of belonging is limited to the self, and not easily extended to civil society or to the 'civilised community'. The state that flows from Nozick's theory is minimal, because its function is to protect minimal natural rights to life, liberty and property. Its role is to protect against violence, theft and trespass and to ensure the enforcement of contracts between rational market actors who are entitled to what they create. The free market as a mechanism for protecting individual private property structures individual honour, labour and belonging in the libertarian account. Compulsory taxation to provide welfare is equivalent to taking someone's property and partially enslaving them. Redistribution is dishonourable and dishonouring because it trespasses on the sovereignty of the territorial self.

– DETERMINING THE SELF –

The distinction between liberals with a territorial view of the individual and those who stress the importance of self-determination can, to some extent, be mapped onto a distinction between pro- and anti-capitalist liberals. The shift between pro-capitalist and anti-capitalist liberalism is not always an unbridgeable divide; the two are dynamically related to each other and can sometimes grow out of each other. For example, in his earlier works, Mill followed Bentham in stressing the importance of security for persons and property as shared social interests for the poor as well as the rich. He saw the inviolability of property as a way of protecting an individual's way of life and of developing their character and individuality. Later, Mill changed his attitude. Rather than focusing on the individual and his property in the person, he drew attention to the concentration of wealth, the problems created by poverty and the relationship between property and power. He identified the excessive protection of property rights with the anti-reformers, with the fetishism of conservative attitudes to property. Mill recommended the redistribution of the burden of taxation, the abolition of some types of inheritance and the taxation of some forms of unearned income.

Within liberalism, property as a concept has a variable and sometimes ambiguous role. It can underpin not only free-market values, and a conception of human identity, society and the state strongly associated with the market, but also the redistributive variant of liberalism criticised by Nozick. Liberalism that is not libertarian operates with a different conception of the individual, the market and civil society. The market remains a central category, but it emerges as a political and cultural as well as an economic institution. It is 'embedded with peculiar political power relations' rather than appearing to be neutral and value free.[39] Once this is recognised by liberals, they begin to consider the political concepts that affect self-determination and the 'civilised community', and in particular to promote the values of equality and sociability.

For liberals who focus on the development of a self-determining subject, human beings are both rational and sociable. Freeden argues that, like socialism, the 'Millite core' of liberalism includes a notion of reason and harmony, based on the natural sociability of human beings and their concern for general welfare and co-operation, and drawing on the French Revolution trinity of liberty, equality and fraternity.[40] For Freeden, sociability and the general interest are core concepts of liberalism, along with liberty, individualism, progress and rationality. Anti-capitalist liberalism can move quite some way from the market, and especially from self-interested, instrumental and purely rational market actors. The core status of sociability is clear in the writings of T. H. Green, for example, whose view of human nature as developmental emphasises the importance of human rationality and self-realisation, and connects them to Hegelian notions of 'rational freedom'. Within this framework, property is not only a matter of economic efficiency, but is intrinsically connected to personality, self-determination and recognition. The capacity for sociability is an individual ethical attribute, a part of personality and of the self-determining subject. The human self is social, and as a moral agent, the individual is concerned with the common good and conscious of his or her ends as a member of the community – and not only as a market actor and a rational contractor. Green worked with a conception of the common good that merged the general interest and sociability, moral agency and individuality.[41] The result is a much thicker description of civil society that draws out the ways in which property functions in a moral space. In this account, property is less about freedom and more about belonging to the civilised community.

Green attacked the narrow focus on freedom of contract by pro-capitalist liberals as assuming equality of choice, but attaching it to inequalities of power. Contract as a device was able to respect people's wants, but not the common good. The territorial vision of the self, with its emphasis on separateness and self-interest, saw the market as an economic mechanism and failed to recognise its cultural and political roots. By emphasising competition over co-operation, it lost sight of self-determination and social recognition. Green argued that the property rights embedded in contract risked encouraging people to treat each other as means rather than ends, undermining the Kantian principle of individuality and equality. According to Green, society should secure for everyone the power of getting and keeping 'the means of realizing a will' directed to the social good.[42] This is a rationale for property that develops Hegel's ideas in a liberal direction. It links the right to a free life with a right to property, seeing property almost as process, a way of constantly realising the will and so working towards self-determination, always with social recognition and a shared concept of the social good as crucial components. This is a strand of liberalism that stresses property as the basis for self-respect, self-determination and social recognition, rather than as a means of exclusion or separation. Rather than stressing efficiency and entrepreneurship in the market place, this version of liberalism is implicitly linked to sociability and community. Some private possessions are vital to the individual's capacity for self-realisation, but there is an important distinction between conspicuous consumption and 'employment of goods as part of a rational plan of life'.[43] Consumption indicates enslavement to impulse and passion, while the rational use of property implies the possibility of social recognition, and of using property to develop a sense of belonging to a civilised community.

Freeden argues that within this more anti-capitalist strand of liberalism, private property has been demoted and marginalised as concept, particularly during the twentieth century, when he identifies a shift towards welfare and away from self-ownership.[44] Attaching property to concepts of welfare and redistribution contradicts the idea that individuals are only entitled to their own self-generated holdings, and cannot have any property rights in other people. This modern variation of liberalism is in some ways an 'assault on freedom of contract and on the sanctity of property rights' – the guiding lights of the pro-capitalist, territorial strand of liberalism.[45] The core notion of sociability bolstered these ideas of community and welfare, of shared human interests, at the expense of the traditional liberal, Lockean, intrinsic connection between property and the person. This strand of liberalism relies on a particular, moralised version of freedom understood in terms of emancipation and human flourishing. Rationality and self-determination are given a communal and welfare context, and liberalism has come to be seen as centrally concerned with social justice. Once the focus of liberalism shifts to social justice, it becomes less self-evident that the freedom of the individual, understood in terms of exclusion, is the highest political value.

– RAWLS AND EQUALITY –

The shift to social justice is clearest in the theories of John Rawls. For liberals, and especially those like Rawls who believe in the value of social co-operation, the market is a complex and ambiguous mechanism. In an efficient market the costs of consumption of goods and leisure and the value of what an individual adds by his or her own efforts are reflected in the net benefit of their contribution to the community. However, where talents are not distributed equally, and abilities as well as preferences are unequal, the market generates inequalities that are not defensible or fairly distributed. It turns out that people do not have different amounts of wealth just because they have different preferences: the cleaner, the professional golfer and the brain surgeon are not (always) the same person making different choices. People's wealth is affected by their inherent capacities, and by luck and accident, as well as by a whole raft of distortions based on power and privilege. In other words, 'the market produces both the required and the forbidden inequalities'.[46] In response, the broadly anti-capitalist liberal with an interest in equality and community membership is tempted to reform the market through a scheme of redistribution. For them, the problem with the more libertarian and market-based approach is that the 'overall result of separate and independent transactions is away from and not toward background justice'.[47] As Michael Lessnoff puts it: 'The Rawlsian contract stipulates that everyone starts equal, then seeks to show how far away from equality we may move without injustice.'[48]

Rawls sets out to show how liberty and equality can be brought together within a liberal framework that can deliver both self-determination and a civilised community. To do so, he focuses on co-operation rather than competition, and on inclusion and belonging as well as on freedom. He is concerned with how to make the 'basic structure' just. By the basic structure he means how the political constitution, the forms of property, the legal system and the economy fit together into a system that assigns rights and duties to individuals, and determines probable outcomes.[49] For Rawls, this has to be a system based on justice, co-operation and equality. To arrive at fair terms of social co-operation, Rawls uses the hypothetical devices of the original position and the veil of ignorance to model the terms of the agreement about how far away from equality society may move without injustice. The original position is a hypothetical situation in which rational persons behind a veil of ignorance choose the principles of justice which should govern the basic structure of society. Behind the veil of ignorance, no one knows their own conception of the good, their social situation or their individual talents and abilities. The parties in the original position are 'men and women with ordinary tastes, talents, ambitions, and convictions, but each is temporarily ignorant of these features of his own personality, and must agree upon a contract before his self-awareness returns'.[50] Individuals in the original position and behind the veil of ignorance cannot function as territorial selves because they know nothing about the 'rational inside'.

The original position and the veil of ignorance are used to 'eliminate the bargaining advantages that inevitably arise within the background institutions of any society from cumulative social, historical, and natural tendencies'.[51] This is what Nozick opposes: the history of holdings is converted into cumulative tendencies that have taken us away from equality, and created an unjust distribution. Rather than respecting, the history of holdings needs correcting. For Rawls, the mechanisms for correction are the original position and the veil of ignorance. They remove the sense that individuals as self-owners are entitled to their self-generated holdings. Rawlsian liberals work on the conviction that 'the fact that we occupy a particular social position is not a good reason for us to propose, or to expect others to accept, a conception of justice that favors those in that position'.[52] Rawls's conception of justice as fairness uses a fundamental organising idea of 'society as a fair system of social cooperation between free and equal persons viewed as fully cooperating members of society over a complete life'.[53] Nozick's position, on this view, is fundamentally unfair. As Singer points out, according to Nozick, 'if a starving man drags himself to our house, where we are entertaining our friends with a sumptuous banquet, we are perfectly within our rights to send him away without a crust'.[54] This conclusion is unacceptable to Rawlsian liberals whose focus is on co-operation and cohesion rather than competition and conflict, and on equality and belonging as well as on freedom.

Rawls argues that the individuals in the original position and behind the veil of ignorance would come up with two principles of justice as the foundation of society. These principles would then become publicly recognised rules to inform the basic structure of society and to guide its institutions. Institutions would be just when they conformed to the two principles of justice. The first requires the greatest equal liberty compatible with a like liberty for all. The second principle requires that social and economic inequalities should satisfy two conditions. First, they must be attached to offices and positions that are open to all under conditions of fair equality of opportunity. Second, the 'difference principle' permits 'only those inequalities in the distribution of primary economic and social advantages that benefit everyone, in particular the worst off'.[55] Inequalities, rather than being given a history and left alone, must be reordered so that they are to the greatest benefit of the least advantaged members of society. The principles are lexically ordered (like the ordering of words in a dictionary), with the first coming before the second, and the first part of the second coming before the second part of the second ('a' before 'b', 'babble' before 'babe').

Taking equality as constitutive of liberalism, Rawls argues that the justice of social institutions is measured 'by their tendency to counteract the natural inequalities deriving from birth, talent, and circumstance, pooling those resources in the service of the common good'.[56] The common good is measured in terms of basic benefits to individuals: personal and political liberty, economic and social advantages, and self-respect. The fair terms of social co-operation specify rights and duties and regulate the arrangements of 'background justice' over time. Each person's rational advantage, based on what they are trying to achieve from their own perspective, is integrated into a well-ordered society aimed at the general good. The relation between citizens is expressed by principles of justice that regulate a social world in which everyone benefits, 'judged with respect to an appropriate benchmark of equality defined with respect to that world'.[57] Rawls admits private property as a liberty 'by giving a new sense to the requirement that the right to hold property must be equal.' He does not require that property should be held in common, or that separately owned property should be equal in amount. He requires that the rules governing the acquisition and disposition of property and the scope of property rights should be the same for all.[58] He uses the difference principle to minimise the inequalities generated by this interpretation of equal property rights. The problem for Rawls is that fair background conditions are gradually undermined even though no one acts unfairly.

The difference principle applies to all the features of the basic structure of society, including the system of money and credit, property rights and the laws governing inheritance, taxation and the provision of public goods. Those with talents that are much in demand will receive less in a society governed by the difference principle than they would if they were competing in a free market. These people are being asked to accept less than they might otherwise have had, 'and there is a clear sense in which they will be asked to accept these smaller shares "for the sake of others".'[59] They are expected to do so because their well-being, as well as everyone else's, depends on social co-operation. This is clearly not about securing and defending the territory of the self from invasion by others, or about using the market to protect entirely self-generated holdings. The basis of Rawls's conception of social co-operation lies 'in the idea that economic institutions are reciprocal arrangements for mutual advantage in which the parties cooperate on a footing of equality'.[60] The difference principle is underpinned by the idea that the basic institutions of society 'are a co-operative enterprise in which the citizens stand as equal partners'.[61] This co-operative enterprise means that the productive skills and capacities of individuals and material productive assets should not be considered to be the self-generated private property of individuals in any absolute sense. Rawls's approach assumes the common ownership of society's accumulated productive resources, and that no one deserves their greater natural capacity. This assumption is central to Rawlsian liberalism, and in some ways it brings debates about property to the heart of modern liberalism. It is this idea of common ownership that is most clearly contested by Nozick and libertarians, and by communitarians.

Rawls's difference principle is a strong kind of patterned end-state principle, and Nozick objects to Rawls's quest to privilege co-operation. To Nozick, Rawls's view seems to be that everyone has some entitlement to or claim on the totality of natural assets, without anybody having a differential or prior claim. For Nozick, this has to involve rejecting a system of natural liberty and entitlement, and undermining principles of justice. The debate is in part about the different conceptions of self-ownership and individualism at work in their accounts of justice. The territorial vision of the self is designed to guarantee an individual's sovereignty over themselves and their rights to their separate, self-generated holdings. It involves, as we have seen, a degree of separateness and a particular conception of independence. For Nozick, the assumption that individual talents, capacities and abilities are held to some extent in common, that sovereignty can be pooled, undermines this particular conception of independence. In Nozick's view, Rawls's principles of justice can only be said to rule out the tendency to regard individuals as means to another's welfare if 'one presses *very* hard on the distinction between men and their talents, abilities, and special traits'.[62] Property and the person have been pulled too far apart, and Rawls (in his opponents' view) abandons self-ownership in favour of welfare.

To investigate this claim, we need to explore Rawls's theory of property. It turns out to be much closer to the self-determination model than to despotic, territorial dominion. Rawls sees property as one of the basic institutions of society, part of its basic structure. The mechanisms of property need to follow a sensible scheme of rules. In order for these rules to be sensible, they should not exceed the capacity of individuals to grasp and follow them, or burden them too heavily with requirements of knowledge and foresight, meaning that they would need to understand the ramifications of their actions and how they might affect future circumstances in too much detail. This view of property is based on the premise of a society that produces and reproduces itself, its institutions and its culture over generations, and in the process moves society away from the baseline situation of equality. Rawls uses the example of the cumulative effects of the purchase and sale of landed property and its transmission by bequest over generations. He argues that it is 'obviously not sensible to impose on parents (as heads of families) the duty to adjust their own bequests to what they estimate the effects of the totality of actual bequests will be on the next generation, much less beyond'.[63] As a result, income and inheritance taxation need to be written into the basic structure to even out the ownership of property, rather than being left to the private judgement of individuals. The basic structure requires a set of rules enforced through the legal system and framed to leave individuals and associations free to act without excessive constraints. Following this account, property rights need to be clearly defined, clearly assigned and legally enforceable. It makes no sense to associate property rights with the minimal state and freedom from government. Property is a complex set of rules enforced by the state, and implies 'the dependency of the individual on the collectivity'.[64]

As Stephen Holmes argues about the situation in post-communist Russia, one of the functions of the liberal state is to allow property owners to believe in the future by predictably enforcing known and stable rules.[65] This seems to me to reinforce the role of property and to link it, as Bentham does, to the security of expectations. A fair distribution can be arrived at only through the actual working of a fair social process over time, using the principles of justice to alter the system of entitlements and earnings so that 'there are no unannounced and unpredictable inter-ferences with citizens' expectations and acquisitions'.[66] Men and women, in Rawls's account, can use property to underpin their selfhood. The scheme of basic liberties includes the right to hold and to have the exclu-sive use of personal property. The role of this liberty is to allow 'a suffici-ent material basis for a sense of personal independence and self-respect, both of which are essential for the development and exercise of the moral powers'.[67] This is language that echoes Green's ideas about sociability as an ethical attribute and property as a means of realising a will, and Godwin's insistence on the sacredness of property. Rawls stresses the fundamental importance of self-respect, rooted in our self-confidence as a fully co-operating member of society capable of pursuing a worthwhile conception of the good over a complete life, secure in our own value and with a 'firm conviction that our determinate conception of the good is worth carrying out'.[68] This self-respect depends on and is encouraged by features of basic institutions. Our sense of our own value depends on the respect and recognition of others, and on our dependence on the collec-tivity: 'If the equal basic liberties of some are restricted or denied, social co-operation on the basis of mutual respect is impossible.'[69] When fair terms are not honoured, those who are mistreated will feel resentment or humiliation, while those who benefit will feel guilt. Such feelings undermine the conditions of self-respect, honour and self-determination as the basis of sovereignty over the self.

For Rawls, retaining self-respect, the moral power to have a conception of the good, means retaining a certain level of material and social well-being, and so is inextricable from property. His notion of civil society involves balancing prosperity, civility and liberty through mechanisms of trust, co-operation and inclusion, and through the framework of the rule of the law. The aim is to achieve a balance of secure expectations, freedom and belonging. For Rawls, being a citizen, a full member of society, is an active enterprise. Like the Levellers, Rawls's theory expresses a belief in the positive value of society, a sense of a 'community of enterprisers' – in its broadest sense, meaning social, spiritual and intellectual as well as economic – who all recognise the ultimate value of living together.[70] This is different from the full-blown possessive individualism of the libertarian and pro-capitalist strands of liberalism, but it is not a socialist anti-capitalism based on substantive equality and equal shares. His theory works with a particular version of self-ownership as self-determination rather than as territorial defence, and with a version of civil society that goes beyond the free market.

– Freedom and Belonging –

In order for this version of civil society to function as civil, civilised and cohesive, Rawls works with a particular fundamental idea of the person as someone who can take part in social life, be a citizen, 'a normal and fully co-operating member of society over a complete life'.[71] Within such a society, citizens have two moral powers: a capacity for a sense of justice, and a capacity for a conception of the good. In addition, citizens have the powers of reason – judgement, thought and inference. For Rawls, 'their having these powers to the requisite minimum degree to be fully co-operating members of society makes persons equal'.[72] It is a prior principle that citizens' basic material needs are met, giving relative priority to social primary goods, wealth and liberty: to a very poor person, nothing is more important than provision for his material needs. It is a constitutional essential that 'below a certain level of material and social well-being, and of training and education, people simply cannot take part in society as citizens, much less equal citizens'.[73] Not everyone is automatically a member of the civilised community, and there is a risk that the poor will remain trespassers and fugitives.

As citizens, they are the opposite of slaves who suffer social and civil death. For Rawls, the opposite of slavery is membership of the political community, rather than the freedom of self-ownership. Free citizens are capable of taking responsibility for their ends and of counting as the source of legitimate claims on the community. Rawls's conception of the person is thus tied up not only with rationality and self-possession, but also with sociability and citizenship, and so with property relations beyond those involved in owning the self and a property in the person. Rawls argues that his theory is liberal 'because it takes the capacity for social co-operation as fundamental and attributes to persons the two moral powers which make such co-operation possible'.[74]

H. L. A. Hart argues that this assumption of the priority of co-operation 'harbour[s] a latent ideal' of 'a public-spirited citizen who prizes political activity and service to others as among the chief goods of life and could not contemplate as tolerable an exchange of the opportunities for such activity for mere material goods or contentment'.[75] The latent ideal is also of belonging to a civilised civil society, and to a polity that is 'disciplined, virtuous, self-sacrificing, productive, far-seeing and wise'.[76] In the past, this ideal required self-possession, and was 'inextricably linked to its unfortunate shadow, the gendered, almost always racial question of "fitness for self-government"'.[77] In its explicitly racialised and gendered construction in the early nineteenth century, the public good rested on a homogeneous polity based on reflection, restraint and self-sacrifice and demanded extraordinary moral character. Rawls makes his requirements for citizenship minimal, but the ideas of having the moral power to have a conception of the good, and of regarding society as a co-operative enterprise, raise questions of fitness and unfitness for self-government. They require that we as individuals learn to govern ourselves in particular ways.

Uday Mehta argues that that liberal theory is based on exclusion: 'Behind the capacities ascribed to all human beings, there exist a set of social credentials that constitute the real bases of political inclusion.'[78] Universal claims can be made because they derive from certain characteristics that are common to all human beings. The idea that everyone is free, equal and rational is taken as an anthropological minimum, but it is under constant threat from individuals who may not have the innate moral principles required to govern themselves, to co-operate effectively or to recognise in others a power to have a conception of the good. We need to be alert to the history of exclusions behind the idea of being a normal and fully co-operating member of society. It takes us back to David

Goldberg's double-bind: 'Subjects assume value ... only in so far as they are bearers of rights; and they are properly vested with rights only in so far as they are imbued with value.'[79] Race and gender often serve to define an individual's capacity for self-ownership and self-direction, and also for co-operation and citizenship.

Liberals tend to approach gender as politically irrelevant. Any polity truly committed to liberal principles of equality should work to counter discrimination by granting women equal rights with men and enabling women to participate equally with men in the public sphere. Equality is a matter of freedom and belonging. Gender differences are viewed as social constructions, created and perpetuated in the interests of men. Liberal feminists accept that the liberal ideal of equality is gender neutral: 'if women are in practice not equal with men, this is as a result of contingent distortions of the ideal of neutrality', of having moved away from equality and the background conditions of justice. Again, the emphasis is not on the history of holdings, or on the justice of individual acquisitions and transactions, but on determining the values of a civilised community and the basis of inclusion. The rational response is to pursue the ideal of neutrality, 'to hold liberalism accountable to its own professed ideals'.[80] In her response to Rawls, Susan Moller Okin contends that the basic structure of society needs to be extended to apply to women by applying the principles of justice to the family. She argues that justice in the public sphere is impossible without justice in the private sphere. If women are to become fully co-operating, normal members of society, they must be equal within the family. Her extended version of justice as fairness eliminates the sexual division of labour that allocates primary responsibility for housework and child rearing to women. This would require fundamental cultural change, and significant changes to state policies on childcare, parental leave and the balance between private and public commitments.[81] These fundamental changes would be required in order to guarantee to women membership of the thicker version of civil society, the civilised community that can underpin a notion of the individual based on self-determination. Okin's critique shows that Rawls's theory has smuggled in assumptions about the civilised community, and about property, labour, honour and belonging.

Membership of a community of enterprisers becomes a crucial consideration as individuals attempt to find a footing with others. Ronald Dworkin argues that each citizen is a member of a community 'and ... he can find, in the fate of that community, a reason for special burdens he can accept with honor rather than degradation'.[82] The community offers the individual the opportunity to lead a life that is of value through active membership. Individuals identify with the future of their community where they have some power to shape it and help to guarantee its prosperity and where they feel that they belong to a community for which it would be worthwhile to make sacrifices. As a member of such a community, the human self is a social, moral agent concerned with the common good and conscious of his or her ends. Property becomes a process that brings together sociability and moral agency, honour and degradation into a system of social recognition. The connective tissue of property, a level of material and social well-being, enables individuals to find their footing with others within this version of liberalism

– NOTES –

1. Dan Avnon and Avner de-Shalit, 'Introduction: Liberalism between Promise and Practice', in Dan Avnon and Avner De-Shalit (eds), *Liberalism and Its Practice* (London and New York: Routledge, 1999), p. 5.
2. Brendan Edgeworth, 'Post-property? A Postmodern Conception of Private Property', *University of New South Wales Law Journal* 11, 1988, p. 88.
3. John Stuart Mill, 'On Liberty', in John Stuart Mill and Jeremy Bentham, *Utilitarianism and Other Essays*, ed. H. B Acton (London: Penguin, 1991), p. 78.
4. John Day, 'John Stuart Mill: *On Liberty*', in Murray Forsyth et al. (eds), *The Political Classics: Hamilton to Mill* (Oxford: Oxford University Press, 1993), p. 209.
5. Jennifer Nedelsky, 'Law, Boundaries and the Bounded Self', *Representations* 30, 1990, p. 168.
6. For further discussion of the 'territorial self', see Laura Brace 'Imagining the Boundaries of a Sovereign Self', in Laura Brace and John Hoffman (eds), *Reclaiming Sovereignty* (London: Pinter, 1997).
7. Avnon and de-Shalit, Introduction, p. 3.
8. Michael J. Sandel, 'The Procedural Republic and the Unencumbered Self', in T. B. Strong (ed.), *The Self and the Political Order* (Oxford: Blackwell, 1992), p. 85.
9. Avnon and de-Shalit, Introduction, p. 4.
10. Chandran Kukathas, 'Liberalism, Multiculturalism, Oppression', in Andrew Vincent (ed.), *Political Theory: Tradition and Diversity* (Cambridge: Cambridge University Press, 1997), p. 152.
11. Alan Ryan, 'Liberalism', in Robert E. Goodin and Philip Pettit (eds), *A Companion to Contemporary Political Philosophy* (Oxford: Blackwell, 1993), p. 298.
12. Richard Bellamy, *Liberalism and Modern Society: An Historical Argument* (Cambridge: Polity, 1992), p. 43.
13. R. H. Tawney, *Equality* (London: George Allen and Unwin, [1931] 1979), p. 69.
14. Ryan, 'Liberalism', p. 302.
15. Howard Warrender, *The Clarendon Edition of the Philosophical Works of Thomas Hobbes*, Vol. III: 'De Cive', English version (Oxford: Clarendon Press, 1983), p. 42.

16. Michael Freeden, *Ideologies and Political Theory: a Conceptual Approach* (Oxford: Clarendon Press, 1996), pp. 276, 278.
17. See below, Chapter 7 on conservatism and E. H. H. Green, *Ideologies of Conservatism: Conservative Political Ideas in the Twentieth Century* (Oxford: Oxford University Press, 2002). Libertarianism appears in this chapter to highlight the role of property in the debate between Rawls and Nozick.
18. Freeden, *Ideologies and Political Theory*, p. 280.
19. Ibid. p. 285.
20. Ibid. p. 287.
21. Roger Scruton, *England: an Elegy* (London: Pimlico, 2000), p. 50.
22. Freeden, *Ideologies and Political Theory*, p. 297.
23. Ibid. p. 305.
24. T. M. Scanlon, 'Nozick on Rights, Liberty and Property', in N. Daniels (ed.), *Reading Rawls* (Oxford: Blackwell, 1975), p. 123.
25. Hillel Steiner, 'Slavery, Socialism, and Private Property', in J. R. Pennock and J. W. Chapman (eds) *Nomos XXII: Property.* (New York: New York University Press, 1980). For alternative definitions of slavery to do with social death and exclusion from the community, see Chapter 8.
26. Robert Nozick, *Anarchy, State and Utopia* (Oxford: Blackwell, 1974), p. 171.
27. C. B. Macpherson, *The Political Theory of Possessive Individualism* (Oxford: Oxford University Press, 1962), p. 153.
28. Nozick, *Anarchy, State and Utopia* , p. 154.
29. Amy Gutmann, *Liberal Equality* (Cambridge: Cambridge University Press, 1980), p. 157.
30. Ibid. p. 158.
31. Peter Singer, 'The right to be rich or poor', *New York Review of Books* 22:3, 6 March 1975, http://www.nybooks.com/articles/9252
32. Nozick, *Anarchy, State and Utopia*, p. 180.
33. Singer, 'Right to be rich or poor', p. 3.
34. Ibid. p. 4.
35. Nozick, *Anarchy, State and Utopia*, p. 172.
36. Steiner, 'Slavery, Socialism, and Private Property', p. 256.
37. Singer, 'Right to be rich or poor', p. 5.
38. Nedelsky, 'Law, Boundaries and the Bounded Self', p. 172.
39. Li Xing, 'The market-democracy conundrum', *Journal of Political Ideologies* 6 (1) 2001, p. 77.
40. Freeden, *Ideologies and Political Theory*, p. 150.
41. Ibid. p. 185.
42. Ibid. p. 191.
43. Bellamy, *Liberalism and Modern Society*, p. 42.
44. Freeden, *Ideologies and Political Theory*, p. 208.
45. Ryan, 'Liberalism', p. 294.
46. Ronald Dworkin, *A Matter of Principle* (Oxford: Clarendon Press, 1986), p. 196.
47. John Rawls, *Political Liberalism* (New York: University of Columbia Press, 1993), p. 267.
48. Michael H. Lessnoff, *Political Philosophers of the Twentieth Century* (Oxford: Blackwell, 1999), p. 246.
49. 'A Rawls Glossary', http://info.bris.ac.uk/~plcdib/rglos.html
50. Ronald Dworkin, 'The Original Position', in Daniels, *Reading Rawls*, p. 17.
51. Rawls, *Political Liberalism*, p. 23.

52. Ibid. p. 24.
53. Ibid. p. 9.
54. Singer, 'Right to be rich or poor', p. 4.
55. Thomas Nagel, 'Rawls on Justice' in Daniels, *Reading Rawls*, p. 3.
56. Ibid. p. 3.
57. Rawls, *Political Liberalism*, p. 17.
58. H. L. A. Hart, 'Rawls on Liberty and its Priority', in Daniels, *Reading Rawls*, p. 236.
59. T. M. Scanlon, 'Rawls' Theory of Justice', in Daniels, *Reading Rawls*, p. 198.
60. Ibid. p. 199.
61. Ibid. p. 204.
62. Nozick, *Anarchy, State and Utopia*, p. 228.
63. Rawls, *Political Liberalism*, p. 268.
64. Stephen Holmes, 'Can Weak-state Liberalism Survive?' in Avnon and de-Shalit, *Liberalism and its Practice*, p. 42.
65. Ibid. p. 42.
66. Rawls, *Political Liberalism*, p. 283.
67. Ibid. p. 298.
68. Ibid. p. 318.
69. Ibid. p. 337.
70. Macpherson, *Political Theory of Possessive Individualism*, p. 157.
71. Rawls, *Political Liberalism*, p. 18.
72. Ibid. p. 19.
73. Ibid. p. 166.
74. Ibid. p. 370.
75. Hart, 'Rawls on Liberty', p. 252.
76. Matthew Frye Jacobson, *Whiteness of a Different Color: European Immigrants and the Alchemy of Race* (Cambridge, MA and London: Harvard University Press 1998), p. 26.
77. Ibid. p. 26.
78. Uday S. Mehta, 'Liberal Strategies of Exclusion', *Politics and Society* 18:4, 1990, p. 429.
79. David Theo Goldberg, *Racist Culture: Philosophy and the Politics of Meaning* (Oxford: Blackwell, 1993), p. 37.
80. Judith Squires, *Gender in Political Theory* (Cambridge: Polity Press, 2000), p. 119.
81. Ibid. p. 155.
82. Dworkin, 'Why Liberals Should Care about Equality', in *A Matter of Principle*, p. 210.

CHAPTER 6

Socialism

In 1755, Jean-Jacques Rousseau argued:

> The first man who, after enclosing a plot of land, saw fit to say: 'this is mine', and who found people who were simple enough to believe him, was the true founder of civil society. How many crimes, wars, murders, sufferings and horrors mankind would have been spared if someone had torn up the stakes and filled up the moat and cried to his fellows: 'Don't listen to this impostor; you are lost if you forget that the earth belongs to no one, and that its fruits are for all.'[1]

For Rousseau, this exchange formed the basis of a fraudulent social contract, under whose terms the rich convinced the poor that they were in need of protection. Without the institution of private property, the rich argued, disorder and chaos would reign and we would all be trapped in a war of all against all, a state of nature that was also a state of war. Rousseau argued that such a situation was not a natural state, but a corruption of human nature. The fraudulent social contract that upheld this particular form of property was an artificial and conventional institution, based on force and power relations that were then consolidated and imagined as natural and fixed. The naturalness of private property, in other words, was an illusion, sustained not only by the powerful rich, the impostors, but also by the poor – those simple enough to believe the lies of the rich. Private property emerged clearly as a relationship between people, and in particular between rich and poor. At the same time, it becomes clear from following his argument how much weight the concept of human nature has to carry in any conception of property, and how deeply ideas about progress, change and property implicate each other.

Of all the major ideologies explored here, it is socialism that most clearly calls into question the naturalness of private property and connects property to progress, change and moral regeneration through its abolition. The idea of property is unstable, contestable and, following Rousseau, is understood by socialists as a relation between rich and poor, based on force and an illusion of consent. The socialist tradition builds on the legacy of the Enlightenment and emancipation, looking forward to a bright new future when humanity, released from mystification and illusion, ushers in an undivided and classless society. The relationship between socialism and property is a difficult and complex one to draw out. In *The Communist Manifesto*, Karl Marx famously summed up the revolutionary project as the abolition of private property, and for many years public ownership of the means of production was the definitive and institutionalised socialist tenet. Socialism as an ideology is generally understood to have grown up in opposition to capitalism, and so on one level, it appears to be an anti-property ideology (or at least anti-private property). For some strands of scientific socialism, 'the assumption is that there is only a single structural principle that matters, the replacement of private property by public property in the means of production, and that all else may be derived in practice from that'.[2]

However, the place of property in socialist thought is more complicated than a simple private-versus-public ownership dichotomy, particularly once the different strands of socialism are taken into account. There are always at least two concepts of equality working within socialist traditions. One maintains that people have an equal right to own property, and that inequalities are acceptable as long as they are based on productive use. The other calls on individuals to pool their property rights and hand their property over to the community. The problem is whether the community then owns not only the goods of its members, but also exercises a degree of ownership over their persons as well. In a different guise, this returns to the problem of partial ownership by others raised by the libertarian critique of welfare liberalism. Socialism in its response to the French Revolution shifts about between equality, liberty and fraternity as constitutive principles and carries property with it, sometimes attempting to solve the problem of how to create a self-determining subject, and sometimes attempting to preserve the territory of the self. It aims at a synthesis between the self-direction offered by the productive use of property and the egalitarian implications of communism.[3]

Property thus has a complex role in socialist ideology, closely associated with its core values. Property has to be understood as the relation between an agent and an object, and it has a crucial bearing on the values of community and equality at the socialist core. Equality, class, labour, reason and human nature are all concepts that are crucially inflected by ideas about property and ownership. Once property is understood as a relation between people, a carrier of power, and a distribution of freedom and unfreedom, it becomes clear that ideas about property must be crucial to socialism, and in particular to its critiques of exploitation, alienation and imperialism. At the same time, ideas about property are at the heart of socialism's discontents, its battles with justice, and struggles with morality, change, emancipation and the workings of a socialist society. The claim that socialism is non-capitalism, for example, raises questions about the escape from poverty, the importance of abundance, and the character of human flourishing, as well as about liberty and equality. Steven Lukes identifies a paradox in Marxism that informs its treatment of property. On the one hand, morality is rejected as a form of ideology. Abstract, universal principles are illusory: on closer examination they will turn out to be historical, relative and determined by class interests. On the other hand, Marx's writings are full of moral judgements about alienation, exploitation and degradation. Marxism, argues Lukes, is 'both anti-moral and moral'.[4] This is bound to affect how socialism as an ideology deals with property as both a moral and an economic question, and the paradox surfaces particularly clearly in the divisions between utopian and scientific socialisms.

The paradox is resolved in the first instance by making a distinction between the morality of *Recht*, an ideological and anachronistic form of morality based on the rights of man (and particularly private property), and the morality of socialist emancipation. The rules of *Recht* depend on the rights of man as a member of civil society, and they are about strangers remaining strangers. The individual living by these rules owns a property in the self and in his own labour, with an entitlement to the exclusive use of his body and his labour. For socialists this means that he is egoistic and separated from his community. Society appears to him as an external framework and he becomes a restricted individual, withdrawn into himself, divided between the public and the private. The morality of *Recht*, socialists argue, is inherently ideological and conflictual, and its practical application is private property.[5] *Recht* is the morality of 'market friendship', within which sovereignty over the self is the basis of limited government, individual liberty and the capitalist economy.

The conditions of *Recht* are scarcity, egoism, conflicts of interest and, socialists argue, a lack of perfect information and understanding. The rational, self-interested, contracting individual who emerges from the vision of pro-capitalist liberals and libertarians is not the spontaneous product of a state of nature, but of specific historical and material conditions. Under capitalism, scarcity arises from material relations and from maldistribution. For socialists, as opposed to conservatives and libertarians, there is no hard core of intractable selfishness within individuals; people's mercenariness is apparent rather than real. Conflicts of interest and competing conceptions of the good, generated by living under the conditions of *Recht*, imply that social relations are necessarily and always antagonistic. The conditions of Rousseau's fraudulent social contract are being constantly reproduced within the structure of society, but the power relations underpinning the contract have been obscured under an illusion of choice and consent. Under these circumstances, where we are all constrained to act as competitive egoists, principles of distributive justice are required, and rights and duties need to be specified 'to protect us from one another's depredations and abuses'.[6] Everything to do with conflicts of interest and basic inequalities, as we have seen, is understood by liberals to be a question of justice. For socialists, this focus on justice is bound to prove distorting and distracting. *Recht* promotes class compromise and delays revolutionary change, hence Marx's demand 'to give up illusions' about the rights of man and justice.[7]

These illusions about the rights of man and justice operate in the sphere of exchange and circulation, differentiated by Marxist theory from the sphere of direct production. In the sphere of circulation the worker is regarded as the owner or seller of his labour power, and engages in free contracts of mutual advantage with others who own their labour. It is, as Marx put it in Volume I of *Capital*, 'a very Eden of the innate rights of man', the sphere of Freedom, Equality, Property and Bentham.[8] As such an Eden, it is an ideological appearance, an illusion 'veiling and mystifying the transfer of surplus value'.[9] The question is whether we can simply assign property to this sphere, assume that is a principle of *Recht* and expect it to wither away along with class and the state. Lukes draws attention to the danger this presents of ignoring injustices and violations, such as the sexual division of labour, the politics of globalisation and environmental concerns, and missing their connections with property.

– UTOPIAN SOCIALISM –

Utopian socialism focuses on the connections between liberty and equality, with a conception of freedom understood in terms of emancipation and human flourishing that is close to the anti-capitalist strand of liberalism concerned with self-determination. While exploitation might be overcome by material abundance, for utopian socialists that might not be enough to guarantee real freedom. Their argument is that capitalism entails alienation as well as exploitation, and so the equation of socialism with anti-capitalism involves more than simply guaranteeing material abundance. For utopian socialists, freedom involves a degree of control over the circumstances and conditions of our lives. Capitalism sets material power above us, making us all dependent and helpless – while making us appear to be independent self-owners. Personal dependence on particular other individuals, such as existed under feudal social relations or under slavery, is replaced by this universal dependency. People living under capitalism appear to be independent of one another 'because their mutual dependency assumes the unrecognizable form of relations between commodities'.[10] Property relations based on force and fraud are disguised as relations between individuals and their things. Competition and the division of labour mean that people rely on an illusory community that rests on concealed and repressed power relations between persons. Civil society, driven by the principles of *Recht*, is not a community but an association of strangers. For utopian socialists, the promise of socialism as anti-capitalism has to involve overcoming this illusory community of strangers and replacing it with a more fraternal and nurturing version of community. Socialism's focus on human flourishing includes a conception of the individual as 'a (potentially) self-directing being who achieves self-realization in mutual identification and community with others.'[11]

For utopian socialists, private property was understood as the basis of capitalist exploitation, but that picture is complicated by the idea that owners could be obliged to put their property to productive use. The focus on labour and creativity means that socialism, particularly in its utopian formations, has always had strong support from artisans who emphasised the virtues of private property, especially in a craftsman's own tools and in the skill reflected in his apprenticeship. Rather as T. H. Green and other liberals suggested, utopian socialists were prepared to argue that it is possible to employ goods as part of a rational plan of life. There is a distinction, for them, to be made between non-productive and productive use. Utopian socialists understood property relations as functioning within a contested moral space, and some of their arguments came close to advocating improvement as a moral principle. Pierre-Joseph Proudhon argued that Roman law introduced a version of absolute ownership when it defined property as the right to use and abuse a thing within the limits of the law: 'The proprietor has the power to let his crops rot underfoot, sow his fields with salt, milk his cows on the sand, turn his vineyard into a desert, and use his vegetable garden as a park.'[12] In this scheme, use and abuse were indistinguishable: the owner could enjoy and dispose of his property, and his right over things was absolute. It was this absolutism, despotic dominion, backed up by the force of the law, to which utopian socialists objected.

The crucial distinction, for Proudhon, was between possession and property. Possession, he argued, was a fact, enjoyed by tenants, farmers and shareholders. Property was a legal power, backed up by force and fraud, granted to owners and heirs. The possessor was responsible for the thing entrusted to him and used it in conformity with general utility. He had the power to preserve and develop it, but not to transform, diminish or change its nature. It was possible to make this kind of possession permanent 'under the supervision of society and subject to the condition of labour and the law of equality', bringing property under the moral law, and returning to the principle of usufruct.[13] For Proudhon, public law and security required that only *possession* should be protected. In establishing *property*, by contrast, the law created a right outside society that sanctioned violence, immorality and poverty. In a clear echo of Rousseau, Proudhon argued: 'The right of property was the origin of evil on earth, the first link in the long chain of crimes and miseries which the human race has endured since its birth.'[14]

For Proudhon, property and society were irreconcilable with one another. In his conjectural history, people originally lived in a community without property. The increase in possession gradually forced them to labour for their support, and they agreed amongst themselves that the labourer should be the sole proprietor of the product of his labour. For Proudhon, this meant that 'they simply agreed that thereafter none could live without working'.[15] Equality of subsistence required equality of labour, and only labour could sustain property and equality together. An individual could clear a field, cultivate the land, build a house and support his family, and then he could own the field as a possession. He could possess it by first occupancy, by labour or by agreement, but none of these would make it his property. Property was created by state legislators who passed positive laws turning possession into property. They extended ownership to include the perpetual and absolute right to retain property by alienating it, leasing it, exchanging it for profit, investing it, using and abusing it. For Proudhon, property was a wholly artificial right, preserved by the intention of the legislators rather than underpinned by natural rights based on labour or occupation or sociability. Legislators were naïve not to foresee that property would lead to exclusions, sanction egoism and destroy equality. Property had become the 'cornerstone of everything that exists and stumbling-block of everything that should be'.[16] It was part of absolutism, tyranny, intolerance and privilege. Very like Gerrard Winstanley and Rousseau, Proudhon argued that property was upheld by force and violence. Justice was 'always invoked as the guardian angel of sovereigns, nobles and proprietors'.[17] It was part of kingly power. The French Revolution, which had ultimately left property intact, was unfinished and unconsummated (in the same way as Winstanley and other radicals argued that the English Revolution was).

While property was part of an artificial superstructure for the utopian socialists, possession created by labour could be legitimate. Whoever laboured became a proprietor, not simply of his salary or wages but of the value which he created through his labour. Even after receiving his wages, the labourer retained a natural right of property in the thing he had produced. It did not disappear. Like John Locke, Proudhon argued that labour was a possession that could not be taken from the labourer, even if the products of it were expropriated from him: 'As a labourer I have a right to the possession of the products of nature and my own industry, but as a proletarian I enjoy none of them.'[18] This dichotomy formed the basis of the socialist approach to property, and in particular of the utopian socialist strand that insisted on the possibility of productive use and legitimate possession based on labour. The Lockean right to own your own labour and to create value with it, was coupled with a critique of private property, and of capitalism in particular. Unless the whole society laboured, possession was distorted into property and so harmed others, excluding the poor and encroaching on other people's rights.

Once this tight connection between labour and property in the product was broken, the space for exploitation and alienation was created. Pulling them apart opened up the possibility of distinguishing between righteous labour and drudgery, and of owning others' labour. The master profited from the value of the labourer's labour: 'Just as the commoner ... once held his land by the munificence and at the pleasure of the lord, so today the worker holds his labour at the pleasure of the master and proprietor.'[19] It no longer belonged to him in any recognised or recognisable sense. As soon as the labourer finished making his product, society claimed it. Proudhon contested the idea that the worker made a contract with his employer on an equal footing, and simply exchanged his labour for wages. He argued against defining the wage relation as an 'exchange', since 'in every exchange there is a moral obligation that neither of the contracting parties shall gain at the expense of another'.[20] Proudhon insisted that to be legitimate, all exchanges had to be exempt from all inequality and be voluntary.

The socialist argument was that commerce or exchange must always be understood as a social act, not as an abstract transaction between two equal individuals. For socialists, any economic transaction was informed by the power relations between unequals:

> The negro who sells his wife for a knife, his children for some bits of glass, and finally himself for a bottle of brandy, is not free. The flesh merchant with whom he negotiates is not his associate but his enemy.[21]

In the same way, (but always in contrast to the 'negro'), the 'civilised labourer' who built a palace and slept in a stable was not free. He produced everything and did without everything. Such an arrangement could not be characterised as a free exchange, and in the process his employer became his enemy and not his comrade. Under these circumstances, John Rawls's view of society as a co-operative enterprise in which the citizens stand as equal partners was an impossibility. For utopian socialists, property dissociated individuals from one another, making them enemies and not comrades, and so it could never provide the ground on which people could meet each other on an equal footing.

Proudhon argued that in order for the producer to survive, the labourer's wages must be enough for him to be able to buy back the product he had made. Under the current system, if a worker received three francs a day for his labour, his employer sold the day's labour of his employee in the form of merchandise for more than three francs. The worker could not then repurchase what he had produced for his master, and so when they bought the products of other people's labour, in effect 'they must pay more for their own labour than they get for it'.[22] In this situation, to satisfy property, the labourer had to produce beyond his needs and beyond his strength. The inadequacy of wages forced workers to monopolise their labour and to compete with one another, 'before being destroyed by scarcity, to destroy each other by competition'.[23] Under these conditions, the labour of one worker harmed others and encroached on their rights. The natural right to labour was not sufficient to guarantee either material abundance or human flourishing.

Socialists emphasised the *social* character of production, and in particular workers' claims to the benefits of their work: their right to participate in controlling the production process and the right to work. When the whole society laboured, it produced for the whole society. The problem was that if the worker's wages were not enough to cover the purchase of his product, it followed that the product was not made for the producer, but for the richer consumer, and so for only a fraction of society. Under these conditions, where only part of society consumed, 'sooner or later a part of society will be idle' and masters and proprietors would live off the drudgery of others.[24] Property pitted men against another: 'Whoever takes by force or cunning what is not the product of his labour, destroys his sociability; he is a brigand.'[25] Like the aristocrat in the liberal account, the master or proprietor was a parasite, living off property that was undeserved and unearned. Socialists moved from there to a critique of idleness. Winstanley, Proudhon and Marx all agreed on the universal obligation to labour. As Winstanley put it, there should be no idle person or beggar in the land. The socialist view of human nature held that humans were essentially productive. They were actors engaged in praxis, and they expressed themselves through work and labour.

This is in part about the socialist conception of human nature and the centrality of sociability and creativity to humanity. For Proudhon, and the utopian socialists, social instinct and moral sense were common to all people and animals. Humans were characterised by their reflective and reasoning powers, and it was injurious to others and to ourselves 'to resist the social instinct which governs us and which we call justice'.[26] This echoed Winstanley's arguments about how the original 'evenness' between humans was destroyed by covetousness and private property, and Rousseau's insistence that private property overlaid and distorted rather than expressed human nature. The selfish man, the robber, sinned against this original nature. The idler or the rogue who enjoyed the social product without performing any social task 'should be charged as a thief or a parasite'.[27] Idleness should be punished. As Richard Pipes points out, utopias often rest on harsh discipline and are strictly controlled enterprises.[28] For Proudhon, we owed it to ourselves to give the idle person nothing, to put him under surveillance and make him work. For socialists, practising justice meant giving each person an equal share of wealth under equal conditions of labour – 'it is to act socially'.[29] Property represented the failure of the social instinct. It was not a binding process; it did not and could not represent the connective tissue between individual human beings. Civil society, understood as a loose association of rational market actors relating to each other through contract, was a distortion, and ultimately a destruction, of sociability and equality and so of humanity.

The entanglement of the core concepts of socialism with each other and with property means that as property suppresses the social instinct it also represents a restriction on freedom. A. Sivanandan describes what he calls the 'unspoken morality' of socialism:

> a simple faith in human beings and a deep knowledge that, by himself or herself, the individual is nothing, that we need to confirm and be confirmed by each other, that only in the collective good our selves can be put forth and grow.[30]

It is this sense of the self as constituted by the collective good and by the social instinct that is directly contradicted by the institution of private property and the radical individualism of civil society and market rationality. Private property is part of the structure of morality, and utopian socialism provides a moralising critique of the prevailing conditions under *Recht* and capitalism. Overcoming alienation involves 'a reintegration of the self and, hence, a re-establishment of control by the individual over that self'[31] and a resurgence of the collective good.

This positive view of freedom, requiring other people, was at the heart of the utopian socialist vision. Proudhon's analysis of property, equality and labour described the problem of how property and possession had been pulled apart, and property had extinguished the social instinct. The question for socialists was how to overcome the egoism and the damage of property, recover the social instinct, reintegrate the self and bring equality and labour back together. George Crowder describes how in the thought of the classical anarchists this sense of self-mastery, reintegration of the self and perfectibility was linked to an assumption about the ultimate harmony of the universe. The utopian socialists saw the universe as an orderly system, within which people could live together without conflict. Society had been dislocated by capitalist industrialism, and (rather as conservatives argue about individualism) had proved to be fundamentally disorientating. It had been divided between occupations: agriculture had been set against manufacturing, and artisans against the factory labour force. It could, however, according to the utopian socialist account, all be brought back into harmony through association, community and co-operation. People working together in small groups would experience solidarity, combination, common living and identity through their participation in clubs, friendly societies and small workshops. Some of their schemes and experiments were modest and small scale, and many of their key values 'were derived from the artisan experience', and in particular the rejection of large-scale mechanisation.[32] They seem to be describing an idealised version of Hegelian civil society: a series of harmonious associations rather than a battlefield tearing individuals from their social ties. Through such associations, members of different social classes would become aware of their common interests, rather than inevitably finding themselves in conflict.[33] The productive and rational use of property could be humanising and, according to the utopian socialists, could help people to overcome the disorientation at the heart of modernity. Utopian socialism addressed itself to the disorientating problems of dehumanisation, powerlessness and loss of community, and attempted to apply ethical principles to these new problems.

Utopian socialism primarily concerned itself with alienation in its critique of capitalism, and focused on the possibility of human flourishing and issues of moral principle. Socialism as non-capitalism was, for them, about recapturing the social instinct and repairing the dislocations that had forced people apart. Possession, as opposed to unearned property, could be reclaimed and put to productive use. French socialism was undialectical, with no account of how capitalism would transform itself and generate socialism and equality. This strand of socialism is based on a moralising critique, within which the socialist society is built from the outside and 'theory is developed independently of the world'.[34] Changes in ownership, the organisation of work and the remuneration of labour would bring about a new type of society without violent upheaval. Such a reclamation required deliberate action and moral regeneration and not only structural changes to the social reality. In part, the utopian socialist case is about opposition to the selfishness and disorientation generated by modern commerce and the possibility of replacing it with the socially unifying 'spirit' of virtue through institutional reform and moral regeneration. For utopian socialists, a person could abandon private property in favour of mutualism through acts of authentic moral will, by recognising and valuing in others 'the distinctively human dignity he finds in himself.'[35] This is an interesting echo of the conservative plea for property structures that will sustain and express a 'shared dignity'. The difference lies in the socialist and anarchist belief in the possibility of wholesale reconstruction, and in a contentious 'perfectionist conception of freedom'.[36] For them, as there was for William Godwin, there was a moral truth inherent in the laws of nature, and hence the possibility of universal agreement on the ends of life and the best way to achieve them. Freedom was conceived as moral self-direction, the possibility of acting in accordance with the authentic self, governed by 'stringent, critical reason' and by virtue derived from natural law.[37] It is possible to argue, as Carol Gould does, that a concept of positive freedom is at the heart of socialism.[38] Where does that leave equality?

– SCIENTIFIC SOCIALISM –

While utopian socialism emphasised deliberate action and moral regeneration in its opposition to capitalism, classical Marxism tended to brush aside issues of moral principle. In direct opposition to the utopian socialists, scientific socialists argued that their theory did not develop independently of the world, or out of a desire to apply ethical principles to new problems. Scientific socialism arose out of the economic conditions: 'Marxism presented itself to itself from its inception as the consciousness of a struggle within the world, rather than as a set of ideals proposed to the world to which the world was required to adjust itself.'[39] With its focus on economics and the dynamics of history, classical Marxism saw equality as emerging through and as a result of history. In this framework, equality was understood to be unavoidable: capitalism carried it in its womb, and would give birth to it. The transformation would be brought about through the agency of the proletariat, acting as midwives, and not by moralists engineering solutions from the outside. Solutions grew in and out of problems, like an embryo gestating in the womb. Birth may be difficult and painful, but there was no other way out, no 'answer that comes from beyond the question'.[40] As G. A. Cohen terms it, this was an 'obstetric doctrine'.[41]

The dialectical idea held that every thing 'develops by unfolding its inner nature in outward forms and, when it has fully elaborated that nature, it dies, disappears, is transformed into a successor form precisely because it has succeeded in elaborating itself fully'.[42] Human industry led to growth in productive power until the economic structure perished. Capitalism destroys itself by perfecting itself. Its capacity to develop and reproduce meant that it both destroys and transcends itself, resulting in equality and communist society. Marx and Friedrich Engels argued that 'capitalist competition abolishes itself by creating enterprises of implicitly social character in which the capitalist becomes obsolete, so that little but his removal is needed to establish socialism'.[43] Marx criticised utopian socialists for trying to develop theories independently of the world, and for seeing 'in poverty nothing but poverty' rather than recognising the economic dynamic and dialectics of capitalism.[44] For scientific socialists, as long as the proletariat were fully aware of the conditions under capitalism, of the gravity of the task facing them and of the meaning of revolution, the transition to socialism was inevitable. For the defenders of the scientific version of socialism, utopian socialism was a precursor, a less advanced stage of socialism. Unlike the utopians, scientific socialists claimed to be able to understand the place of their project in the world and in history, because 'enough history has unfolded'.[45]

For scientific socialists history had its own dynamic logic and formed the bridge between the current cultural constraints of capitalism and the socialist future. Those who expected material abundance to guarantee socialism needed only to wait and organise for the post-revolution abolition of property. In the meantime, they treated private property as a mere bourgeois indulgence, an outgrowth of capitalism, self-interest masquerading as a right and a freedom. If this was so, then questions about distribution, injustice and violations related to property risked being shunted off into the future and ignored in the present. In the scientific socialist account, equality was guaranteed by the rise of an organised working class acting as the agent of change, and by the development of productive forces. Unlike the utopian socialists, with their suspicion of mechanisation and industrialisation, scientific socialists argued that industrial production gave human beings the power to transform nature for their benefit and to sustain material abundance. The processes of industrialisation could be harnessed in order to overcome the maldistribution of resources which made it appear as though capitalist society inevitably produced scarcity for some.

In the scientific socialist account, replacing scarcity with abundance would be enough to make it 'possible to supply what everyone needs for a richly fulfilling life'.[46] Marx's ideal society required conditions of abundance, and he argued that abundance would bring with it full self-realisation and a new form of social unity based on the abolition of private property and of the division of labour. The transformation would be total: socialism was anti-capitalism, and the reality of socialist abundance was the opposite of the illusion of capitalist scarcity. In this abundant society, socialised men who were no longer dissociated from each other by the structures of private property and the division of labour would become 'associated producers' who could bring nature under control through rational regulation. The problem with this approach was that it set up a narrative of dichotomy. The gap between abundance and scarcity became unbridgeable, and it was then impossible for socialists to admit the possibility of scarcity in socialist societies. The closed circuitry of the argument suggested that scarcity takes us straight back to capitalism. For Marx, anything short of abundance, any hint of scarcity, would lead to a struggle for necessities, social conflict and so a return to class society.

The crux of the question about property and socialism was how to deal with the conditions of *Recht*, and the sphere of exchange and circulation where the worker was an owner and seller of labour power, able to make free contracts and pursue mutual advantage. For the utopian socialists, primarily concerned with human flourishing and freedom, the exchange relation had the potential to be equal, reciprocal and genuinely voluntary. Proudhon argued that commerce could exist among free men, with transactions carried out without violence or fraud, as long as neither of the contracting parties gained at the expense of the other. This was not only a critique of the prevailing conditions under capitalism, it also raised the possibility that under other conditions, property relationships were possible and non-damaging. On Marx's reading of Proudhon, this approach related only to the superficial form of property and not to the underlying questions of alienation and exploitation. For Marx, human selfishness was ineradicable where scarcity existed and conflicts over resources might arise. Such conflicts could not be resolved through commercial exchange; that would bring us straight back to conflictual social relations based on class. Property relationships, for scientific socialists, could not be non-damaging or humanising.

As Cohen argues, the scientific socialist attitude towards material abundance was simultaneously pessimistic and optimistic: anything short of abundance was fraught with danger, while material abundance took us straight to rich and fulfilled lives. This optimism was reflected in the vision of the communist society of the future that it brought with it. In communist society, the principles of *Recht* were assumed to have withered away. The necessity for labour would decrease, and there would be time for the free development of individuals. For associated producers, work becomes a free activity and the product belongs to the worker. Marx tended to see self-interest as tied to civil society and private property, rather than as part of the hard core of the individual. Egoistic man was separated from other men and from the community, like the fragmented self described by Sivanandan: 'a small, selfish inward-looking self that finds pride in lifestyle, exuberance in consumption and commitment in pleasure – and then elevates them all into a politics of this and that'.[47] Capital fragmented the self as it fragmented society, and communism as non-capitalism ended the false opposition between the particular and the common interest, between self-preservation and common preservation. For scientific socialists, the abolition of private property would end alienating social relationships and exploitation. Supply and demand would dissolve into nothing as people gained more control over exchange, production and social relations.

For scientific socialism, the morality of emancipation was based on setting people 'free from the pre-history of human bondage'.[48] The dynamic logic of history and of social reality, rather than our own moral regeneration and individual reason, would take us from the past into the future. Emancipation entailed the abolition of the contradiction between separate individual interests and the common interest, bringing with it the development of higher forms of humanity. Emancipation and enlightenment enabled individuals and collectivities to determine their true interests, and to release themselves from forms of coercion based on mystification and illusion. Rather than feeling themselves 'unroofed' or robbed of harmony by the power of modern enlightenment, socialists 'find a liberating force in the recognition that any social role can be held up to human criticism and that no such necessities are dictated to us by nature'.[49] In a communist society, the transient nature of structures, ideas and beliefs would became clear, and people would transcend the limitations that class interests had placed on human association.

As we have seen, scientific socialists argued that the abolition of private property would bring with it the abolition of the division of labour. For them, wherever labour was divided and workers were dissociated, the interests of one and the interests of the whole were brought into conflict and turned into a division between one class and another. However, the simultaneous abolition of private property and the division of labour would, for scientific socialists, bring about the recovery of an undivided and classless society. For Marx, since private property was the negation of the personality in every sphere, communism was 'the universalization of the condition of propertylessness'.[50] Propertylessness automatically entailed classlessness. The new communist society would be a non-acquisitive society of material abundance and plenty. Without the distortions of private property and class, decisions about distribution and justice would be made collectively.[51]

Unlike the moral regeneration of the will required by utopian socialism, scientific socialism expected equality and classlessness to emerge from the collapse of capitalist relations. They relied on historical inevitability and an evolutionary view of progress that took very little account of the morality of the individuals involved. They did, however, need to provide some picture of 'what kind of beings human beings are and might one day become, and more particularly [of] what limitations they have and how these might constrain the feasible shapes of an alternative future'.[52] Norman Geras argues that this required scientific socialists to make a 'quite remarkable leap' that takes us from people we know to people freed from familiar human faults and vices, and 'improved ... beyond recognition'.[53] For Cohen, the obstetric conception of change has proved to be false and damaging. It carried the risk of assuming that the concrete analysis of a concrete situation would disclose to you what your political intervention should be. For scientific socialists, the solution simply issued from the problem. History unfolded itself: dissociated producers associate, conflictual individuals make collective decisions and particular interests dissolve into the common. Under these conditions, Steven Lukes argues, 'you do not expect and therefore do not face the uncertainties and hard choices with which a responsible politics must contend'.[54] In other words, scientific as well as utopian socialism failed to recognise that 'we have to start from where we are, therefore from the realities of human motivation, of moral weakness as much as moral strength, with which we are familiar, and not simply fly towards a speculative ideal' either of an ultimate harmony or of classlessness.[55]

– EXPLOITATION AND NEED –

Historically, scientific socialism has been characterised, as we have seen, as a struggle on behalf of working people to create a world in which there are only workers. The proletariat is, by definition, a set of people who both create the wealth and end up with very little of it. A worker can say, 'I made this: I produced the goods and they were taken from me' and 'I need this: I have been left with nothing, and I have nothing to lose.'[56] As a labourer I have a right to my products, and as a proletarian I enjoy none of them, and I suffer as a result. Cohen argues that this connection between exploitation and need is crucial to a scientific understanding of socialism, and that it can no longer hold together. Those who produce the wealth and those in need are no longer the same set of people. It is no longer (if it ever was) only working people who suffer. Even under conditions of material abundance, the permanently unemployed, the unemployable, disabled people and carers remain in need. The optimism of the scientific socialists, the idea that equality was inevitable, guaranteed by the rise of an organised working class and the development of productive forces, has proved unfounded. It has failed to deliver what everyone needs to live a rich and fulfilling life. This means that we can no longer rely on material abundance to achieve equality, and so property relations have begun to raise particular problems for socialism because they ' have to seek equality for a context of scarcity'.[57]

In this new context, exploitation and need are in a different and potentially contradictory relationship. Marx's initial problematic was about the problem of surplus value, and it was this concern that locked exploitation and need together. The idea that those who made the wealth had very little of it was central to capitalism's capacity for modernisation, industrialisation and investment, and to the issues these raised about commodity production, classes and property relationships. Frederic Jameson argues that these are problems specific to modernisation that have disappeared in late capitalism:

> Capitalism may well have triumphed, but its outcome is increasingly marked by dizzying paper-money speculation on the one hand, and new forms of 'immiserisation' on the other, in structural unemployment and in the consignment of vast tracts of the Third World to permanent unproductivity.[58]

In the new global context of scarcity and abundance, the problem of inequality cannot be solved by the development of the productive forces, or by the organised working class. The problem is not just that those who produce the wealth have very little of it, but what happens to those who are not deemed productive, who are excluded from the world of workers and so cannot belong.

Modern socialism needs to take into account the impact of these new forms of pauperisation and structural unemployment. Two-thirds of the world is hungry 'while the affluent are titillated with ever more sophisticated - and often environmentally destructive – consumer goods'.[59] The richest fifth of the world has over 90 per cent of the world's income, while the poorest fifth has just 0.25 per cent, making an income inequality ratio of 400:1.[60] In the richer countries, capital does not have to import cheap labour any more. It moves instead to the 'captive labour pools' of the poor countries, choosing its locale of exploitation.[61] The burden of extracting surplus value has shifted from workers at the centre to people at the periphery, who are a different kind of worker, not needed on a long-term basis and working in countries without a social wage below which labour cannot fall. Poor countries are desperate to end unemployment, and so they remove labour laws and trades union rights in order to offer cheaper and cheaper deunionised, female and child labour to the capitalists. The realities of uneven development mean that centres and peripheries are polarised less in terms of their rates of industrialisation, and more in relation to productive social co-operation. Even where exploitation and need are reconnected, the development of the productive forces and the organisation of the working class are not part of the social reality on offer. Rather than being able to organise themselves in opposition to capitalist expansion, those in need are fragmented and pauperised.

For some modern Marxists, the overarching conflict is 'between the class interests that impose globalization and the discontented masses'.[62] According to this analysis, the US and other dominant imperial powers rely on coercion and economic power to keep other countries under their control and influence. This new phase of capitalism destroys the environment, makes violence endemic and impoverishes the masses of the world. According to this argument, new 'postmodern economies' have emerged, concentrated in the informal sector sustained by globalisation and technology. These diverse economic activities, including street vending, flea markets and garbage scavenging, are undertaken by the underemployed 'and the discarded sectors of society'.[63] Cain, the shut out of the earth, has indeed (as Winstanley argued) become a scavenger in a world of freelance hustlers. As the meaning of work and labour has shifted, so have the meanings of ownership and the sites of exploitation and need. Capitalists have found that it is no longer necessary to be the direct owners of the means of production. The class struggle has been transformed by sourcing and contracting out. The cheaper labour zones such as Singapore, Malaysia and Hong Kong provide sweatshops in the electronics industry and subcontracting creates a new transnational labour market. Within this labour market, there is a new structural logic of core and periphery, where the core labour is high skill, high wage and guaranteed, and peripheral labour is low wage, low skill, informal and casual. These low-wage sectors create 'a veritable "Third World" within the overdeveloped countries'.[64]

The complexity of these new relationships and markets ruptures the link between exploitation and need. Once the link is broken, socialism can no longer confine itself to dealing only with class. The scavengers and the freelance hustlers, those who are permanently unemployed and those who work in the service industries and as care providers will often turn out to be 'discarded' or excluded on the basis of race and gender as well as class. Women frequently make up 80 per cent of the workforce in the Asian 'free zones' and are paid $2 a day.[65] The traditional division between the factory and the household is no longer straightforward. Service and domestic-sector employment in the core nations has been growing, and so has paid industrial homework – production contracted out to the household. At the same time, the association between women and care work persists, and the distinction between paid and unpaid labour is attached to the division between women and men. [66] The processes of constituting labour power, deciding what counts as labour, are central to the inequalities created and sustained by modern capitalism. Labour is a 'value-creating activity'. It may be creative and dignifying for the individual, but it is also always linked to 'questions of social value'.[67] As such, it cannot be separated from gender as a carrier of social value. Class turns around the experience of inferiority, and as a category is always 'contingent and embodied, as always necessarily having to realize and specify itself by way of the categories of gender and race'.[68]

Once these contingencies and embodiments are taken into account, it is possible to see inequalities and injustices that persist in the new context of scarcity. This means that scientific socialism can no longer claim to be 'anti-moral', and define itself straightforwardly in opposition to the moralising stance of utopian socialism. Lukes argues that 'marxism [sic] has from its beginning exhibited a certain approach to moral questions that has disabled it from offering moral resistance to measures taken in its name'.[69] It is unable to offer an adequate account of justice and rights, and this is particularly clear in its struggle with the contested moral space of property, where it intersects with labour and belonging. For Lukes, the problem is that socialism's focus on the future tends to rule out 'the interests of persons in the here and now', before they are improved beyond recognition.[70] The danger is that this means ignoring current injustices and violations being visited on human beings with limitations, faults and vices. Property becomes a problem with a future solution, rather than an expression of actually existing social relations, injustices and inequalities. The focus on the universal obligation to labour at the heart of socialism risks reproducing the distinction between righteous labour and drudgery, and leaving it inseparable from questions of belonging and exclusion. Those who are underemployed and discarded, whose labour does not count as righteous and creative, are left to struggle with the morality of *Recht* without having even the potential to become 'associated producers', self-directing beings who achieve self-realisation in community with others.

– Notes –

1. The History Guide, 'The French Revolution and the Socialist Tradition; Early French Communists (1)' (2000), quoting Jean-Jacques Rousseau, 'Discourse on the Origin of Inequality', http://www.historyguide.org/intellect/lecture19a.html
2. Anthony Wright, *Socialisms* (Oxford: Oxford University Press, 1986), p. 80.
3. George Crowder, *Classical Anarchism* (Oxford: Clarendon Press, 1991), p. 102.
4. Steven Lukes, *Marxism and Morality* (Oxford: Oxford University Press, 1985), p. 25.
5. Lukes, *Marxism and Morality*, and Chapter 4 above.
6. Lukes, *Marxism and Morality*, p. 33.
7. Ibid. p. 35.
8. Ibid. p. 53, quoting Karl Marx, *Capital*, Vol. 1.
9. Ibid. p. 54.
10. Derek Sayer, *Capitalism and Modernity* (London and New York: Routledge 1991), p. 64.
11. Lukes, *Marxism and Morality*, p. 78.
12. Pierre-Joseph Proudhon, *What is Property?*, edited and translated by Donald R. Kelley and Bonnie G. Smith (Cambridge: Cambridge University Press, [1840] 1994), p. 35.
13. Ibid. p. 66.
14. Ibid. p. 75.
15. Ibid. p. 57.
16. Ibid. p. 65.
17. Ibid. p. 31.
18. Ibid. p. 36.
19. Ibid. p. 92.
20. Ibid. p. 103.
21. Ibid. p. 103.
22. Ibid. p. 144.
23. Ibid. p. 145.
24. Ibid. p. 145.
25. Ibid. p. 172.
26. Ibid. p. 174.
27. Ibid. p. 177.
28. Richard Pipes, *Property and Freedom* (London: Harvill Press, 1999), p. 41.
29. Proudhon, *What is Property?*, p. 177.
30. A. Sivanandan, *Communities of Resistance: Writings on Black Struggles for Socialism* (London and New York: Verso, 1990), p. 58.
31. Michael Freeden, *Ideologies and Political Theory: A Conceptual Approach* (Oxford: Clarendon Press, 1996), p. 443.

32. Keith Taylor, *The Political Ideas of the Utopian Socialists* (London: Frank Cass, 1982), p. 19.
33. Ibid. p. 35.
34. G. A. Cohen, *If You're an Egalitarian, How Come You're So Rich?* (Cambridge, MA: Harvard University Press, 2000), p. 74.
35. Crowder, *Classical Anarchism*, p. 103.
36. Ibid. p. 4.
37. Ibid. p. 10.
38. Carol C. Gould, 'Democratic Egalitarianism', in James P. Sterba (ed.), *Social and Political Philosophy: Contemporary Perspectives* (London and New York: Routledge, 2001).
39. Cohen, *If You're an Egalitarian*, p. 102.
40. Ibid. p. 68.
41. Ibid. p. 64.
42. Ibid. p. 46.
43. Ibid. p. 48.
44. Ibid. p. 52. The quotation is from Marx, 'The Poverty of Philosophy'.
45. Ibid. p. 74.
46. Ibid. p. 114.
47. Sivanandan, *Communities of Resistance*, p. 44.
48. Lukes, *Marxism and Morality*, p. 29.
49. Bernard Williams, 'Necessary Identities', in Tommy L. Lott (ed.), *Subjugation and Bondage: Critical Essays on Slavery and Social Philosophy* (Boulder, CO and Oxford: Rowman and Littlefield, 1998), p. 21.
50. Iain Hampsher-Monk, *A History of Modern Political Thought* (Oxford: Blackwell, 1992), p. 509.
51. Ibid. p. 560.
52. Norman Geras, *The Contract of Mutual Indifference* (London: Verso, 1997), p. 103.
53. Ibid. p. 103.
54. Lukes, *Marxism and Morality*, p. 76.
55. Geras, *Contract of Mutual Indifference*, p. 103.
56. Cohen, *If You're an Egalitarian*, p. 106.
57. Ibid. p. 115.
58. Frederic Jameson, 'Actually Existing Marxism', in Saree Makdisi et al. (eds), *Marxism Beyond Marxism* (New York and London: Routledge, 1996), p. 22.
59. P. Self, 'Socialism', in Robert E. Goodin and Philip Pettit (eds), *A Companion to Contemporary Political Philosophy* (Oxford: Blackwell, 1993), p. 339.
60. Kai Nielsen, 'Socialism and Egalitarian Justice', in Sterba, *Social and Political Philosophy*, p. 207.
61. Sivanandan, *Communities of Resistance*, p. 180.
62. Roger Burbach et al., *Globalization and its Discontents* (London and Chicago: Pluto Press, 1997), p. 2.
63. Ibid. p. 154.
64. Kenneth Surin, '"The Continued Relevance of Marxism" as a Question: Some Propositions', in Makdisi et al., *Marxism Beyond Marxism*, p. 185.
65. Ibid. p. 187.
66. Anne Phillips, 'What has Socialism to Do with Sexual Equality?' in Jane Franklin (ed.), *Equality* (London: IPPR, 1997), p. 117.

67. Kathi Weeks, 'Subject for a Feminist Standpoint', in Makdisi et al., *Marxism Beyond Marxism*, p. 92.
68. Jameson, 'Actually Existing Marxism', p. 43.
69. Lukes, *Marxism and Morality*, p. 141.
70. Ibid. p. 146.

CHAPTER 7

Conservatism

Conservatism hopes to use property to overcome the disorientation of individualism and to counter the dangers of abstract equality. Where socialists seek for humanity and shared dignity in the abolition of property, conservatives want to overcome the contingency and instability of property relationships by anchoring property firmly in nature and the imagined community. They aim not to set freedom loose, but to find authenticity and permanence in specific forms of belonging. They manage the conflicts of private property by emphasising anchorage over endowment, and by connecting liberty to property and to the idea of a civilised life, as well as to the nation and the state. Property as a political concept takes on a very specific meaning within conservative discourse, acquired not only through its relationship with other concepts and ideas – the family, individualism, civil society and the state, for example – but also through its relationship to conservatism itself. Property can be understood as conservatism's organising concept, drawing together the conceptions of history, security, independence and human nature that underpin conservatism. The idea of property itself becomes a kind of 'bridging mechanism' converting a variety of options into certainty and political identity. The fluid morphology of conservatism crystallises around its notion of private property – its 'primary fetish' as Roger Scruton describes it. It is the conservatives' 'tenacious regard of property – along with rank in polity [that is] their most obsessive and durable heritage'.[1]

As an ideology, conservatism offers no universal prescriptions of principles, ideals and institutions. It is 'procedural or methodological rather than substantive'.[2] Theorists have, however, attempted to identify a substantive core of beliefs that characterise conservatism. Anthony Quinton identifies three central doctrines: traditionalism, a sceptical view about political knowledge and a conviction that human beings and society are not susceptible to abstract theorisation. Similarly, the 'Oakeshottian core' emphasises stability and safety, respect for tradition and practices and the conviction that human beings are naturally embedded in their immediate social environment. For Scruton, the core is definable in opposition to the liberal emphasis on individual autonomy and the natural rights of man. One major conservative target is the idea that human beings are perfectible and infinitely malleable, a notion that they diagnose as being at the heart of both liberalism and socialism. This conflicts with the basic conservative attitude which 'seeks above all for government, and regards no citizen as possessed of a natural right that transcends his obligation to be ruled'.[3] Property, for conservatives, cannot belong to a state of nature or to an original position. It cannot be detached from the inequalities and relations of power, or from the idea of belonging to a particular community. Any attempt to impose an abstract order on the world is bound to be unnatural and destructive. For conservatives, it is never possible to rise above the concrete and particular, or for the individual to exist outside the social order. The conservative social order will turn out to be based on natural inequalities, on exclusion, power and privilege, and on freedoms that do not interfere with private property.

– PROPERTY AND INHERITANCE –

Property is 'almost sacred to conservatives: the accumulation of property, and its passing down through the family are seen as natural developments, vital to social stability'.[4] Property is 'above anything else in civilization, the very condition of man's humanness, his superiority over the entire natural world'.[5] In direct contrast to the socialist claim that property undermines the natural social instinct, in conservative thought property is integral to human nature. Conservatism takes us back to G. W. F. Hegel, to the connection between property and personality and to a whole web of attachments. The mature individual 'lives in the web of three kinds of opposition: he is set up against nature, himself and others'.[6] These oppositions are basic existential conflicts that cannot be abolished, but they can be contained. Property can contain or minimise the opposition between humans and nature. It creates a direct link to parts of nature and secures the individual against society.

For conservatives, without property it is impossible to see any part of the world as connected to or shared with anyone else, and there can be no common understanding of the world. Instead, the world 'remains alien to each of them, and a battleground for both'.[7] Once property is properly instituted, objects become the focus of rights and obligations and so self-consciousness becomes possible. Individuals take possession of their property, and of themselves. Through ownership, they relate to each other and to themselves, creating a social existence and some common ground. Social existence, for conservatives, presupposes proprietorship. Property bears 'the imprint of human social relations, and reflects back to its owner a picture of himself as a social being'. As we have seen in the discussion of Hegel, property has to be embodied and recognised by others. It has an integral social dimension. Once individuals are recognised as persons and as property owners, the world ceases to be a battleground and the property owner 'is now at home where before he was merely let loose'.[8] This notion of being 'at home' in the social world is crucial to conservatism, and owning property is essential to attaining it.

The conservative notions of property and of 'home' are heavily inflected by the idea of inheritance. Superiority over the natural world and the idea of continuing to master it take property beyond the individual, and stretch the threads of the web beyond a single lifetime. The distinction between being at home and being let loose rests on ideas of peace and permanence, and of rootedness. This makes the family a crucial component of conservative thought. Inheritance depends upon and expresses the strength of family life, and reinforces the connection between family and property which is part of human nature and of conservative 'natural' politics. For conservatives, there is a deep connection between property and self-realisation and between the sense of property and the sense of home as 'the place where private property accumulates, and so over-reaches itself, becoming transformed into something shared'.[9] Sharing is the essence of family life, and private property reinforces the primary social bond, and enables men to move beyond it, to transcend the family and reach the unity of the state. Women, according to this account, are expected to find their substantive destiny in the family, and not to aspire to move beyond or transcend it. Their role is to foster affection and morality: 'to love the little platoon we belong to in society is the first principle (the germ as it were) of public affections', the first link in the series of bonds by which we proceed towards a love of country and of mankind.[10] Family and property are deeply intertwined and it is a distortion to prise them apart: 'It is no accident that the ... concept of property is coupled to a ... notion of home-ownership, a form of property which provides the bastion of physical security, privacy, and self-containment for the family.'[11]

Property is central to this process of creating the social bond. For conservatives, it connects history, life and nation and is embedded in the social order through both custom and performance. The archetypal English gentleman, for example, brought his money home from the City and the colonies to his country retreat, 'to embellish the house, the landscape and the gardens with the trappings of peace and permanence.'[12] As a property owner, the individual is connected to the past through his ancestors, and to the present institutional order by the duties and responsibilities imposed on him by ownership. Scruton uses the example of the country house, where the squire employed farm hands and house servants and contributed to local agriculture, industry, employment and markets. In contrast to the conflictual rural property relations described by E. P. Thompson, Scruton insists that 'hierarchy was softened by neighbourliness, and wealth by mutual aid.'[13] Ownership was bound up with privileges like hunting rights, jury membership, and having a voice in the state. Property was experienced as personal honour, forging an intimate connection between the self and ownership, so that property is tied up with subjectivity. Subjectivity is in turn linked to privilege, and privilege is consolidated through financial and social distance. Certain forms of property in need of protection by conservatives are of a kind 'that many non-owners have no chance whatever of acquiring the means to possess'.[14] Property becomes something beyond the individual, an accumulation of experience, something transcendent in its incompleteness. It takes on an almost mystical life of its own, but even in its transcendence it remains firmly attached to particular sorts of owners; it belongs to the squires rather than to the farm workers and their neighbours. Property, for conservatives, is firmly attached to inequalities of power and is always about hierarchy, softened or otherwise. It determines the boundaries of belonging, fixing people (farm workers, servants and women) in their dependence and in their social roles.

Robert Nisbet argues that the dogmatics of conservatism emphasise the family character of property, its concreteness and connection, defined in opposition to the uncertainty and transitoriness of individual possession. Where liberalism is understood as the theory of the modern individual, conservatism has a much more ambivalent relationship both to modernity and to the individual as a social category. As we have seen, for conservatives the family is the primary unit of property and both are under threat in the modern world. For conservatives, the abolition of entail and primogeniture in the French Revolution inaugurated modernity and throughout the nineteenth century and beyond conservative ideas about property remained steadfastly pre-modern, emphasising its connections with duty, interdependence and stewardship. The conservative ideal of property ownership 'is agricultural, even feudal', epitomising an earlier mode of relating to the world.[15]

Conservatism is, by definition, resistant to democracy and to egalitarianism and it crystallises around opposition to the notion that it is possible entirely to refashion a people, to bring them into line with a set of preexisting abstract principles. This means that it is directly opposed to particular forms of individualism. Jeremy Bentham was identified as the primary offender, for his reliance on centralised authority, reason, bureaucracy and permanent reform, his 'icy rationalism with respect to all human arrangements'.[16] Conservatives distrust rationalism and stress the need to recognise the role of prejudice, feelings, emotions and experience as well as pure logic in reaching private judgements. Authority and wisdom, for conservatives, can be expressed through prejudice and tradition as well as through reason. They object, for example, to a moralised conception of property that identifies ownership with rational improvement. Edmund Burke and others direct conservative attention towards pre-rational common sense and away from the 'internal imperialism' associated with political rationalism and with some forms of individualism.[17] For conservatives, the revolutionary disposition, with rationalism at its heart, rests on 'the Cartesian illusion that one can clear the ground and start all over again'.[18] The rejection of this illusion is bound to affect conceptions of property. Property becomes part of common sense, associated with prejudice, custom and emotion, entangled with the pre-rational and the pre-modern. Richard Pipes, for example, includes acquisitiveness in his 'hard core' of human nature, so that it is not just part of human conduct. It is not available for refashioning. It cannot be cleared away: it is part of the densest undergrowth. It is not an accident that the metaphor Kenneth Minogue chooses to convey the impossibility of the Cartesian illusion is 'clearing the ground'.

Michael Oakeshott argues that modern rationalism set itself up as an enemy of authority, prejudice, tradition, custom and habit. A modern rationalist is sceptical, questioning and optimistic about the power of universal reason, common to all mankind. He or she endures the past as an encumbrance, and his or her intellect is insulated from external influence; 'he has no sense of the cumulation of experience' to counter the illusion that the ground can be cleared and humanity refashioned.[19] For the icy rationalists, politics becomes a technique, a puzzle to be solved by the application of reason. They imagine, for example, that they can find a rational and abstract formula for discovering how far a given society can move away from equality without injustice. Conservatives are deeply sceptical about the notion that all rational preferences are bound to coincide, or that a precise formulation of the rules will bring us to the best form of government. For Oakeshott, devices such as the original position and the veil of ignorance reinforce the idea that 'there is no knowledge which is not technical knowledge'.[20] For Oakeshott, this means that rationalism is preoccupied with certainty and with its own certainty in particular. It becomes 'a self-complete sort of knowledge' that is 'taught best to those whose minds are empty'.[21] Such empty minds, according to conservatives, are corrupted by the authority of technique, and so have no power to correct their own shortcomings or to recognise the limits of their knowledge. The kind of idealist reasoning to which conservatives object treats abstractions such as facts, values, concepts, ideas and relationships 'as though they were the whole of what is to be understood and made sense of, the whole of reality'.[22] For conservatives, this is a fundamental error and risks mistaking the appearances and illusions of property for the reality. They emphasise instead the importance of ambiguity, partiality, of the practical realities that are resistant to understanding and inadequately captured by thought. They hope to recapture a 'sense of incompleteness'.[23] Property is understood as a practical reality, but also as essentially incomplete. It can never be finished because passing it on is part of its essence. There is no escaping from it; 'enough' history can never unfold. The essence of inheritance is that it cannot be contained.

The conservative instinct is not to prevent change 'but to guard the essence which survives it'.[24] This includes guarding the essence of property, understood as the principle of inheritability, from those who seek to clear the ground, abolish property and start afresh. Inheritance may undergo changes to its institutional structure, or even to the constitution, but such changes can be rendered safe as long as the essence of inheritance is strengthened. Conservatives worry that the interests of 'absent generations' are 'jeopardised by too much democracy.'[25] Not only the excesses of the French Revolution, but also John Rawls's conception of the original position and the veil of ignorance threaten too much democracy by failing to represent these absent generations. Only the hereditary principle will guarantee 'to place the long-term view at the heart of politics',[26] and so effectively counter the forces of 'ignorant democracy.' Conservatism relies on a version of property that is not self-contained or self-generated, but stretches across the generations and strengthens the threads of connection.

For conservatives, 'the illusion that we can escape from our past is entirely crippling' and so is a theory of history based on imaginary evolutionary progression.[27] They reserve particular distaste for emancipatory and popular movements that attempt to overcome 'natural' inequalities and introduce freedoms that will interfere with private property. For conservatives, with their distrust of modernity, mass movements of the 'swinish multitude' are dangerous and bound to be destructive of property and order. Conservatism favours a view of history based on gradual change, and the connection of the future to the past. The future cannot be understood as 'the abstract expression of some entirely new and self-contained existence' in the way that those who believe in revolutionary change suggested.[28] It is crucial to avoid reading the past in terms of the present, seeking to discover a single plot line, a pattern leading us forward, progressing inexorably from the past towards the future. A conservative view of history, and of property, tends to emphasise the role of contingency, and of continuity rather than change driven by discernible laws of historical development.

Against what they saw as the abstraction and mechanisation of Enlightenment thinking, Romantic conservatives drew upon the knowledge that came out of community, family, intuition and inner experience. Conservatism stresses the importance of culture – history, life and nation - in giving an individual an understanding of his social nature. They argue that social and political practices are embedded in the social organism through custom and tradition. In their version of traditionalism, custom, ceremony and participation in institutional life are enacted and not designed, and it is this enactment and performance that 'makes history into reason' and allows the individual to relate himself to something transcendent.[29] For conservatives, unlike liberals, custom is not necessarily opposed to dynamism or change, and history has to take us beyond a theory of the individual.

These processes of participation and performance need to take account of political reality. Conservatism insists on the value of common sense, and on the validity of the concrete and the practical. The emptiness and certainty of the revolutionary principle meant that it could find no concrete institutional or constitutional form. Its abstract 'frenzy of virtue', connected to the natural rights of man, but disconnected from concrete political reality, destroyed the settled virtues of constitutional government necessary for the enjoyment of liberty, property and civilised life.[30] These three principles are the foundation of a conservative civil society, and together they form a kind of trinity, inseparable from each other. The conservative concept of liberty attacks the principle of abstract equality, declaring that human beings are unequal in their nature. Conservatives warn against the dangers of abstract equality disconnecting individuals from each other, from history, from nature and from their inner selves to create an 'internalised anarchy' and chaos. Individualism would bring with it dissociation and disorder. Instead, conservatives argue for the possibility of a fundamental design, a growing self-awareness 'which originates, just like the experiencing of property, in an earlier mode of relating to the world'.[31]

The series of bonds that take us from the family, through civil society to the nation are based, according to Burke, on two principles – 'the spirit of a gentleman, and the spirit of religion'.[32] A society infused by these spirits will be able to sustain the trinity of liberty, property and the civilised life. Burke's argument was a defence of the aristocratic social hierarchy against the forces of individualism. Without the nobility and the clergy, we would be in danger of creating 'a nation of gross, stupid, ferocious, and at the same time, poor and sordid barbarians, destitute of religion, honour, or manly pride'.[33] Rampant individualism can only hope to create barbarians, the polar opposites of civilised gentlemen. For conservatives, individuality has to be filled out by participation in the common life, the cultivation of inbred sentiments and duties and by the appeal to tradition. The only self we can discover that is not a barbarian is a social self. The individual 'should seek and find his completion in society', and it needs to be a civil, civilising and civilised society to ensure that the self he finds is a honourable and manly gentleman, and not a poor and sordid barbarian or a scavenging freelance hustler.[34] The key mechanism for guaranteeing civility is private property. Conservatism counters barbarianism with an emphasis on organic change, limited power and the 'idea of a self-motivated individual, exercising independence and force of character shored up by private property'.[35] Such an individual is subject to the laws of human nature and civilisation: 'the laws of property, of inequality, and of obedience'.[36] For conservatives, property cannot be detached from the structures of inequality and obedience. Liberty, property and the civilised life require a fixed hierarchy to sustain them.

– CONSERVATISM AND CIVIL SOCIETY –

The risks involved in decoupling individuals and their property from the structures of obedience were made clear during the French Revolution. The earlier mode of relating to the world, and the vision of a society resting on the foundation stones of liberty, property and civilised life, were under attack. Traditional mediating groups such as guilds, monasteries and corporations had been condemned as divisive by Jean-Jacques Rousseau and in 1791 all guilds were abolished. In 1792 marriage was declared a civil contract, grounds for divorce were made available, and primogeniture and entail were set aside. The revolutionaries aimed to destroy the link between property and corporate organisations such as the family, the church, the guild and the monastery, 'individualizing as far as possible the rights of ownership'.[37] In order for rights of ownership to be individualised, property would have to be pulled out of the undergrowth by the roots, and the link between hierarchy and order broken. Once it had lost its anchors in experience, custom and social performance, the ground was cleared for property to be equalised, levelled or abolished. Levellers, in the conservative view, can 'only change and pervert the natural order of things'.[38] This natural order is bound to include inequality. Individualising property risks implying an equal right to it.

The conservative response to the dangers of fixing property in the individual is complex, and not a straightforward rejection. Conservatism argues that universal selfishness – the hard core of human nature – means that humans are not naturally sociable. They follow Hegel in arguing that civil society is bound to be full of conflicts, a battlefield of economic competition. Like the pro-capitalist liberals, conservatives see competition and conflict as fundamental to the human condition, but unlike them, they argue that civil society has to be ordered politically, subjected to the state, in order to remedy its injustices and synthesise its particular interests into a universal political community.[39] For conservatives, civil society acts as a restraint on the passions and ambitions of individual men. For Burke, it thwarted the inclinations, controlled the will and brought the passions into subjection. Conservatism tends to work with a particular view of freedom and duty that relies on civil society for its fullest expression, and this means that the individual cannot be a territorial self. For conservatives, liberty requires restriction and the nature of men means that this 'can only be done *by a power out of themselves*'.[40] Family, religion, the local community, the guild and other intermediate groups reinforce liberty by shoring up corporate and communal rights as the basis for a conservative view of freedom, inextricable from belonging. Property itself acts as a kind of buffer, allowing strangers to remain strangers to one another, enabling them to trust each other without reducing the distance between them. It forms the basis of politeness.[41] Social institutions such as the church, the family, the school, the club, the business and private property are 'the foundation of a proper civility'.[42]

These conservative visions of property and civil society rest on an 'organicist conception of social structure.'[43] This means that they see society as a living whole and not as an aggregate of individuals, in opposition to liberal individualism and socialist collectivism. According to this strand of conservatism, society is an organic whole, and individuals are social animals, members of groups and communities, with a hard core of shared human nature, interdependent but distant and separate in important ways. The relationship between individuals and society is understood as symbiotic. Individuality can be expressed only through familiar rules and customs, social interactions, laws and norms. E. H. H. Green argues that this 'organicist conception of society served to provide the Conservatives with a distinctive social philosophy that differentiated it in crucial ways from classical Liberalism and Socialism'.[44] The problem was that not all conservatives held this organicist conception in its strongest form, and so while it differentiated conservatives from liberals and socialists, it also divided conservatives amongst themselves. For some, it is this 'organicist tenet' that was abandoned by libertarian conservatism, and in particular by the Thatcherite conservatives who embraced liberal market economics. This pro-capitalist strand of conservatism works with a notion of active self-proprietorship that is shared with pro-capitalist liberals. It plays with the risks of individualising property and of detaching individuals from the universal state. It is prepared to deal with separate individuals, rational market actors making contracts with one another. This approach directly contradicts the idea of society as an organic whole.

Organicist conservatives reject the notion of radical separation implicit in the libertarian claim. They bring the ideas of intimacy and connection to bear against the abstractness of human relationships in the capitalist world and argue, as we have seen, that 'property is the reflection of rootedness'.[45] Rootedness requires security and a sense of belonging to be valued above independence. According to Scruton:

> A citizen's allegiance requires fixed expectations, a settled idea of his own and others' material status, and a sense that he is not the victim of uncontrollable

forces that might at any moment plunge him into destitution or raise him to incomprehensible wealth.[46]

Property ownership brings with it not only the physical security of concrete expectations, but also the possibility of being able to make sense of the world by finding a place in it, rather than merely being set loose on the battlefield of civil society. Some of the conservative opposition (from both organicists and libertarians) to socialism and welfare liberalism is based on the conviction that they will undermine this notion of security. The Rawlsian focus on redistribution means that a central distributor of property is required, equality between individuals is presumed and the 'natural lottery' of inequalities is understood to be unjust. From the conservative perspective, welfare liberalism allows the state to take on the role of protecting private property and the public good, and in the process security as a concept is redefined. This process of redefinition rests, argue conservatives, on the idea of 'social rights', guaranteeing not only protection for the individual's own property, but 'access to the property of others gained with the help of the state'.[47] Against such social rights, all conservatives bring to bear the right to property that is based on exclusion, and that has to include the right to exclude the state.

– CONSERVATISM, PROPERTY AND THE STATE –

The relationship between property and the state in conservatism is a complicated one, and it brings us back to questions of how conservatism deals with modernity and change, and so to the French Revolution. Property, for conservatives, is in essence about inheritance, tradition and the social order, and so it is inseparable from politics and political change. Conservatism can in part be understood as an extended reflection on the revolution in France and a rejection of its goals and strategies. Karl Mannheim argues that the disjunction between liberal and conservative thinking at the turn of the nineteenth century was directly connected to concrete political and philosophical debate about the French Revolution, and in particular the conceptions of history and property underpinning the notion of revolutionary change. Burke argued that the revolutionaries in France had acted with little regard for the security of property. Conservatives looked back to the French Revolution and saw it as an attempt to undermine the power and influence of traditional groups within civil society such as guilds, monasteries and corporations. By abolishing these mediating institutions, the revolutionaries had interfered with private property and free enterprise, and attempted to narrow the range of things open to private ownership, bringing them under the control of the state. They disrupted the social order, and closed off some of the spaces where a natural aristocracy could flourish. For conservatives, possession carries responsibilities as well as rights, and widely diffused property fosters independence and self-reliance, and strengthens the family and the agencies of civil society against the power of the state.

According to conservatives, people's aims – defined as peace, security, fame, power, love – all rest on property, 'since they require the ability to assert a massive right against intrusion'.[48] The desire for property is inseparable from the desire for security, status and power. For conservatives, liberals have fundamentally misunderstood property by reducing it to a series of human agreements, in the same way as they have fundamentally misunderstood the state by reducing it to a partnership agreement. Instead, property needs to be understood as an institution, realised and protected in the forms of the state and as a right conditional on allegiance. Conservative rejection of the social contract as a way of understanding the constitution of the state is inextricably bound up with a conservative view of property. Burke in his *Reflections on the Revolution in France* carefully contrasted the French experience to England's Glorious Revolution of 1688. He argued that the Glorious Revolution was made to preserve ancient laws and liberties and the ancient constitution of government: 'It has been the uniform policy of our constitution to claim and assert our liberties, as an *entailed inheritance* derived to us from our forefathers, and to be transmitted to our posterity.'[49] Society 'exists through authority, and the recognition of this authority requires the allegiance to a bond that is not contractual but transcendent, in the manner of the family tie'.[50] Society requires forms of allegiance and a recognition of authority that transcend any contractual bond: 'the state ought not to be considered as nothing better than a partnership agreement in a trade of pepper and coffee'.[51]

Burke's argument was that we receive, hold and transmit our government and our privileges in the same manner as our property and our lives. By preserving and sustaining the natural rhythms of decay, fall, renovation and progression in the conduct of the state and property, conservatives claim that we can bring our artificial institutions into conformity with nature. It is centrally important that men should not act as if they are the 'entire masters' either of their own property or of the state. They must take account of both their ancestors and their posterity, the absent generations, and 'they should not think it amongst their rights to cut off the entail, or commit waste on the inheritance, by destroying at their pleasure the whole original fabric of their society'.[52] Cutting off the entail or laying waste to the principle of inheritance risks leaving a ruin instead of a habitation to those who come after them, and breaking the whole chain and continuity of the commonwealth by assuming that it was a partnership agreement. Under such conditions, 'no one generation could link with the other. Men would become little better than the flies of summer'.[53]

Scruton makes a similar point about property and the dangers of undermining the principle of inheritance. Death duties and capital transfer tax, he argues, use the taxation laws to attack hereditary wealth and undermine the transfer of wealth between generations. They constitute an attack on property, family and friendship and so risk breaking continuity 'when men take from their parents nothing but the fact of birth, and nothing tangible passes from generation to generation except by stealth'.[54] Property requires stability, and the dead have an enduring interest in our respect for them. It has to be a settled principle to enable parents to speculate in the education of their offspring and to develop habits, customs and a sense of honour. Without stability in property holding, the commonwealth 'would, in a few generations, crumble away, be disconnected into the dust and powder of individuality, and at length dispersed to all the winds of heaven'.[55] For conservatives, our natural instinct is to secure property and to preserve communities, not to take pleasure in the destruction or ruin of the institutions of the state. Scruton argues that it is reverence for the dead that has formed the basis of institution building. Schools, universities, hospitals, orphanages, libraries and churches are often created on the basis of trustees respecting the bequests of the dead and continuing their purposes by respecting their wishes. Trusteeship rests on respect for the dead; 'remove the dead from the equation, and you remove the unborn'.[56] Property is the cable that connects the past and the future, and the social order cannot include freedoms that interfere with it.

The conservative outlook is concerned with the long-term effects of social customs and political institutions and with the 'web of attachments' into which men are born and which are sustained by the institution of property.[57] These attachments have the potential to overcome the disconnection and disorientation of individualism. Society needs to be understood as a 'great primaeval contract', in Burke's famous formulation, 'not only between those who are living, but between those who are living, those who are dead, and those who are to be born'.[58] Living individuals are suspended between their ancestors and their posterity, and it is property that can connect them to both and form the threads of the web of attachments. Property also connects the individual to the state, and the foundation of good order involves balancing the subject's power of acquisition against the demands of the state. 'The strong struggle in every individual to preserve possession of what he has found to belong to him and to distinguish him, is one of the securities against injustice and despotism implanted in our nature.'[59]

This struggle within the individual to preserve her property against the state is also a struggle within conservatism. There were at least two conservative responses to the revolutionary move to abolish the voluntary associations and civil organisations that underpin civil society, and the differences between these responses reverberate through the development of modern conservatism and the divisions within it. One response was to emphasise the need to strengthen the autonomy of civil society, to develop forms of social and civil association which are not part of the state apparatus, and which indeed can act as a buffer against a despotic or authoritarian state. According to these conservatives, civil society is set up as against the state, a crucial line of defence against authoritarianism. The argument is that without civil society to act as a buffer, the state will gain too much power. In fascist Italy and Nazi Germany, for example, conservatives argue that the state had become the owner of last resort. Under these regimes, private property became a privilege bestowed by the state and the common good took precedence over self-interest. Private property and civil society withered away under the authoritarianism of the state.[60] Under these conditions, society is 'uncivilised' by too much government: 'In this world turned upside down by despotic governments, (potentially) self-determining and sociable individuals become lost, causes and effects appear reversed, and states represent themselves as the real and proper source of property, power and prestige.'[61] This is an argument with liberal elements about how individuals live and survive as independent beings in a free, industrious society. In the face of state authoritarianism, it transmutes into a strand of conservative argument, setting the effectiveness of self-determining individuals with rights and duties against overarching state power.

The danger of limiting the autonomy of civil society and allowing the state to determine the public good is obvious to conservatives, who emphasise individuals as the source of property and power. It creates the conditions for state regulation, centralised planning and political dependence. State institutions take over providing public utilities and services, and the government monopolises education, health care and social welfare. Under this 'administrative suffocation of civil society', the modern state transforms its citizens into passive subjects who are expected to trust the state as a benevolent power.[62] This development has to be combated by the growth of civil associations beyond the control of the state, nurturing 'local and particular freedoms' and providing a check on the power of the state.[63] Conservative attitudes to property leave a wide range of things open to private ownership, and not in public or communal ownership. The expectation is that by pursuing her own interest the individual will frequently promote the interests of society more effectively than she would if she set out to promote the common good. Conservatives create a larger private sector than socialists or social democrats and 'more of the activities of the society are a matter of buying and selling, and of buying and selling competitively'.[64] Diffusing property involves making a wider range of things open to private ownership, strengthening the freedom to acquire, hold and conserve property, and entrenching inequalities. The effect is that the conservative society 'enlarges the total of what is distributed according to the ability to pay, and decreases the total of what is distributed according to need'.[65] This strengthening of individual property is seen as a way of guaranteeing liberty, property and the civilised life by limiting the role of the state. Individuals are left to buy and sell, free from violence, theft and trespass, and to resist being uncivilised and made passive by too much government.

Conservatives, however, are bound to be ambiguous about a change that advocates a weak state and the sovereignty of the private and the individual. For organicist conservatives, this threatens to unbalance the trinity of liberty, property and the civilised life by removing the structures of inequality, obedience and inheritance that sustain it. According to this argument, strengthening individual property risks weakening the stable institutions that a conservative social order requires. The organicist conservative response rejects the individualism implicit in advocating the autonomy of civil society, and insists instead on the universality of the state. Scruton argues that conservatism in its organicist version originates in an attitude to civil society. The social-contract vision that comes out of revolutionary rationalism fails to capture the authority of the state, an authority that rests on shared institutions and a shared conception of human nature – without which the contract would be impossible to imagine. In this concern for legitimacy and authority, there is the sense of an ability to recognise a transcendent bond, outside the sphere of individual choice and consent. This 'bond of society', as we have seen, is transferred by the citizen from his family to place, people and country.[66] For Burke, it was this bond that had been broken by the French revolutionaries. These turbulent, discontented men of quality, puffed up with personal pride and arrogance, acted out of selfish ambition, and in doing so showed 'a profligate disregard of a dignity which they partake with others'.[67] This shared dignity, which should have formed the basis of the social bond, was sacrificed to ignoble and inglorious ambition. For more modern conservatives, the same danger is inherent in libertarianism. In the context of English civil society, this shared dignity ought to form the basis of bonds of honour between gentlemen, a belief in respectability and the crucial concept of trust. These are all bound to be undermined by any doctrine that bases itself on a complete break with the continuity of the past, and on a belief in individuals as the owners of their own self-generated holdings and the authors of their own morality. Conservatives have struggled to find a balance between individualising rights of ownership to strengthen independence and force of character, and developing social bonds that can conserve a shared dignity and a universal state.

– PATERNALIST AND LIBERTARIAN CONSERVATISMS –

Like liberalism, conservatism has had to deal with the general shift away from self-ownership towards welfare. The welfare state has two purposes. The first is redistributive or compensatory, and it attempts to enhance social justice. The second is functional: it sets out to deal with market failure and to enhance economic efficiency. Conservative opponents of the welfare state object to the way this smuggles in planning for economic growth, but their demands for deregulation and privatisation and the lowering of costs are not primarily based on economic arguments. For these critics, the welfare state 'diminishes the productive readiness of its members'.[68] It is self-destructive because it undermines the moral qualities of its citizens, and in particular their civic spirit. One conservative response is to stress the autonomy of civil society. Those who adhere to the principles of laissez-faire, express their 'almost unlimited faith' in the 'genuine capitalism' of the free-market economy.[69] State welfare, and in particular its remedies for poverty, worked to eliminate self-expression and to create a centralised and authoritarian system. For more paternalist conservatives, the issue was more about the balance between civil society and the state than about the absolute autonomy of civil society 'against' the state. The One Nation group established in the 1950s stressed the Conservative contribution to UK welfare legislation, but they were critical of the universalism of the welfare state that ignored the distinction between the industrious and the idle. The state, they argued, 'had taken on responsibilities better exercised by the citizenry'.[70] They were concerned to restore the 'proper balance' between the power of the state and the rights of the individual, and so to ensure that civil society remained civil while the state did not gain too much power and slip into authoritarianism.

The problem with this balancing act was that it had the potential to undermine the autonomy of civil society, and so the freedom of the individuals within it. These concerns were summarised by Margaret Thatcher in a 1968 lecture. She talked about the problem of reconstruction in the post-war period, with its emphasis on growth, state planning and authoritarianism. Conservative governments had not only failed to reverse socialism, but had in some cases embraced and extended its statism.[71] This, in her view, made it essential to 'roll back the frontiers of the state', stressing the values of personal responsibility, force of character and independence from the state. The agencies of civil society needed to be strengthened so that charity, philanthropy, entrepreneurship and benevolence could flourish in the place of dependency on the state. Liberty, markets and the rule of law offered the only possible way out of the serfdom offered by statism, and in particular by the organic conception of the state. The disposition to charity, for example, goes to the heart of a particular conception of society 'as a duty-bound relation between strangers'.[72] Charitable behaviour becomes a way of emphasising the importance of strangers, and of maintaining the distance between yourself and others, showing that the ties that bind are based on duty and responsibility. This rests on a particular way of imagining the community and the boundaries of belonging that is not to do with fraternity, but with civil distance. Property is a mechanism for holding people apart.

For conservatives, these delicate relationships are bound to be damaged by a welfare state that transforms government into a 'giant mechanism for the redistribution of private assets'.[73] When the state steps in, the argument goes, generosity is restricted. Money is taken away and spent by Government, and 'the blessing goes out of giving and out of the effort of earning to give'.[74] Freedom, property and individual initiative are given less weight than goals of social justice and equality determined by the state. Independence and force of character are not fostered. For conservatives, the emphasis on equality diminishes distance, assuming a consensus that does not exist. It is imposed on individuals through the coercive mechanisms of the state and taxation, and so is bound to require coercion at the expense of liberty and voluntary principles. Here libertarian conservative arguments are very close to Robert Nozick's critique of Rawlsian liberalism. This is where the conservative commitment to privatisation fits in, removing public utilities, public services and essential industries from state control and bringing them into the enlarged sphere of 'buying and selling'.[75] This expands the range of private ownership and free enterprise, and increases the range of resources distributed according to the ability to pay rather than according to need. As Ted Honderich points out, this can be taken as a conservative and not simply a libertarian principle. Burke advised William Pitt the Younger that his government should make food available to the hungry only by selling it for profit, not by distributing it according to need.[76] Property remains attached to the inequalities of power, and to structures that sustain liberty and the civilised life, rather than an abstract standard of equality or welfare.

Libertarian conservatives tend to characterise themselves as 'seeking to preserve what was of lasting value in nineteenth-century Liberalism against the ever-increasing aggression of an authoritarian state'.[77] Laissez-faire liberalism was embraced as a counter-balancing philosophy, a way of preserving and protecting the nineteenth-century liberal gains against socialist encroachment. These gains included a belief in personal liberty, and in the importance of the individual, property owning, free enterprise and fair competition, and these had all been absorbed into Tory philosophy. Thatcher's version of individualism emphasised the polity as an aggregate of individual citizens 'in which individual rights and duties were the fulcrum of social and political life'.[78] There was, as she famously declared, no such thing as society, only individuals and their families.[79]

The more paternalist strand of conservatism accepted the need for state assistance with industrial reorganisation and regeneration, but attempted to avoid state control of either industry or the economy by keeping state intervention to a minimum. The state was expected to act as 'an enabling body', intervening where necessary to correct failings in the economy, but also 'providing opportunities for existing economic agencies to bring about corrections'.[80] The state was supposed to act as a catalyst for change, using its influence to encourage industry to co-operate and interfering directly only as a last resort. This allowed for a degree of conservative planning, and relied on a notion of ends and objectives, such as full employment and modernisation, being shared by the state and civil society. Historically, it was these paternalist conservatives who had supported the regulation of wages and the conditions of work in the 'sweated' trades through the 1909 Trade Boards Act. Employers had no incentive to increase wages and the workers were not in a position to organise themselves into trade unions. For paternalists, the conditions resulting from sweated labour were so bad that state intervention was rendered necessary. From this perspective, it is possible to justify some degree of state intervention. It may sometimes be legitimate for the state to restrict the independence of civil society in order to remedy injustices and inequalities, or to protect the universal interest of the population. The requirements of the public good set some limits on the autonomy of civil society.[81]

Libertarian conservatives argue that even such minimal state intervention works to undermine the conditions of free enterprise and competition. General state interference with wages and conditions would prove counter-productive. The state, they argue, is bound to interfere in the wrong place and at the wrong time, blocking the spontaneous workings of the market and blighting the commercial decisions of rational market actors both as consumers and as producers. For libertarian conservatives, adults have to be treated as able to judge their own interests and make their own decisions about what occupation to follow. They need to be recognised as individuals who are able to live and survive as independent beings in a free, industrious society. Without state interference, they should seek for voluntary ways of protecting themselves, by forming trade unions, guilds and corporations which are bound to serve their interests better than the state. This libertarian strand of conservatism emphasises the 'social value and effectiveness' of the existing agencies of civil society, and views state action as a potential danger, a threat to that effectiveness, rather than as a supplement or an incentive.[82] The problem was that the individualism at the heart of this strand of libertarian conservatism carried its own dangers, an internal logic of individuation that worked to break down rather than enhance the effectiveness of the agencies of civil society. Relying too heavily on the territorial vision of the individual and on the right to exclude others meant individualising property and detaching individuals from the web of liberty, property and the civilised life, transmuting conservatism into libertarianism.

– CONCLUSION –

Conservatism converts a variety of understandings of property and ownership into a variety of political identities that connect property to the self and to the state. For organicist conservatives, from Burke through Hegel to Scruton, property creates social relationships that ensure that individuals are embedded into their environment in particular ways that sustain stability, inequality, hierarchy and obedience. In property, they would argue, we seek above all for government, for security. Property trumps the empty liberty of the radicals, and of the more libertarian conservatives who argue for the autonomy of civil society. It is security of property that can sustain manly sentiment and heroic enterprise, 'that proud submission, that dignified obedience, that subordination of the heart, which kept alive, even in servitude itself, the spirit of an exalted freedom'.[83] Submission and obedience are a prerequisite for belonging, and inextricable from freedom. This strand of conservatism attempts to bring freedom and belonging together, and to attach notions of honour and dignity to membership of a naturalised hierarchy and a fixed social order. The gendered language of manly sentiment and heroic enterprise is not accidental. It reflects the identification of property with the family and inheritance, and with the inequalities of power that are expressed through gender, and fixed as natural by conservatives. Social roles are understood to be rooted in nature, and conservatives worry that a loss of this certainty 'leads to alienation and a feeling that human beings have been unroofed and robbed of a harmony between themselves and the world'.[84]

This notion of being 'unroofed' is central to the debates about property within conservatism, and to the idea that individualism is fundamentally disorientating. For conservatives, the problem is how to deal with modernity and enlightenment, and in particular 'the recognition that any social role can be held up to human criticism'.[85] This suggests that property relationships can be pulled out of the densest undergrowth and attached to independent individuals living in a free, industrious society. Such unroofed individuals may not seek above all for government, and they may understand themselves to be possessed of natural rights to their property. Once they do, they bring 'old-fashioned' liberalism with them into conservatism, and the notion of self-ownership proves deeply disruptive to traditional conservative notions of honour and belonging and to the trinity of liberty, property and the civilised life.

– NOTES –

1. Robert Nisbet, *Conservatism* (Milton Keynes: Open University Press, 1986), p. 15.
2. Anthony Quinton, 'Conservatism', in Robert E. Goodin and Philip Pettit (eds), *A Companion to Political Philosophy* (Oxford: Blackwell, 1999), p. 247.
3. Roger Scruton, *The Meaning of Conservatism* (2nd edition) (London and Basingstoke: Macmillan, 1989), p. 16.
4. Roger Eatwell, 'The Nature of the Right, 1: Is There an "Essentialist" Philosophical Core', in Roger Eatwell and Noel Sullivan (eds), *The Nature of the Right: European and American Politics and Political Thought since 1789* (London: Pinter, 1989), p. 50.
5. Nisbet, *Conservatism*, p. 56.
6. R. N. Berki, *On Political Realism* (London: J. M. Dent and Sons, 1981), p. 168.
7. Scruton, *Meaning of Conservatism*, p. 99.
8. Ibid. p. 100.
9. Ibid. p. 101.
10. Edmund Burke, *Reflections on the Revolution in France*, ed. Conor Cruise O'Brien, (Harmondsworth: Penguin, [1790] 1969), p. 135.
11. Michael Freeden, *Ideologies and Political Theory: A Conceptual Approach* (Oxford: Clarendon Press, 1996), p. 390.
12. Roger Scruton, *England: an Elegy* (London: Pimlico, 2000), p. 238.
13. Ibid. p. 239.
14. Ted Honderich, *Conservatism* (London: Hamish Hamilton, 1990), p. 92.
15. Quinton, 'Conservatism', p. 258.
16. Nisbet, *Conservatism*, p. 43.
17. Ibid. p. 34.
18. Kenneth Minogue, 'Revolution, Tradition and Political Continuity', in Preston King and Bikhu Parekh (eds), *Politics and Experience* (Cambridge: Cambridge University Press, 1968), p. 306.
19. Michael Oakeshott, *Rationalism in Politics and Other Essays* (Indianapolis: Liberty Press, 1991), p. 6. While I have neutralised some of the pronouns, it is not accidental that conservatives rarely use gender-neutral language.
20. Ibid. p. 15.
21. Ibid. p. 16.
22. Berki, *On Political Realism*, p. 74.
23. Ibid. p. 75.
24. Scruton, *Meaning of Conservatism*, p. 52.
25. Scruton, *England*, p. 187.
26. Ibid. p. 189.
27. Minogue, 'Revolution, Tradition and Political Continuity', p. 283.
28. E. H. H. Green, *Ideologies of Conservatism: Conservative Political Ideas in the Twentieth Century* (Oxford: Oxford University Press, 2002), p. 284. The quotation comes from R. A. Butler in 1961.
29. Scruton, *Meaning of Conservatism*, p. 40.
30. Arthur Aughey, 'The Moderate Right: the Conservative Tradition in America and Britain', in Eatwell and Sullivan, *The Nature of the Right*.
31. Karl Mannheim, *Conservatism: a Contribution to the Sociology of Knowledge* (London and New York: Routledge and Kegan Paul, 1986), p. 95.
32. Burke, *Reflections on the Revolution in France*, p. 173.

33. Ibid. p. 174.
34. Scruton, *Meaning of Conservatism*, p. 66.
35. Freeden, *Ideologies and Political Theory*, p. 355.
36. Ibid. p. 357, quoting W. H. Mallock, 1880.
37. Nisbet, *Conservatism*, p. 9.
38. Burke, *Reflections on the Revolution in France*, p. 138.
39. John Keane, 'Despotism and Democracy: the Origins and Development of the Distinction Between Civil Society and the State, 1750–1850', in John Keane (ed.), *Civil Society and the State* (London: Verso, 1988), p. 53.
40. Burke, *Reflections on the Revolution in France*, p. 151.
41. Scruton, *England*, pp. 50, 151, 158.
42. Aughey, 'Moderate Right', p. 104.
43. Green, *Ideologies of Conservatism*, p. 286.
44. Ibid. p. 287.
45. Eatwell, 'Nature of the Right', p. 50.
46. Scruton, *Meaning of Conservatism*, p. 96.
47. Richard Pipes, *Freedom and Property* (London: Harvill, 1999), p. 246.
48. Scruton, *Meaning of Conservatism*, p. 102.
49. Burke, *Reflections on the Revolution in France*, p. 119.
50. Scruton, *Meaning of Conservatism*, p. 45.
51. Burke, *Reflections on the Revolution in France*, p. 194.
52. Ibid. p. 192.
53. Ibid. p. 193.
54. Scruton, *Meaning of Conservatism*, p. 109.
55. Burke, *Reflections on the Revolution in France*, p. 194.
56. Scruton, *England*, p. 187.
57. Scruton, *Meaning of Conservatism*, p. 201.
58. Burke, *Reflections on the Revolution in France*, pp. 194–5.
59. Ibid. p. 245.
60. Pipes, *Property and Freedom*, pp. 218–22.
61. John Keane, 'Despotism and Democracy', p. 45.
62. Ibid. pp. 58–9. Keane is summarising Alex Tocqueville's argument.
63. Ibid. p. 61.
64. Honderich, *Conservatism*, p. 103.
65. Ibid. p. 89.
66. Scruton, *Meaning of Conservatism*, p. 33.
67. Burke, *Reflections on the Revolution in France*, p. 135.
68. Herfried Münkler and Karsten Fischer, 'Common Good and Civic Spirit in the Welfare State: Problems of Societal Self-description', *Journal of Political Philosophy.* 10:4, p. 425.
69. Green, *Ideologies of Conservatism*, p. 248, quoting from the speeches of Enoch Powell between 1965 and 1968.
70. Ibid. p. 247.
71. Ibid. p. 250.
72. Scruton, *England*, p. 128.
73. Pipes, *Property and Freedom*, p. 228.
74. Green, *Ideologies of Conservatism*, p. 277, quoting from Thatcher's 1977 Ian Macleod Memorial Lecture.

75. Honderich, *Conservatism*, p. 103.

76. Ibid. p. 93.

77. Green, *Ideologies of Conservatism*, p. 252, quoting Nigel Birch in 1949.

78. Ibid. p. 258.

79. For further discussion, see Nigel Meek, '"Society" Does Not Exist: (and) If It Did It Shouldn't', *Political Notes* 144, http://www.libertarian.co.uk/lapubs/polin/polin144.pdf

80. Green, *Ideologies of Conservatism*, p. 265.

81. Keane, 'Despotism and Democracy', pp. 53–4.

82. Green, *Ideologies of Conservatism*, p. 269.

83. Burke, *Reflections on the Revolution in France*, p. 170.

84. Bernard Williams, 'Necessary Identities', in Tommy L. Lott (ed.), *Subjugation and Bondage: Critical Essays on Slavery and Social Philosophy* (Boulder, CO and Oxford: Rowman and Littlefield, 1998), p. 21.

85. Ibid. p. 21.

CHAPTER 8

Slaveries and Property:
Freedom and Belonging

The connections between slavery and property are not as straightforward
as they may initially appear, and they return us to issues of honour and
degradation, belonging and exclusion as well as drudgery and righteous
labour. The idea of slavery folds back to John Locke and to G. W. F. Hegel,
to the unequal possession of the earth and to the distinction between civil
and human society. Defining slavery has proved to be fraught with
problems and ideological dispute. This is in part because any definition is
multi-layered. The dictionary definition, for example, mentions that a
slave is the legal property of another, that he or she is bound to absolute
obedience and and that he or she will engage in exhausting labour. As
Robin Blackburn argues, our common definitions of slavery capture both
legal property and hard labour as its constituent elements. This is bound
to mean that the legal and the economic are woven together and pulled
apart, emphasised by different commentators in different ways at different
times. In terms of this book and the idea of property, the threads constituting slavery take us back to Locke, self-ownership and freedom and to
Hegel, recognition and belonging.

A slave occupied a certain place in society, a status defined by rights
and liabilities, by the privileges and powers that others could exercise over
her. As Richard Hare argues, this legal status did not exhaust the definition of a slave. Slavery is also a relation to a master: the slave is the slave
of another person. The problem of defining slavery itself as an absolute
condition and a fixed status has exercised many scholars over many years,
especially since it is often argued that in order to understand liberty and
autonomy, we need to know how to recognise their opposites. For liberals
this has meant striving to draw bright lines between slavery as a wrong or

a logical impossibility and individual autonomy as a good and a right. For socialists, the concept of slavery is more flexible, blurring into servitude and blending into exploitation. The idea of slavery is thus central to liberalism and to socialism: it has become the emblematic state of unfreedom and inhumanity and has taken on a 'mythic potency' that takes it beyond the facts and experience of history.[1] It is important to remember that, unlike the lived experience of slavery itself, slave *status* was a myth and an illusion, sustained by tales and stories as much as by political theories and ideologies. Slave status was a social construction and not a natural essence, and so it had to be constantly produced and perpetuated. In this, it is not unlike the concept of property itself, and it brings us to the limits of what or who can count as property, and what it might mean to be possessed as a thing. In the process (since why should we imagine that a person could be owned as an object?) slavery exposes some of the ways in which property itself relies on 'appearances and illusions' to sustain itself.[2] Slavery both as a legal status and as hard labour relies on the politics of property.

Slavery brings us back to the intersection between what is understood as social and what is understood as natural, and to the boundary between self and other. The issue of slavery makes clear how property functions as a moral and political space as well as an economic relationship, and emphasises just how fraught and contested that moral space can be. One approach to slavery would assume that the opposite of slavery is freedom. On this account, it is the slave's inability to own herself and to exclude others that makes her a slave. A slave is someone unable to exercise self-ownership, to act as a rational, self-interested and competitive individual. Their exclusion from the market and from civil society means that they cannot own property. As Robert Miles argues, this means that the wage labourer can be constructed as a free and active subject who owns his labour power as a form of private property and so is understood to be relatively autonomous when compared to a slave. His ability to alienate his own labour, to decide how and where to sell it, 'gives to the wage labourer an area of personal determination within the limits set primarily by market conditions.'[3] Without this area of personal determination that functions as a sphere of discretion, slaves cannot use property as a means to distance themselves from others, to make themselves strangers. They do not have property as a means of separation from others, and so they are vulnerable to the use of force, caught in the war of all against all where the absolute autonomy of the master relies on extinguishing the autonomy of the slave. The slave is often defined as an individual whose person is the property of another person. The enslaved person is understood to be unable to exercise free will: her will is subject to her owner's authority and her labour or services are obtained through coercion. Under this kind of definition, slavery is a fixed status, and once the individual is detached from their property in the person it raises the possibility of being owned by someone else and so becoming an object of property, a commodity. As Alan Hyde puts it: 'The essence of slavery is that the body *is* property, just not the property of the person inside it.'[4]

Another, perhaps more comprehensive, approach to property makes closer connections with the idea of men as masters of themselves, and between property, liberty, consent and self-government. According to this approach, slavery is less fixed, more open textured, and its definition does not need to rely on the illusion that a person could be a commodity. Once we place slavery in the context of a set of powers, claims and privileges, we are back to Laura Underkuffler's discussion of moral importance. Property is supposed to generate duties for others, and so has to involve recognition by others. It becomes collective as well as individual. On this account of property, the opposite of slavery is belonging rather than freedom. For the slave, the collective context has broken down and her legitimate interests have gone unrecognised. On this account, the injustice of slavery is not the lack of self-ownership by the slave but the way in which slave interests in material well-being, autonomy and dignity are not recognised as significant, and are only 'marginally and insecurely protected'.[5] This more communitarian approach to property, slavery and freedom emphasises the insecurity (rather than the unfreedom) of the slave. The slave is caught in the war of all against all not because of a lack of self-ownership, but because he or she is constructed as unable to leave the state of nature and to find a footing with others. They do not have property as a means of connection with others, the assurance that their rights and interests will be granted significance and protected. They cannot move beyond the 'precarious and shifting balance of power between masters and slaves', and it is the way in which they are incorporated into the legal and political system *as slaves* that defines their status.[6] In other words, those who contrast slavery to belonging tend to focus on the role of the state and the legal system, rather than on labour, in order to define slavery.

The slave is the opposite of a Lockean individual, able to lead their own life, responsible for themselves, their reason, their conscience and their labour. Slaves are hopelessly dependent on another's will. They are subjects who are not bearers of rights and are not imbued with value. They do not have the capacity to exclude others, and so are constituted as living outside the moral space of property. Their outsiderness is double pronged: they are understood as unable to act as self-determining agents, and so as somehow incapable of freedom. Their lack of self-determination also means that they are understood as unable to belong to the imagined community of free and active subjects. Slaves are defined as outsiders, as enemies, foreigners and strangers, and also as lazy, irresponsible and irrational. Slavery, then, is opposed both to freedom and to belonging.

– DEFINING SLAVERY –

Slavery was defined by the Slavery Convention of the League of Nations in 1926 as 'the status or condition of a person over whom any or all of the powers attaching to the right of ownership are exercised'.[7] This twentieth-century definition, as David Turley points out, covers the ownership of slaves by individuals, temples, the public or the state. 'Chattel slavery' is a fuller term for the most traditional form of slavery, defined as 'the complete ownership of one human being by another'.[8] The chattel slave was regarded as an animate piece of property, and that status as property was heritable, passed on from one generation to another. People were born or sold into the possession of another, treated like property. In theory, the slave was then the extension of the will of another, a being without rights. The chattel slave was unable to make a will, to bring formal criminal charges against others or to appear as a witness in most civil cases. He had no right of petition, no property and no right of appeal. A slave's evidence was acceptable in court only if it had been extracted by torture.[9] Under the system of chattel slavery, it was almost universally agreed that a slave could be bought, sold, traded, leased, mortgaged, bequested, presented as a gift, pledged for a debt, included in a dowry or seized in a bankruptcy.[10] For some, this makes the relationship between property and slavery straightforward: the slave is the property of his or her owner. One of the central illusions of property and slavery has been the notion that it is possible to be both a person and an object owned by another. This formulation captures a basic ambiguity. Legal systems generally found it impossible to act consistently on the premise that people were property. Slave codes treated slaves as people capable of committing crimes, for example, and the law often granted slaves theoretical protection against murder and grievous bodily harm. Orlando Patterson declares that no legal code has ever attempted to treat slaves as anything other than persons at law.[11]

Slaves were, and are, inescapably human and in order to own them the slave holder required the support of the law and of myth. The idea that a person was property could only be sustained by appearance and illusion; it could not be established as a matter of natural fact.

This brings us back to the League of Nations definition, 'the status or condition of a person over whom any or all of the powers attaching to the right of ownership are exercised'. As Blackburn points out, this definition refers to 'any' as well as 'all' powers attaching to the right of ownership. Some claims and powers associated with ownership can clearly be made and exercised over people who are not slaves. For example, employers, spouses and football clubs all exercise some of the powers attaching to the right of ownership over their employees, spouses and players.[12] Once we recognise that absolute ownership is a fiction, and that property is not about the ownership of a thing, it becomes clear that a person can possess and exercise some property powers over their spouse, their servant, their employee or their land, and not only over their slave. As Blackburn argues, it is 'the *comprehensive* extent of the property rights claimed by the slave owner which distinguish [*sic*] slavery'.[13] This is a useful approach to the problem of defining slavery, one that makes clear its continuities with other forms of ownership and exploitation as well as its distinctive status.

This definition involves paying attention to the power, claims and privileges that individuals exercise over other people, and to the degree of protection and security they are offered in exercising their power over others. For Patterson, it is here that we can see where property intersects with slavery. The slave could not claim or exercise direct powers of property. Even where slaves were understood to own property, they did so without security. Patterson concludes that 'the slave was a slave not because he was the *object* of property, but because he could not be the *subject* of property'.[14] This is a useful distinction because it draws attention to the relative powerlessness of the slave. Rather than representing the slave straight-forwardly as an object or a commodity, focusing on the idea that a slave cannot own property opens up the possibility of exploring how far the slave could act as an agent and how far a slave could have legitimate interests in material well being, autonomy and dignity. The slave's inability to own property was part of their wider 'social death'. Slavery, for Patterson, can be distinguished from other social relationships by its constituent elements of force, dishonour and permanence: '*slavery is the permanent, violent domination of natally alienated and generally dishonored persons*'.[15]

This definition means that slavery is not simply about the legal system or hard labour. It also has to be about individuals' relations to each other, their imagined communities and their sense of personhood. Turley argues that 'whatever the basis of slavery, once individuals or groups had acquired that status they were considered degraded and shamed figures'.[16] The slave was compelled to undergo dishonouring rituals and to acknowledge the master's total possession of him, often symbolised by renaming the slave. Where slaves were not physically distinct, they were often deliberately marked, branded, pierced or fettered to make their status as others and outsiders unmistakable. For Patterson, these elements of honour and dishonour are a universal feature of slavery as an institution and a relationship. He argues that the experience of mastership generated a strong sense of honour, balanced by the slave's experience of its loss. The slave had, by definition, chosen life over honour: he had chosen to submit and live rather than to die unvanquished. For Patterson, this was a primal act of submission: 'The dishonor the slave was compelled to experience sprang ... from that raw, human sense of debasement inherent in having no being except as an expression of another's being.' Patterson makes clear that for the slave owner there is a sweetness in his mastery that comes from the slave's debasement, a 'lightening of the soul' at having his sense of honour and mastery personified in another person whose resistance has been overcome.[17]

This understanding of slavery as centrally connected to honour and degradation focuses attention on the origins of slavery in force, violence and an act of war. The association of slavery and violence is one of the constituent features of slavery. For the Greeks, as Bernard Williams argues, slavery was about ill luck imposed by force. It was an 'arbitrary calamity' for someone to become a slave; it required force imposed from the outside.[18] Once imposed, it could only be sustained by continued violence and it was this that made slavery inherently dishonouring and degrading. It was uncivil, its arbitrariness and violence placed it outside 'a more or less well-defined pact between the social and natural order, and between one group and another.'[19] Slavery was not a natural condition, and it could not be easily mapped onto preexisting structural inequalities. The social being of the slave could be altered at any point by his master: his status could be overturned by the will of another. The processes of capture and manumission that bounded the experience of slavery were not fixed or even predetermined. Slavery was, and is, inherently random and despotic, and in this randomness and despotism issues of self-ownership, honour, labour and race are easily tangled up.

– Slavery and the Social Contract –

As Charles Mills points out, the reality of slavery means that we cannot start our political theories, social contracts or property histories from the assumption that in general all humans have been recognised as persons. Instead, we have to begin from the 'historical reality of a partitioned social ontology'.[20] Mills goes on to argue that white male philosophy is predicated on taking personhood for granted, until the whiteness and the Eurocentrism of the outlook become second nature.[21] In his introduction to Locke's *Two Treatises*, Peter Laslett points out about Locke that 'slave labour in no way peturbs him', although 'a modern believer in the enormity of personal servitude' is likely to find that reading the First Treatise leaves them feeling 'very uncomfortable, if not indignant'.[22] He leaves the matter there, and the political theory of property and slavery often gets us no further than this sense of discomfort and indignation. Slavery is not really allowed to peturb Locke's theory of limited government, or the wider liberal tradition of self-ownership and the social contract. Liberals tend to declare that persons simply cannot be property, and move on.

This lack of disturbance is in part made possible by the ways in which liberal theory theorises slavery as outside civil society and politics. Conquest, colonialism and African slavery are not understood as part of the ethical, cultural, intellectual or political inheritance of the West or of European modernity. Slavery is not regarded as internal to 'our' property history. To try and draw out how this positions slaves as shadow members of society, and as subpersons who can exist only outside the social contract, this section concentrates on Locke's theory of slavery. Locke argued that the origin of slavery lay outside the social contract. Slaves were the opposite of citizens, lacking the connective tissue of property to anchor their freedom or their membership of the political community.

Slavery is set up as a sort of logical impossibility for liberalism. An individual cannot sell him- or herself into slavery, or use their freedom to give up their freedom. It is impossible for an individual to enter into a contract which puts him under the absolute, arbitrary power of another who can take away his life when he pleases, and so confirms that he is unable to preserve or defend himself. It was central to Lockean liberalism that every individual had a right to natural freedom, not to be subjected to the will or authority of any other man, and that 'no Body can transfer to another more power than he has in himself; and no Body has an absolute Arbitrary Power over himself, or over any other, to destroy his own Life, or take away the Life or Property of another'.[23] Locke equated slavery with absolutist power, and absolute rule violated personality and rights. The attempt to subject anyone to absolute power was understood as an attempt on that person's life, and as an attempt to claim more rights over an individual than individuals themselves possessed under the law of nature. Such regimes could not be legitimate. Locke used the example of slavery to argue that the criteria of legitimacy existed outside political society, so that it was possible to make judgements about whether political power was properly constitutional and based on the consent of rational men. In his theory, injustice and the state of war could take place in what appeared to be civil society, and illegitimate coercion sometimes tried to pass for political power.[24]

Locke used the device of a state of nature as a moral code, a set of rules which men were morally obliged to obey when they had not contracted with each other to modify their behaviour. Locke's state of nature was governed by the law of nature that restrained men from invading others' rights and doing harm to one another. Men were all the workmanship of one infinitely wise maker, and everyone was bound to preserve themselves and to preserve the whole of mankind. Equal, rational and independent individuals found that they were each given responsibility for executing the law of nature. Those who transgressed the law of nature, according to Locke, broke 'the tye which is to secure them from injury and violence'.[25] A man who had transgressed the law of nature became degenerate, and declared himself an outsider, a person who had abandoned the principles of human nature. By breaking the law of the nature, he no longer lived under the ties of common law and reason, and so had 'no other Rule, but that of Force and Violence, and so may be Treated as Beasts of Prey.'[26] It was to avoid the dangers and pitfalls of such a state of insecurity and war that men put themselves into society and consented to government. The aim of such government was the preservation of all, a society of 'Rational Creatures entred into a Community for their mutual good'.[27] These rational creatures managed to escape the state of war and the state of slavery by becoming members of a civil and civilised society, governed by standing rules and not by the arbitrary impositions of another's will.

From Locke onwards the liberal tradition holds that the opposite of slavery is civil society and the social contract. Slaves who had been taken captive in a just war and found themselves legitimately subject to the absolute dominion and power of their masters forfeited their lives, liberties and estates and so could not be considered rational creatures with the capacity to enter into the community or become members of civil society. Instead, they were in the '*State of Slavery*'.[28] Being in the state of slavery made them incapable of owning any property. They lost both their self-ownership and their capacity to belong. Slaves remained in the state of nature, with no decisive power to appeal to, and no judge on earth to redress their injuries. Having forfeited their lives, liberties and estates and been stripped of all their property, they were like the subjects of an absolute monarch, as inconsistent with civil society 'as if he were degraded from the common state of Rational Creatures'.[29]

The state of slavery was not a state of nowhere, or an abstract state of nature in a mythical past. It existed in the plantocracies of the West Indies. In the *First Treatise*, Locke discussed the powers of a planter in the West Indies. Like a feudal lord, he had the personalistic power to use his slaves to make war on others. Slaves and slave owners lived outside civil society, and the planter was not a sovereign because he could not direct the force of the state and he did not have the consent of his subjects. He had the power of making war or peace without any political supremacy or legitimacy, and so the state of war continued.[30] Under these circumstances, outside the bounds of civil society, the slaves were 'to be looked on as a Herd of inferiour Creatures, under the Dominion of a Master, who keeps them and works them for his own Pleasure and Profit.'[31] They were the opposite of citizens. Their degradation was complete, and the slave was the opposite of the rational creature who could make himself a member of the imagined community.

The members of a herd of inferior creatures, part of a family only because they had been purchased, were outsiders not only because they were not members of a properly constituted civil society but also because they were not properly connected to their families. The ties of law and reason had been broken, and these included the ties of family. Patterson argues that one of the constituent elements of slavery was that the slave is a person without natality. The slave's natal alienation meant that he 'ceased to belong in his own right to any legitimate social order.'[32] He had no claims or obligations to his parents, his blood relations or to his descendants. Patterson terms such slaves 'genealogical isolates', living outside the social relations of the community within which they lived, and culturally isolated from the social heritage of their ancestors.[33] Slaves were not 'allowed freely to integrate the experience of their ancestors into their lives, to inform their understanding of social reality with the inherited meanings of their natural forebears, or to anchor the living present in any conscious community of memory'.[34] Patterson's argument is not that slaves had no social relations amongst themselves, but that such relations were never recognised as legitimate or binding. Slave couples could be forcibly separated, they had no custodial claims over their children and the master had the power to remove the slave from his or her local community. Slaves constantly had to live with the fear of separation as part of the experience of living with the arbitrariness and ill luck of slave relations. Patterson uses the term 'natal alienation' to capture slaves' outsider status, their apartness, because it focuses on their forced alienation, their loss of the ties of birth and attachment. Natally alienated slaves had to live without the bond of society identified by Burke, and so lived outside the structures of family, place and country. Without ties to the past or to the future, and without property, slaves could not make sense of the world by finding a place in it and making themselves at home in the social world. As Patterson argues: 'Not only were they natally alienated from their ancestors, and often from their community of origin, but also from their descendants.'[35] Slaves who had been captured and sold were disconnected: 'The slave's origins were entirely effaced and there was no continuing link.'[36] They were, in Edmund Burke's terms, little better than the flies of summer.

The captive whose life was spared owed his life to the slave holder, and as he forfeited his life, liberty and estates, he could no longer draw his identity from his kinship relations, his ancestors, his society of origin. Slavery, as Blackburn argues, annulled their prior rights and identity, and slaves became 'shadow members of society'.[37] As shadow members of their new societies, slaves were marginal and vulnerable, 'replaceable and interchangeable'.[38] Recognition and integration were arbitrary since the slaves' value lay in their detachment from family structures, their alienability from social relations, their isolation, and their 'almost infinite vulnerability to the will of others'.[39] The slave, as David Brian Davis argues, was a symbol of extreme dependency, objectifying other people's fears of being effaced and of losing their continuing links and their home in the social world. They also symbolised the dangers of not being protected by the social contract. They personified the dangerous consequences of being stripped of property and the protections and security that property brings with it. Not to be the subject of property meant lacking substance and free will. The natally alienated slave had no identity of his own, 'it was the shadow cast by the owner.'[40]

Natal alienation and the sense of being a shadow member of someone else's society were closely connected to the dishonour of the slave. Patterson, as we have seen, argues that the slave is a person without honour. He or she has no power except through another, no independent existence and so no public worth. Their marginality, vulnerability and shadow status meant that slaves as individuals did not compete for honour and were not expected to do so. For Patterson, this is the clearest marker of their outsider status. Pride and shame, honour and dishonour are, he argues, fundamental to the sense of belonging to a community.[41] The inherent dishonour of slavery was connected to the origins of slavery in defeat and capture, and to its continuing basis in violence. As Blackburn argues, slave status was 'defined by, and saturated with, violence to a greater extent than any other social relations'.[42] Slavery as an institution and as a relation between individuals was, and is, maintained by direct violence. Slave-holding societies existed outside the social contract. The pact that handed over to the state the power and authority to direct the force of each individual had not been made: master and slave remained in the state of nature and continued the state of war. Terror was used as a device to symbolise and preserve the inequalities of power and as an incentive to increase the effort and productivity of the slaves.[43] In both these uses, it was fundamentally dishonouring, reinforcing both the slave's unfreedom and her outsider status, with no family ties to protect her from random violence or to avenge her systematic ill treatment.

The violence of slavery placed the slaves outside the complex web of esteem, shame and envy that structured the social membership of the imagined community. Part of the common ground between the members of an imagined community is the publicly recognised right of the wronged person to redress. When that right to redress is denied, the slave is clearly outside the moral community. Honour, William Ian Miller argues, is about sensitivity to the experience of humiliation and shame, and the honourable person is 'one whose self-esteem and social standing is intimately dependent on the esteem or the envy he or she actually elicits in others'.[44] People live partly in the estimation and opinion of others, and as Jean-Jacques Rousseau argued, individuals have an unremitting rage to distinguish themselves from others and to have that distinction recognised. Personhood is established 'in a context that takes place before witnesses'.[45] Slaves have no legitimate witnesses to their struggle for self-consciousness. Instead, 'the slave becomes *fixed* in his dependence on the master for his life'.[46]

Patterson argues that the interactions between slaves and masters were fundamentally structured by honour and dishonour. He disagrees with the

Hegelian argument that the slave stood between the master and the world, so that their relationship was defined by what the slave produced. He points out that in many slave-holding societies, slaves produced nothing and were economically dependent on their masters.[47] Patterson's argument that generalised dishonour is the central structure of slavery ties him to an understanding of slavery that hinges on recognition and belonging. Slavery as a form of social death is less about exhausting, hard labour than it is about powerlessness and loss. As a social system, slavery is characterised for Patterson by marginality and exclusion, dishonour and degradation. The slave has no community, and so no security. His lack of property epitomises his lack of connection to others, the way in which he is forced to operate outside the normal network of kinship, dependency, obligation, privilege and social standing.[48]

– SLAVERY, SELF-OWNERSHIP AND LABOUR –

For Patterson, there is nothing in the nature of slavery that requires the slave to be a worker. They can be used as a worker, and indeed their natal alienation will make their exploitation particularly effective, but 'this does not in any way mean that slave necessarily implies worker'.[49] For others, however, the relation of slavery to the surplus is definitive. Slavery is regarded as the opposite of free wage labour and of individual autonomy and as part of an economic system of exploitation. G. E. M. de Ste. Croix, for example, argues that slavery and other forms of unfree labour are primarily forms of extraction of labour for the master. For him, the distinguishing feature of a mode of production is 'how the dominant propertied classes, controlling the means of production, ensure the extraction of the surplus, which makes their leisured existence possible'.[50] The slaves' lack of property is about their lack of property in their person and in their labour.

There are problems with setting up slavery as either about social exclusion or about labour, and with insisting that it has to be understood either as the opposite of belonging or as the opposite of freedom. This dichotomous approach risks losing sight of the ways in which property both connects individuals to one another, and holds them apart from each other. It misses the connections and continuities between labour, morality and honour and between self-ownership and community. In order to understand the intersections between property and slavery, we need to pay attention to the overlaps and to the complexity of what it means to be a shadow member of society. That shadow status is likely to turn out to concern the slave's incorporation into market and civil society as well as into kinship networks of privilege and honour. When Patterson discusses the dishonour of slavery, he focuses on the inability of the slave to defend himself or to secure his own livelihood, and both self-defence and securing a livelihood are difficult to disentangle from the concept of self-ownership (and indeed imply that slavery does necessarily have something to do with work). I want to try and draw out some of these connections by exploring how slavery, race, self-ownership and labour interact with one another.

Race, as Mills argues, is a marker of entitlement or dispossession and of normative inclusion or exclusion.[51] However, as Turley points out in his discussion of slavery, the power to define who was marginal and who could be enslaved 'was not always tied to stable markers of difference and inferiority'.[52] As I argued in Chapter 1, both blackness and whiteness are fluid and unstable. The authority of the powerful extended to the power of definition and redefinition, shifting and redefining who counted as a person and who was allowed to belong to the community and the polity. Normative inclusion and exclusion are not clearly separable from issues of labour and self-ownership. Unstable boundaries and identities can be shifted and defined by economic processes. In certain historical circumstances, 'the appropriation of labour power is accompanied by a process of racialization'.[53] Race is not an independent variable, a natural, biological fact, but a historically contingent belief: it formed a useful part of the social, political and ideological relations of power needed to underpin and sustain slavery. It is important not to expect the markers in the process to be stable and fixed, and risk losing sight of the class and power relations involved. As Robert Miles puts it: 'It is never "whites" who dominate, but a ruling class, itself composed of various fractions.'[54]

This fracturing by class, and the instability of marking inferiority should remind us of the qualities of the subperson defined by Mills. Slavery is not about being excluded altogether from the categories of personhood and self-ownership, but about being granted only a qualified self-ownership and a limited rationality. It is not a process that turns an individual into an object, or even a beast of burden, but one that constructs slaves as individuals who can be encroached upon with impunity, whose rights and interests will be at best insecurely protected and who will be understood as outsiders and others. This is in part about the self-definition of those who are not outsiders, who have the power to define others: the ability of the Greek male, for example, to distinguish himself from 'barbarian, woman, slave'.[55] The image of the slave was a counterpoint to his own white self-image, but it is, as Mills points out, important to remember that this was more than a contrast. It was not just that slaves could not be imagined as belonging to the community, but that the community could not be imagined without slaves.

Personhood was connected to subpersonhood and to self-definition through the notion of self-ownership. It is central to self-ownership that the individual should be the active proprietor of their own person and capacities, and fully in charge of directing their own labour, at least in the sense of choosing how to alienate it. The wage labourer is by definition responsible for himself. Slaves cannot be: it is part of their unfitness for self-government, part of what makes them a herd of inferior creatures rather than rational members of the imagined community. The notion that slaves are by nature lazy and require compulsion in order to work is crucial to their symbolic status as well as to their lived experience. Within the ideologies sustaining slavery identified by Turley, the derogatory stereotype of the slave centres around the idea that the slave was concerned with the material and sensual aspects of life. This concern meant that he was morally deficient: 'Thus slaves were thought of as cowardly, dishonest, lazy and amoral when not downright immoral.'[56] They were also regarded as passive, irrational and lacking in self-control and so as incapable of initiative and improvement. Slaves by definition belong to the category of the idle and the listless; they are the opposite of the industrious and the rational. Stereotyping involved social distancing as well as labour discipline. The whip was a badge of slavery, a symbol of the servile state. As Patterson concludes about all his comparative data: 'There is no known slaveholding society where the whip was not considered an indispensable instrument.'[57] The whip was required because slaves were understood to have no moral impulse to labour. They required external discipline, other people had to take responsibility for them. In Greece, 'the barbarian slave had only the capacity to perform tasks as directed by others'.[58] Their capabilities and capacities had to be directed to functions defined by their masters, and this is a central part of the degradation and humiliation of being a slave.

It is here that the connections between slavery and colour were forged and reinforced. The Atlantic sugar economy hinged on African slaves, and the myth of slave labour easily transformed itself into the idea that slaves, in need of direction and compulsion, were only fitted for certain kinds of labour. Africans were supposed to be naturally suited to harsh physical labour in tropical conditions. Planters and slave traders built on this spurious environmental assertion to argue that Africans and their descendants were uniquely fitted by their physiological characteristics for labour in the sugar fields.[59] Their skin, their hair, their features were understood to mark them out for slavery, as beasts of burden who could undertake back-breaking field work and hard labour. As James Walvin argues, 'slavery generated and bequeathed a number of important myths about black humanity; most notably the idea that blacks were in essence lazy and would work only under compulsion'.[60] They needed to be disciplined through a regime of threats, violence and rewards. Slave owners declared 'Negroes' to be inefficient, useless, indolent and incorrigibly lazy.

This degradation and derogation of dignity needs to be understood as connected to labour and to self-ownership, as well as to honour and social standing. Slaves were constructed as not owning a property in the person, as not having the right not to be invaded or usurped by others. They had no right to exclude others, to resist punishment, or to protect their own physical security. Within the self-ownership discourse, as C. B. Macpherson argues, this right to exclude others is part of what makes a man human and gives him despotic dominion over himself. The construction of slaves as subpersons, in Mills's terms, was not only about rationality and outsider status; it was also about their inability to exclude others. Their self-ownership was so compromised that it could not form the basis for their own labour or independence. It was not only that slaves did not belong within the imagined community, but also that they were understood to belong *to* their masters.[61] Some of this was, of course, part of the myth and illusion of slavery, the idea that an individual could lose their being and become nothing more than an extension of their owner's will, a conscious being transformed into a dependent consciousness. The way that this myth robbed slaves of their agency and self-ownership was important, and served the interests of the slave owners. Slave owners and the wider slave-owning ideology constructed black slaves as unable to live and survive 'as independent beings in a free, industrious society'.[62]

Independent beings in a free, industrious society were understood to own their own labour as a commodity and a form of private property. The wage labourer was able to participate in exchange relationships and to take responsibility for her own reproduction as a worker. Her arena of independence was constrained by the market and by her overwhelming need to find an employer, but she was able to choose her exploiter, and the wage system gave her the incentive to increase the quality and quantity of her labour power and to engage with notions of skill and flexibility.

The wage labourer was always potentially a pauper, but she was also to some extent a free and active subject, with relative autonomy. The slave, by contrast, did not own her labour power as a commodity, or participate in the market. She had no incentive to develop her skills or talents and so lost even the relative autonomy of the wage labourer that lay in the potential for honourable labour and a property in membership. She was provided directly with the means of subsistence and survival, and so rather than struggling to control the material world, 'the slave is maintained', like a farm animal or a tractor.[63]

It is difficult, though, to construct a definition of slavery that is based on labour as its defining feature, and the complex relationship between slavery and property cannot be understood as simply residing in labour and the violent extraction of the surplus. All those who were defined as idle and listless were subject to corporal punishment and to harsh discipline, including branding and mutilation. Not only slaves, but also vagabonds and vagrants, the undisciplined, the lazy and the unemployed lived within social relations saturated by violence and structured by a compromised version of self-ownership. It is difficult to use violence as a way of distinguishing slavery from other forms of unfree labour and servitude, and considering slavery as a social relation will always draw us back to the question of belonging. Part of the complexity stems from the fact that slave operations worked best where slaves were not only punished, but also given incentives to work and granted 'spheres of independence'.[64] Walvin points to the significance of slaves' own plots, gardens and homes. They spent their free time growing food, tending animals, improving their homes and, crucially, selling, bartering and consuming food, timber, animals and clothes. In the Caribbean and in America, slaves participated in slave markets and expressed their energy, initiative and enterprise within a slave economy and a material culture that was tolerated by the plantation owners, who granted certain liberties, such as days free from work, to allow the slaves' independent world to exist. Sunday was market day, and slave women sold their produce, ranging from cattle, fruit, vegetables and fish to clothing, pottery, baskets and bedding in the local market, for cash. The slave owners found that there were advantages to owning slaves who were committed to property and connected to a local way of life.

However much slaves were constructed as outsiders, as objects of property and dependent consciousnesses, many of them were part of the local cash economy. Walvin points out that in Jamaica in 1774 it was calculated that slaves owned 20 per cent of all the cash in circulation.[65] It is important to recognise that slaves' status as outsiders and enemies did not necessarily mean that they did not participate in the market or in the local economy. They did, to some extent, have an arena of consumption and a (highly circumscribed) potential to produce for themselves. For many slaves, it was not the case that they were only maintained like a farm animal or a tractor without participating in any market. The freer slaves had the potential to become 'freelance hustlers', not only selling their goods in the local market but also working as washerwomen, domestics and hawkers, moving between the country and the town.[66]

There was a constant slippage between the freedoms and unfreedoms of slaves and unfree labourers. This slippage created complicated layers of incorporation into the economy, relations of production, civil society and the state. The indentured labour system in the seventeenth-century Caribbean, for example, provides a useful case study of how the state reproduced and reformed relations between producers and non-producers.[67] Plantations required 'a good store of hands' to be worth anything, and these hands were shipped out from Britain to the Caribbean and the American mainland in the seventeenth century in the form of indentured labour. The English labour force were paid their passage, fed, clothed and sheltered for between three and ten years in return for their labour. The individual entered a legal contract that exchanged the total product of his labour power for transport, subsistence and reproduction. At the end of their fixed term, they were paid a 'freedom due' of £10, granted a small plot of land or given a quantity of sugar.[68] The planters depended on indentured labourers from Britain for the transition to sugar because they brought with them the skills, basic literacy and familiarity with advanced industrial machinery that were needed to support large-scale sugar production.

The system of indenture in the English West Indies before the 1661 Masters and Servants Act came to be known as 'white slavery', and behind the loadedness of the term was the suspicion that white labourers were being treated as if they too were not only inefficient, idle and listless but also capable of being owned as property. The qualifying term 'white' marks the system out as unnatural and unsettling, not so easily aligned with the prevailing myths and illusions about white humanity. The labourers signed a formal legal contract, but the alternative to indentured labour was often punishment for vagrancy or vagabondage, and a kidnapping system was well organised.[69] The indenture system was regarded as indistinguishable from slavery because of the property rights the planters held in their servants, and the ways in which they were treated as productive capital: 'Pioneer Barbadian planters quite freely bought, sold, gambled away, mortgaged, taxed as property, and alienated in wills their indentured servants.'[70] The system of indentured labour was embedded in the customs of the country, and it was accepted that the planters enjoyed total control over their servants, a control that extended into their non-labouring lives as well as their labouring hours. For example, servants were required to produce a pass in order to be allowed to leave the plantation, and they had to obtain their master's consent to marry. They could not vote, trade with non-slaves or make cash savings, and they were subject to corporal punishment. These elements of control were part of a wider strategy by the planters 'to demonstrate that the servant was not a free person under contractual obligations, but primarily a capital investment with property characteristics'.[71]

Hilary Beckles argues that Barbados planters established this comprehensive set of property rights in their servants in order to maximise output, to ensure the extraction of the surplus. They needed to accumulate capital in order to move into sugar production, and they invested not only in land, but also in indentured labour. The indentured servants became 'the most liquid form of capital on the plantation', and planters sold their servant stock on the open market in order to raise money in the short term.[72] For Beckles, this way of treating labour as a form of capital was a basic prerequisite for slavery. Indentured servants were categorised as property, tied to the plantation as an integral component of its capital assets and listed as alienable property in inventories of sale. It was, as Beckles points out, a logical extension of market values and commodification to use indentured servants as a form of currency. In 1644 Thomas Applethwaite, a Barbados planter, bought a 200-acre plantation and paid for it with twenty-five indentured servants. Beckles carefully distinguishes even this form of indentured labour from slavery. The indentured labourer was bound only for a specified period, and as Miles argues, some of them must have chosen to enter these relations 'in the belief that they might realize some benefit from doing so'.[73] Some constraints prevented masters from using their servants as chattel slaves. The servants were protected under law in the areas of property ownership, sexual abuse, marriage and the family. Unlike slaves, indentured servants kept their status as free individuals 'in abeyance', so that despotic dominion was still available to them when their contracts ended.[74] For Beckles, this is an important distinction, and he stresses the unique permanence and inevitability of the slave's status. Before the 1661 Masters and Servants Act both servants and slaves were used as property, but slaves 'were seen, like animals, as permanent and self-reproductive'.[75] Beckles's conclusion is that the property status is in itself insufficient to allow for a definition of the servant as a slave.

The process of turning a system of indentured labour into a system of slavery hinged on judgements about the character and capacity of labourers and about their incorporation into production. Racism, Miles argues, provided a way of selecting and legitimating whose labour power should be exploited within a particular set of unfree production relations.[76] In the seventeenth-century Caribbean, enslaved African labourers worked alongside indentured European labourers in the sugar cane fields. The white indentured labourers from Britain were gradually replaced by black slaves, first in unskilled field work and then in skilled work. Indentured labour was proving difficult to maintain as the land ran out and emigration from England was discouraged. Slaves proved to be cheaper. The price of slaves remained constant as the price of indentures rose, and the longer period of servitude meant savings for the planters. Plantation owners also reduced costs by providing slaves with small plots of land to grow their own food.[77] Black people entered the slave trade as indentured servants, but during the last decades of the seventeenth century, a whole new set of special restrictions and legal burdens were imposed on them and codified as chattel slavery. The transition from indentured to slave labour was, Miles argues, not part of a grand design, but 'the consequence of *ad hoc* responses to particular circumstances.'[78] Between 1640 and 1700, 134,500 Africans were shipped to Barbados. Their labour was cheaper, longer-term and more intrusively managed than the English indentured labour. Their hereditary lifetime bondage gave them 'a new kind of subjectship' and meant that they were unable to claim the minimal legal protections extended to English servants.[79] They were outsiders and subpersons, lacking full self-ownership, who could be raped and physically assaulted without legal penalties. This subjugation had to be justified, and in response doctrines of racial inequality were established by law. In legislating for black chattel slavery, 'Americans went beyond any explicit provisions in English law and gave legal expression to an increasingly racialized sense of their identity so powerful that the very humanity of these outsiders was denied'.[80] Slaves were forced into a separate sphere, and their exclusion from the community was not only a result of their dishonour and natal alienation, but also of how they were incorporated into the labour force and the relations of production.

Legislation set out the conditions under which labour power could be exploited. Slave labour was never based on a purely private relation of domination and submission: it was constituted, reproduced and enforced by the state. The state, for example, enforced the pass system in the Caribbean and chartered companies to procure and supply human beings to be enslaved.[81] There were important political as well as economic considerations in the English settlement of the Caribbean. The Council of State in 1656 issued an order to apprehend and export dangerous persons, vagrants and idlers to the Americas. The idle and the listless, those hedged out by enclosure and the changing relations of production in England, had become a 'surplus population' who needed to be removed.[82] In Miles's account, the state used political and legal means to bind migrants to landowners and prevent them from establishing themselves as independent producers. The state uses racism to select and legitimate whose labour power counts as improving, rational and industrious and who remains indolent and idle. In the process, it constructs a hierarchy of acceptability and incorporation, within which some are incorporated into servitude and contract labour and others are constructed as foreigners and migrants, on the outside. They are understood as unable to belong to the imagined community, as separate from the nation and as 'natural' outsiders. The state is integral to this process of 'differential incorporation' of indigenous and migrant populations into relations of production.[83] David Brion Davis makes a similar point about incorporation when he describes slaves as the first 'modern' people. Their vulnerability, marginality and incomplete incorporation into the community made them, he argues, 'the prototype for the migratory labor and confused identity that have accompanied every phase of human progress'.[84]

– CONCLUSION: SLAVERY AND DRUDGERY –

The slippages and continuities between free and unfree labour take us back to the moral question of how to define slavery. Thomas Hobbes and Locke both used the term 'slavery' to refer to nonconsensual servitude, and much of their argument turns out to focus on what counts as consensual, and how to maintain a distinction between justifiable and unjustifiable forms of domination and servility.[85] Tommy Lott argues that the difference between their respective concepts of slavery can be represented by a continuum, with slavery at the harsh end and servitude at the benign end. On Hobbes's version there is no overlap between slavery and servitude, since slavery for Hobbes can only mean physical bondage. For Locke, there is room for some small overlap between the most benign slavery and the harshest servitude. This works because Locke sees slavery as being subject to the arbitrary power of another (rather than as simply physical bondage). However, as Lott goes on, Locke cannot account for some forms of harsh servitude that are indistinguishable from harsh slavery. On Locke's version 'the possibility that some forms of slavery were not as harsh as many forms of servitude is entirely concealed'.[86] Lott argues that this is linked to the conceptual and moral argument that slavery is always, by definition, harsher than servitude. For Locke, once there is a contract between the conqueror and the captive, their relationship changes, power and obedience are limited on both sides, 'so that *as soon as Compact enters, Slavery ceases*'.[87] Locke conceded that among the Jews and other nations, men did sell themselves, but, he argued, ''tis plain, this was only to *Drudgery, not to Slavery*'. By this, he meant that the person sold was not under arbitrary, despotical power and his master could not have the power to kill him. Indeed, 'he could not, at pleasure, so much as main him, but the loss of an Eye, or Tooth set him free'.[88]

This insistence on distinguishing so clearly between slavery and servitude, force and contract, places a great deal of weight on the notion of consent, 'a notion that obscures the fact that some forms of servitude involved coercion and legal ownership, and some forms of slavery allowed slaves to own slaves themselves'.[89] The blurriness is revealed by the relationship between slaves and their property as well as between servants and their labour. Slaves' rights to property underpinned their 'spheres of independence' and their economic activity in the markets. They were confirmed by convention and common sense, but not by the state and legislation. Some planters acted as executors to their slaves' wills. At the same time, slave property was easily removed, slave families were easily undermined, and their locale shifted. Their various freedoms, their attempts to make their own lives more tolerable, were all subject to the constant threat of violation. They were based on rights 'which were readily denied, infringed or transgressed'.[90] Slaves had no security, and so no real property. They could not forge an imagined community for themselves in the context of social relations shaped by oppression, arbitrariness and invasion. They could only ever aspire or expect to be 'freelance hustlers', migrant labourers, not fully incorporated into civil society or the state. Slaves who were natally alienated, dishonoured and unable to own property could not feel the 'value of affection' that Jeremy Bentham argued came from property's connection to inheritance from our ancestors and a sense of reward for our own labour. Without property, there was no invisible thread that could be spun into a cable in the social state. The insecurity of their property was inextricable from their compromised self-ownership, and from their dishonour and degradation. As a result, an 'end to slavery often ushered in not freedom, but bondage in its various, adaptable guises'.[91]

Beckles argues that his example of 'white slavery' in seventeenth-century Barbados shows 'the folly of assuming that the categories of "owner" and "owned" have been borrowed from nature or of assuming that "persons" own "things"'.[92] The ways in which the blurriness of property rights and self-ownership undercut a clear distinction between slavery and servitude should also remind us of the problem of contrasting freedom and belonging too starkly. Trying to define slavery without accounting for labour risks losing sight of the continuities between 'compact' and slavery, and in the process making slavery appear somehow both fixed and universal, and unique. Focusing on the violence of the individual master–slave relationship, for example, takes attention away from the wider political, legal and economic relations of dispossession that prevented the 'idle and the listless', both slaves and drudges, from establishing themselves as independent, industrious and rational producers and landowners. The bundles of rights to labour power, both our own and other people's, are 'extraordinarily various' and 'it is surprisingly difficult to draw bright lines between those with full personal autonomy and those without it'.[93]

The problem with Locke's view of coerced consent is that he 'failed to recognize that the overlap of certain forms of drudgery with certain forms of slavery can be explained in terms of power relations that extend well beyond the master's authority over the slave'.[94] The basic power relations that support and perpetuate a dominant class are not questioned. For both Hobbes and Locke, the distinction between slavery and servitude can be understood in legalistic terms, focused on the idea that the slave is the legal property of another and is bound to absolute obedience. The idea that a contract ends slavery relies on a moralistic concern that ignores the possibility that the slave, and any other individual, might have an 'interest in not performing intense, undesirable labor'.[95] Lott argues that an emphasis on the moral and legal aspects of slavery means that abolishing slavery concentrates on 'systematically granting more rights to slaves, including manumission, while maintaining a social arrangement that perpetuates virtually the same power relations of domination and servility'.[96]

This chapter has argued that, instead, we need to pay attention to the complex relationship between slavery and property, to recognise the connections between freedom and belonging rather than setting them up against each other. Honour, self-ownership, race and labour are not easily disentangled, and unequal possession of the self is difficult to separate from unequal possession of the earth.

– NOTES –

1. Robin Blackburn, 'Defining Slavery – its special features and social role', in Leonie Archer (ed.), *Slavery and Other Forms of Unfree Labour* (London and New York: Routledge, 1988), p. 269.
2. Robert Miles, *Capitalism and Unfree Labour* (London: Tavistock, 1987), p. 30.
3. Ibid. p. 25.
4. Alan Hyde, *Bodies of Law* (Princeton: Princeton University Press, 1997), p. 71.
5. Joshua Cohen, 'The Arc of the Moral Universe', in Tommy L. Lott (ed.), *Subjugation and Bondage: Critical Essays on Slavery and Social Philosophy* (Boulder, CO and Oxford: Rowman and Littlefield, 1998), p. 307.
6. Ibid. p. 307.
7. G. E. M. de Ste. Croix, 'Slavery and Other Forms of Unfree Labour', in Archer, *Slavery*, p. 19.
8. Roger Sawyer, *Slavery in the Twentieth Century* (London and New York: Routledge and Kegan Paul, 1986), p. 1.
9. Bernard Williams, 'Necessary Identities', in Lott, p. 5.
10. David Brion Davis, *The Problem of Slavery in Western Culture* (Ithaca, NY: Cornell University Press, 1966), p. 32.
11. Orlando Patterson, *Slavery and Social Death: A Comparative Study* (Cambridge, MA and London: Harvard University Press, 1982), p. 23.
12. Blackburn, 'Defining Slavery', p. 274.
13. Ibid. p. 274. Emphasis added.
14. Patterson, *Slavery and Social Death*, p. 28.
15. Ibid. p. 13.
16. David Turley, *Slavery* (Oxford: Blackwell, 2000), p. 29.
17. Patterson, *Slavery and Social Death*, p. 78.
18. Williams, 'Necessary Identities', p. 8.
19. Blackburn, 'Defining Slavery', p. 264.
20. Charles Mills, *Blackness Visible: Essays on Philosophy and Race* (Ithaca, NY and London: Cornell University Press, 1998), p. 7.
21. Ibid. pp. 9, 125.
22. Peter Laslett, Introduction in John Locke, *Two Treatises of Government* (Cambridge: Cambridge University Press, 1991), pp. 105–6.
23. Locke, *Two Treatises of Government* (Cambridge: Cambridge University Press, [1698] 1991), Second Treatise, §135, p. 357.
24. Iain Hampsher-Monk, *A History of Modern Political Thought* (Oxford: Blackwell, 1992), p. 86.
25. Locke, Second Treatise, §8, p. 272.

26. Ibid. §16, p. 279.
27. Ibid. §163, p. 376.
28. Ibid. §173, p. 384.
29. Ibid. §91, p. 327.
30. Locke, *Two Treatises of Government* (Cambridge: Cambridge University Press, [1698] 1991), First Treatise, §131 & 132, p. 238.
31. Locke, Second Treatise, §163, p. 377.
32. Patterson, *Slavery and Social Death*, p. 5.
33. Ibid. p. 5.
34. Ibid. p. 5.
35. Ibid. p. 331.
36. Blackburn, 'Defining Slavery', p. 266.
37. Ibid. p. 263.
38. David Brion Davis, *Slavery and Human Progress* (Oxford: Oxford University Press, 1986), p. 15.
39. Ibid. p. 18.
40. Blackburn, 'Defining Slavery', p. 267.
41. Patterson, *Slavery and Social Death*, p. 79.
42. Blackburn, 'Defining Slavery', p. 271.
43. Cohen, 'Arc of the Moral Universe', pp. 288–90.
44. William Ian Miller, *Humiliation: and Other Essays on Honor, Social Discomfort and Violence* (Ithaca, NY and London: Cornell University Press, 1993), p. 84.
45. Cynthia Willett, 'The Master–Slave Dialectic: Hegel vs. Douglass', in Lott, *Subjugation and Bondage*, p. 154.
46. J. M. Bernstein, 'From Self-consciousness to Community: Act and Recognition in the Master–Slave Relationship', in Z. A. Pelczynski (ed.), *The State and Civil Society* (Cambridge: Cambridge University Press, 1984), p. 23.
47. Patterson, *Slavery and Social Death*, p. 11.
48. Davis, *Slavery and Human Progress*, p. 15.
49. Patterson, *Slavery and Social Death*, p. 99.
50. Ste. Croix, 'Slavery', p. 20.
51. See Charles Mills, *Blackness Visible*, p. 127 and Chapter 1 of this book.
52. Turley, *Slavery*, p. 29.
53. Miles, *Capitalism and Unfree Labour*, p. 7.
54. Ibid. p. 9.
55. Williams, 'Necessary Identities', p. 17.
56. Turley, *Slavery*, p. 114.
57. Patterson, *Slavery and Social Death*, p. 4.
58. Turley, *Slavery*, p. 115.
59. James Walvin, *Questioning Slavery* (London: Routledge, 1996), p. 32.
60. Ibid. p. 27.
61. Davis, *Slavery and Human Progress*, p. 18.
62. Walvin, *Questioning Slavery*, p. 92.
63. Miles, *Capitalism and Unfree Labour*, p. 28.
64. Walvin, *Questioning Slavery*, p. 136.
65. Ibid. p. 147.
66. Ibid. p. 41.
67. Miles, *Capitalism and Unfree Labour*, pp. 181–2.

68. Hilary Beckles, 'The Concept of "White Slavery" in the English Caribbean during the Early Seventeenth Century', in John Brewer and Susan Staves (eds), *Early Modern Conceptions of Property* (London and New York: Routledge, 1996). See also Miles, *Capitalism and Unfree Labour*, pp. 76–7.
69. Miles, *Capitalism and Unfree Labour*, p. 77.
70. Beckles, 'Concept of "White slavery"', p. 575
71. Ibid. p. 576.
72. Ibid. p. 577.
73. Miles, *Capitalism and Unfree Labour*, p. 175.
74. R. M. Hare, 'What is Wrong with Slavery?', in Lott, *Subjugation and Bondage*, p. 212.
75. Beckles, 'Concept of "White slavery"', p. 580.
76. Miles, *Capitalism and Unfree Labour*, p. 188.
77. Ibid. p. 81.
78. Ibid. p. 81.
79. Rogers M. Smith, *Civic Ideals: Conflicting Visions of Citizenship in U.S. History* (New Haven, CT and London: Yale University Press, 1997), p. 63.
80. Ibid. p. 64.
81. Miles, *Capitalism and Unfree Labour*, p. 183.
82. Ibid. p. 75.
83. Ibid. p. 224.
84. Davis, *Slavery and Human Progress*, p. 15.
85. Tommy L. Lott, 'Early Enlightenment Conceptions of the Rights of Slaves', in Lott, *Subjugation and Bondage*, p. 114.
86. Ibid. p. 116.
87. Locke, Second Treatise, §172, p. 383.
88. Ibid. §24, p. 285.
89. Lott, 'Early Enlightenment Conceptions', p. 116.
90. Walvin, *Questioning Slavery*, p. 156.
91. Ibid. p. 179.
92. Beckles, 'Concept of "White slavery"', p. 583.
93. Ibid. p. 583.
94. Lott, 'Early enlightenment conceptions', p. 123.
95. Cohen, 'Arc of the Moral Universe', p. 303.
96. Lott, 'Early Enlightenment Conceptions', p. 124.

CHAPTER 9

Gender and Property: Mothers of Pearl

This chapter explores the ideal of self-ownership and its connections with gender and class in the eighteenth, nineteenth and late twentieth and early twenty-first centuries. It focuses in particular on the fraught and contested relationship between women, property and self-ownership. The question of how women and property are connected brings us back to questions of power and agency, and of citizenship and social death. Women's relationships to property are mediated by the issues of honour, belonging and labour that help to define slavery. Women, too, find themselves caught between insecurity and unfreedom, and within a precarious and shifting balance of power. Their relation to property raises questions about who can own and who can be property, and emphasises the ways in which property as a contested moral space helps to define both freedom and belonging by telling stories about the unequal possession of the self.

The power of property, as we have seen, arises in complex economic, social and legal ways and social hierarchies are constructed by and reflected in property relationships. In this process of constructing hierarchies, 'property takes on stereotypically masculine characteristics; but at the same time, the object of property is sometimes said to be structurally female'.[1] This correlation between men as the subject of property and women as its object is reflected in the historical ownership of women by men, and in the more general objectification and commodification of women. One approach to women's property history is to concentrate on subordination and patriarchal rule, and to argue that women in the past have been subject to total domination and treated as the objects of property and as slaves. According to this account, the way to understand the relationship between women and property is to think of women as the property of men, exchanged for dowries, sold in wife sales, trafficked for sex. There are, of course, elements of truth to this account, but there are dangers too. It is tempting, once domination is understood as total and subordination as natural, to assign the idea that women are property to the past. A totalising account of men's subordination of women is easily read as belonging to a distant patriarchal past, with little to tell us about women's current relationships to property, personhood and citizenship. It is too easy to assume that it is a past that has been overcome, that does not carry a legacy. At the same time, but from the opposite direction, there is a danger of simply inverting patriarchy, without disturbing its characterisations of the 'natural', or of the categories of men and women. If patriarchy is given too much weight to bear, rather than assuming it has been overcome, it can be seen as timeless, static and inescapable, and the women who suffer from its effects can become passive victims.

This chapter constructs a more nuanced view of the complex and fraught relationship between women and property than one that insists on total domination and women as property. It does so by concentrating on the question of self-ownership and how it is extended to women, especially in the contexts of marriage and work. By focusing on women's historical construction as refuges and dependants and men's role as protectors and improvers, property emerges as a site of struggle and as a historical process. Women as a social category are not static or fixed, and neither is their relationship to property, contract, labour or each other. Women's relationship to property in the self, in their bodies and in their labour is inflected by class and race as well as by gender, and the disruptions these differences cause to the ideal of self-ownership are sometimes as important as the disruptions caused by gender difference. Working-class women are fitted uneasily into the narrative of labour as improving and industrious, and women as carers and mothers are often excluded from the self-sustaining myth of civil society. These complicated and complicating notions of coverture, class and care capture more about the troubled relationship between women and property, self-ownership and the imagined community than a totalising discourse about women's subordination to men is able to do.

– SELF-OWNERSHIP –

Self-ownership, as we have seen, particularly in the discussion of John Locke, is a crucially important concept in the philosophy of property. It is central, as Patrick Day points out, to the theories of Locke, Samuel Pufendorf, Robert Nozick and John Rawls.[2] Pufendorf, Locke and Nozick all refuse to allow the possibility that a person can be unowned. Mankind's radical dependence on God, and the workmanship model which holds that all makers own what they have made, mean that 'everything is owned, or *nothing is unowned*'.[3] The idea that the individual cannot be unowned, and cannot belong to no one, but must belong to himself gives individualism the 'possessive quality' identified by C. B. Macpherson.[4] Seventeenth-century individualism constructed the individual as essentially the proprietor of his own person and capacities, owing nothing to society for them, and exercising a despotic dominion over themselves: 'The relation of ownership, having become for more and more men the critically important relation determining their actual freedom and actual prospect of realizing their full potentialities, was read back into the nature of the individual'.[5]

One of the clearest discussions of self-ownership appears in Richard Overton's *An Arrow Against All Tyrants*, an explication of 'selfe propriety' written in 1646. Every individual was given 'an individuall property by nature, not to be invaded or usurped by any'. The self was an object of possession, 'a selfe propriety', but it also needed someone to possess it. An individual had to be the subject of possession, an owner of himself 'else he could not be himselfe'.[6] Identity was created, protected and sustained by ownership. Any attempt to invade or usurp another individual threatened not only his property rights, but also his right to be himself. The individual's right to his 'selfe propriety', his property in his person conveyed a right to enjoy, use and exclude. This right to exclude that came from owning a property in the person was inalienable. We have already seen through the discussion of slavery that this notion of inalienability, and the whole discourse of exclusion, was problematic for those who were constructed as subpersons, but the idea was that self-propriety could not be given up to others. Macpherson emphasises that 'it is this property, this exclusion of others, that makes a man human'.[7]

If this is the case, it raises the question: what makes a woman human? The language of political theory is very rarely gender neutral, and in this case it is important to consider how the relation of ownership is 'read back' into the nature of men and women in very different ways. The impossibility of being unowned has different consequences for women, in a world and a theory where 'God and Man are the only *significant* self-owners'.[8] The relation of ownership is of critical importance in determining women's freedom and their prospects for realising their full potential, but it works for them in different ways, both in terms of excluding others and in terms of self-determination. The significance of men's proprietorship of their persons was not about passive enjoyment, but about active improvement: 'Men were created to improve, and enjoy by improving their capacities'.[9] Freedom consisted in this active proprietorship of one's person and capacities. There was a moral appeal behind the workmanship ideal, the 'moral thesis that the legitimate basis of entitlement lies in productive action'.[10] Women have had to struggle to be recognised as productive actors, capable of improvement and active proprietorship. Their position as members of the 'industrious and the rational' rather than the idle and the listless was never guaranteed or easy to maintain. They were not constructed as able to live and survive as independent beings in a free, industrious society.

Men who could live and survive independently needed to be 'disengaged' selves, struggling with the external world, appropriating and improving it. They had the potential to achieve self-mastery through their mastery of the world. Their self-ownership was a prerequisite for their agency and their property, and in turn their agency and material property worked to guarantee and reinforce their self-ownership. The model of the 'disengaged subject' which Charles Taylor ascribes to René Descartes and Locke relies on some notion of disembodiment, a transcendent rationality which allows the individual to control both himself and the world.[11] For Immanuel Kant, we give ourselves to the moral law and discover what it is through the exercise of rationality, attached potentially to all persons by virtue of their common humanity. Women have access to humanity, but not to the full personhood guaranteed by the moral law. Instead, women are more clearly identified with their bodies. In the process, man is identified with reason and woman with the irrational. As Raia Prokhovnik argues, men and reason are associated with intended action, consciousness, reflection and choice, while women's lives are understood to be dictated by nature and bodily rhythms associated with 'unintended action'.[12] Women's rationality is understood to operate at a lower level than men's because women are unable to free themselves from their bodies, their feelings or their emotions. They cannot escape their bodies or leave them behind to enter the world of the industrious and the rational; they are not understood as independent beings in the sense of being able to control and govern themselves.

The history of men's self-ownership presupposed a particular relationship between the self and nature. The disembodied individual had overcome his own bodily nature by taking control of the natural world. He had civilised himself by moving out of the state of nature, by being industrious, rational, disciplined and 'improving'. He was able to remake himself through his intended actions; his properties, desires, and habits of thought and feeling could all be 'worked on', husbanded and improved.[13] Women's relationships to embodiment, labour, improvement, civilisation and to 'nature' were different, more clearly entangled with their relationships to others and to their own bodies, and more crippling for their self-sovereignty and for their property ownership. They were more likely to find themselves 'worked on', disciplined and husbanded by others. As Orlando Patterson argues about slavery, it is not that women were the objects of property, but that they could not be the subjects of property. Like slaves, women in the nineteenth century were understood to be socially and civilly dead, but even under the doctrines of marital unity and coverture, women continued to function as individuals. They operated under conditions of relative, rather than total, powerlessness. They were constructed as irrational and incapable of making contracts and rational exchanges, but were still expected to enter the marriage contract. They were constructed as idle and non-industrious, but were still expected to work. Their self-ownership was qualified, and their rationality limited, so that their incorporation was partial and their sense of belonging precarious, but their exclusion was not total. I want to explore how women's freedom and belonging operated through the mechanism of the marriage contract in the eighteenth and nineteenth centuries, and through the idea of domestic work in the late twentieth century.

– MONSTERS AND MOTHERS OF PEARL –

Mary Poovey sees the most basic opposition established by civil and property law in nineteenth-century England as the opposition between subjects, defined as 'those people considered able to determine and act on their own interests, hence capable of binding themselves by contract, and non-subjects, 'who were not considered responsible and therefore not so bound'.[14] Subjects were male property owners and non-subjects were the female representatives of property, in need of protection. Women's material dependence was critical to the symbolic economy, and men's identity as subjects with rights rested on constructing women as non-subjects.[15] A man's identity as a self-determining subject rested on his rationality, his active proprietorship of himself and his capacities, and so on his role as a market actor. His ability to act on his intentions, to reflect and to make decisions and choices underpinned his industrious rationality and a whole system of market relations between equal, self-interested and rational individuals. His honour was connected both to his honourable labour and to his sense of belonging to a community of subjects. As a non-subject the middle-class woman was constructed as a maternal, virtuous figure cloistered in a realm beyond self-interest and the market. She became an alternative to competition, a refuge from the alienation of the market and a guardian of the boundaries of morality. This symbolic role as a refuge and a guardian affected both her relationship to the polity as a citizen and her relationship to personhood and self-ownership. Women were crucial to maintaining the appearances and illusions of both gender and property.

Women marked the boundary of alienating, unsettling and disorientating market relations. The structure of middle-class assumptions constructed them as a forcible contrast and a necessary supplement to the market. Unlike men, they were not supposed to be mercenary, competitive or self-interested and were constructed instead as maternal, virtuous, respectable and self-sacrificing. Such characteristics were bound to affect their relationship to property, personhood and citizenship. Morality and property were brought together by gender and class into a particular constellation in the mid-nineteenth century, focused on the chastity of middle-class women. Chastity became their point of honour, their way of symbolising 'the proper'. Poovey draws attention to the importance of reputation and credit to middle-class property, and argues that the ideology of separate spheres 'both generated and depended upon an arrangement of social and property relations that positioned women as moral superiors *and* economic dependants'.[16] Women's moral superiority was inextricably bound to their economic dependence and both were understood as natural and fixed, as part of the binary of sexual difference. Morality, and particularly the morality of women, was seen as the basis of class as well as gender stability. It was a morality that was closely tied to property and to the integrity of the domestic sphere as a refuge from market relations. As Caroline Norton argued in the early nineteenth century, it was property and not morality that was held sacred, and since men were allowed to be motivated by mercenary self-interest, women – who were not self-interested, active self-proprietors– simply ceased to exist.[17]

This invisibility, or ceasing to exist, was most marked under the institution of coverture that underpinned the marriage contract until the late nineteenth century. Coverture was a legal relation between husband and wife, under which husband and wife were understood to be 'but one person'. Under common law, a woman's legal identity was eclipsed or 'covered' by her husband's. Her situation was most clearly stated by William Blackstone in his *Commentaries on the Laws of England.* The doctrine of the unity of person between the husband and wife meant that 'the very being and existence of the woman is suspended during the coverture, or entirely merged and incorporated in that of the husband'.[18] Her personal property was by marriage absolutely vested in the husband, so that he could dispose of it at any time without her consent.[19]

Coverture was a complex legal, social, political and economic relation that reflected the complexity of women's position in society, and it has been analysed and interpreted in contested ways. For some, coverture as an institution exemplifies women's civil subordination. From the seventeenth century onwards, those who opposed coverture argued that the civil position of a wife resembled that of a slave, and the comparison of wives and slaves reverberated throughout the nineteenth century. Under coverture, the wife explicitly agreed to obey her husband. This made the marriage contract unique by reserving for wives 'the gratuitous degradation of swearing to be slaves'.[20] Writing in 1825, William Thompson drew the analogy with slave contracts in the West Indies: 'Marriage was nothing more than the law of the strongest, enforced by men in contempt of the interests of weaker women.'[21] For Carole Pateman, marriage was straightforwardly about men's power over women, and about the organisation of orderly sexual access. In her account of the sexual contract, to become a 'husband' is to attain patriarchal right with respect to a 'wife', to gain uncircumscribed sexual access to her, and to control her property and her labour. The marriage contract itself institutionalised the law of male sex right. Marriage fixed the wife's dependence on her husband and trapped her in a balance of power that was personal and precarious.[22]

A wife's freedom was contingent on her husband's renunciation of his power. Rape in marriage was not recognised as a crime in Britain until 1990, and the nineteenth-century marriage contract included the woman's promise to submit to her husband's conjugal rights. The ability to consent or to refuse sex is a form of property that women have historically been denied. If property involves power and security, the ability to exclude, not to be invaded or usurped, and the ability to maintain expectations and to exercise exclusive possession, then, 'each of these elements of property ownership corresponds to an absence within a woman's control over her own sexuality'.[23] The relation of ownership was read back into the nature of the wife in ways which revealed the impossibility for women of being unowned. The law of the strongest, the man's power over the woman based on physical force, was rewritten as a legal relation and reconstructed as a contract based on consent.

The wife consented to be a willing slave in return for protection from her husband against the physical threats and dangers posed by other men. If we follow the Lockean argument that 'as soon as compact enters, slavery ceases', it is possible to argue that under these conditions, women continued to own a property in their person and to enjoy the minimal form of self-ownership. Nozick, and libertarians like him, would argue that the most abject proletarian enjoys the relevant rights of self-ownership. Z is abject because she owns no private property, and she will therefore contract on adverse terms with someone who does own some, if she can find a person with property who is willing to contract with her. No capitalist has to strike a agreement with Z in order to survive, and so Z's survival is not guaranteed. In this situation, Z still has self-ownership. She is not a slave, because 'while [she] can do nothing without another's agreement, it is also true that there is nothing which [she] need do without [her] own agreement'.[24] Unlike the slave owner, the capitalist does not have rights of sheer command over Z, grounded in a prior contract to obey. For G. A. Cohen, this means that self-ownership can constitute only 'the bare bourgeois freedom which distinguishes the most abject proletarian from a slave'.[25] It could be argued that the wife (Z) retains the same bare bourgeois freedom under the marriage contract, since she agrees to marry. For Thompson, and for Pateman, it is the prior agreement to obey that turned the wife from a proletarian into a slave.

The relation of protection and obedience was written into the terms of the contract and could not be altered. It was read back into the social categories of husband and wife, and so into the natures of men and women. Pateman argues that through the marriage contract 'women's subjection is secured in civil society'[26] and she points out that 'the slave's status was little different from the subjection for life and the perpetual service required of a wife'.[27] Against this, Ursula Vogel argues that the contract on its own is not enough to account for women's subordination and establish patriarchal rule. In her analysis, it is not so much that individual women swear to be slaves through a series of contracts, but that marriage as a public institution relies on extinguishing the independence of the wife by subordinating it to the public interest. For her, marriage, even after its main focus seemed to have shifted from sacrament to contract, remained embedded in the religious framework which tied the rights and duties of married men and women to procreation. Vogel argues that this discourse took the essence of marriage to be the conjugal bond, and severed this essence from assumptions about individual rights and private autonomy.[28] The ethical love and unity expressed through the marriage contract needed to be enforced by law, and this public interest was expected to take priority over the private interests of the individuals involved. This included emphasising 'the law's prior interest in the unifying effects of the husband's control over matrimonial property. That is, from the higher viewpoint of the public interest, the institution of marriage had to rank above the independence of the wife'.[29] The collective, public interest trumped the formal guarantees of equal agency included in the terms of the civil contract and reaffirmed the husband's rights over the person and property of his wife, fixing her dependence on him.

The husband's rights over the person and property of his wife were expressed in various ways that expressed the extinction of her independence. Coverture underpinned a legal system that treated women as conduits of property, 'nothing but the intervening stage between her father's and her husband's and her son's ownership'.[30] Her legal disabilities, based on her characterisation as irrational, meant that she was categorised with idiots, convicted criminals and infants. The dishonour and degradation of coverture came close to robbing women of their history, not allowing them to belong in their own right to the legitimate social order. A wife was civilly dead, but masters and husbands 'could not help recognize the humanity of their human property'.[31] Like slave owners struggling with the status of their 'living tools', men found it difficult to reduce women to the status of objects of property.

For Pateman, women cannot be 'individuals' because the individual is an inescapably masculine construction, a patriarchal category. To be an individual means to possess and have access to sexual property: the individual is 'a man who makes use of a woman's body'.[32] Donna Dickenson argues (against Pateman) that women were property, but they were simultaneously persons: they had to have enough capacity to enter the civil marriage contract, and so they could not have the status of animals, slaves or property. Coverture was oppressive for women precisely because it represented the absence of contract. For Dickenson, coverture was emphatically not a contract because the doctrine of marital unity 'is the very opposite of the notion of two independent individuals required by contract'.[33]Without the protection provided by contract, women were unable to act as agents, but for Dickenson they did not cease to be individuals and continued to hold a property in their persons.[34] Rather than exemplifying women's position as civil subordinates within the liberal contract, Dickenson argues that it is 'more instructive to see the rigidification of coverture as a form of *backlash* against liberalism's otherwise triumphal progress'.[35] According to Dickenson, Pateman, and others who see women as property, risk essentialism in mistaking the historically specific conditions of coverture for universal and inevitable subordination.

Dickenson insists that we need to recognise property regimes as particular and historical, and so restore women's relation to property as 'a site of struggle'.[36] Under the nineteenth-century conditions of coverture, women were not the subjects of property. They were never appointed overseers of wills, and were hardly ever made trustees of funds, or appointed guardians of children. Their relationship to property was never permanent, their expectations could not be settled. Under the system of coverture, a widow's property belonged to her only until she remarried, handing her property over to another man. She could not use her property as a necessary buffer to the irregularity and caprice of others; it offered her no protection. At the same time, it is important to remember that her freehold property remained hers, and to recognise that often the law of coverture was often ignored or proved unworkable in practice. Amy Louise Erickson points out the disjuncture between theory and practice, and the need to recognise the differences between theoretical individuals and real people making property decisions in their ordinary lives. Both women and men worked hard to find ways around coverture's strictures. While the majority of women married, a large proportion never did, and in practice many wives managed their finances on their own behalf or jointly with their husbands. Many wealthier wives avoided the common-law basis of coverture by making complex marriage settlements enforceable through equity and in the Court of Chancery. Ordinary women, too, employed pre-marital property settlements to protect their property, especially where widows remarried.[37]

The writings of moralists, theologians and theorists of the late eighteenth and early nineteenth centuries did not present the relationship between husband and wife as the straightforward exercise of male sex right over a slave, but instead dealt with property as a more ambiguous moral space. Their more complicated views of the power relationships involved recognised the possibility of tyranny and slavery, but also drew on a rhetoric of rational subjection on the part of the wife, and benevolence and responsibility on the part of the husband. The writers preferred to see themselves and their male readers as rational masters of servants, in a position to husband and to improve, and as part of a system of reasonable subjection which was bound to be more orderly and productive than unlimited liberty. They raised the possibility of freedom in servitude. The possession of the life, liberty and obedience of his wife was presented as the addition of another soul, a heavy duty and ultimately as an enhancement of his freedom. It was not just that women were constructed as moral superiors and economic dependants, but that men were constructed as rational masters and dutiful stewards. The relation of ownership was read back into the nature of individual women as a specific form of dependence that relied on her having a degree of self-ownership and rationality, and into the nature of individual men as a specific form of mastery tied to honour and security.

The careful construction of the relationship between gender and property involved a complex negotiation of the space between being self-owned or other-owned, and of the distinction between property in the person and in the body. Eighteenth-century writers made it clear that the 'natural' inequality between the sexes was bound to have ethical implications. This was not always as straightforward as identifying men with reason and mind, and women with nature and body, because their minds and bodies interacted. Men's robust constitutions and strong limbs enabled them to farm the soil, erect dwellings, set up industries and defend the community. Providence had designed women for a state of dependence by giving them timidity of temper and 'tenderness of make'.[38] According to these moralists, men as law givers had the larger share of reason bestowed on them. Women were better prepared for compliance. Men and women were naturally made of differing tempers, and so their natural, mutual relation was of protection and obedience. Women were the weaker sex and this 'maketh it reasonable to subject [them] to the *Masculine Dominion*'.[39] This was understood as a dominion designed by nature rather than imposed by force, and one to which women willingly consented through the marriage contract and the doctrine of marital unity. In praising Lady Alice Lucy, Samuel Clark described how 'She knew that her taking of a *second self*, was a self-denying work; and therefore she resigned both her *reason* and her *will* unto her *Head* and *Husband*'.[40] Women exercised their reason in submitting themselves to their husbands and to nature.

As rational masters and dutiful stewards, men found advantages in marriage which outweighed the loss of their 'so much boasted Freedom'. There is an interesting parallel here with the exchange of freedoms at the heart of Jean-Jacques Rousseau's social contract. In his account, as men leave the state of nature they give up their natural self-sovereignty, and gain civil and moral liberties that are explicitly linked to self-mastery and to membership of the imagined community. The anonymous author of *The Art of Governing a Wife* argued that through marriage the man 'is put into a better State of Freedom, and is possessed of a Woman who deposites in his Hands, her Liberty, her Will, her Fortune, her Care, her Obedience, her Life, and even her very Soul'. She gave him a dominion over herself that was both material and spiritual. Ownership for men is not constructed as simply about freedom, or about domination. The husband was understood to have lost his freedom, but 'how great a Gainer he is by the Change'.[41] The author of *The Art of Governing a Wife* makes clear that this brings with it a new duty of care and industry that ought to increase proportionally, as it would if he had been given a new farm to improve. He becomes an active proprietor and improver both of himself and of another soul that has been added to his soul. The wife should find that her husband 'giveth you ease without abridging your *Liberty*'. She was in '*rational subjection* to a Prince', which was bound to be preferred to 'the disquiet and uneasiness of *Unlimited Liberty*'.[42]

It was in this context that women's marital infidelity and the bearing of illegitimate children were treated not just as having broken a private contract but also as violating public order and morality. Women without virtue neglected their husbands' interests, and undermined the notion of unity. They broke through 'every Tie that should be held Sacred'.[43] The unfaithful woman undermined the whole notion of rational subjection and freedom in servitude. She was figured as resistant to the social forces of obligation such as shame and fear and so as incapable of being restrained. Female immorality was understood as a form of corruption, a public menace. An adulterous man was not understood to be defiant and unrestrainable in the same way because his offence did not involve the sacrifice of his character. William Foster made this explicit: 'A man cannot sink to a level with an Adultress, *till he has forsaken his Post in Battle*.'[44] A woman's ownership of herself, her sense of honour and her reputation were intimately bound up with her membership of the imagined community. Her freedom and her belonging were both inextricable from her chastity.

The marriage discourse differentiated property in the person and self-ownership along gender lines. As husbands, men's identities were caught up with their roles as responsible protectors, improvers and rational superiors. Men's honour was linked to being not only masters of themselves, but also of their wives. They were self-governing individuals who took responsibility for themselves, for their labour, their conscience and their reason – and for the souls of their wives. The female point of honour was chastity – and only chastity. An adulterous woman took the risk of giving up everything, of abandoning herself. Without chastity women were 'wives no longer, the bond of wedlock is immediately dissolv'd'.[45] They were charged with preserving the honour, reputation and property of the family 'from any Mixture that may bring a Blemish to them'. The disadvantage of the double standard was 'more than recompens'd, by having the *Honour* of *Families* in your keeping'.[46] A woman's modesty was the 'best Portion, the best Estate, and the richest Jewel' she could bestow upon her husband.[47]

A woman's public role was to uphold the reputation of the family, to guard and steward it as her property, protecting it from blemish and dishonour. Chastity was central to her marriage contract, and so to her partial incorporation into the public. It was also crucial to her self-ownership, bringing together her property in her person, her sexuality and her property in her body in ways which were irreducibly gendered. Women needed to be watchful when they were in the company of men in order not to come to harm. They were required to form the appearance of property through the notion of the 'proper person'.[48] Moralists urged them to strive to be like the bee who lived 'in the midst of the Hive full of clinging stuff, yet keeps her wings untoucht with it'. It was important for women to live blameless, almost other-worldly lives so 'as not to partake of the corrupt and sinful humours … as Mother Pearls live in the Sea, not taking in one drop of Salt Water into their Shells'.[49] The performance and public display were taken to reflect an essential truth about women's selves. Women were expected to understand themselves as unrestrainable rather than self-controlled and reflective: 'Your looks, your Speech, and the course of your whole Behaviour, should own an humble distrust of your selves.'[50] Their dominion over themselves was fragile rather than despotic. Ownership was read back into female bodies as distrust and a recognition of the dangers of being unowned, either by self or other.

Women as mothers of pearl were constructed as the chaste guardians of men's property, and in particular of the institution of inheritance. Without security or trust themselves, they were supposed, through their rational subjection, to offer men the guarantee that their expectations were secure. It was women who were seen as spinning the invisible thread of property into a cable, and making it part of the fabric of ethical love and equal dignity. They imparted to property its value of affection by rooting it in the family and in unity. Unlike men, who were defined as separate active proprietors of themselves, owing nothing to society for their persons or capacities, women were seen as part of a moral whole. 'Hearth and rootedness' were understood as 'sacred symbols to all civilized races', as a distinctive part of the bourgeoisie's conception of itself.[51] Both had to be underwritten by women's chastity, understood as essential and natural and as definitive of womanhood. Abandoning chastity meant abandoning humanity, ceasing to be a member of the society of rational creatures and putting the self outside the social contract. It 'ranks you among the Bruits' because 'An Unchaste Woman is look'd upon as a kind of a Monster; a thing divided and distorted from its proper form'.[52] This was women's version of self-propriety, their way of possessing themselves and making themselves human. Self-ownership was read back onto their bodies specifically as chastity, and given its possessive quality by being made to seem essential and natural.

A middle-class woman's 'proper form' was as her husband's second soul. In the eighteenth- and nineteenth-century fabrication of the self 'it becomes clearer that in order for men to exercise and sustain a sense of themselves, women *must* find their primary self as familial'.[53] Only when women found their substantive destiny in the family could men move beyond family relationships to define themselves outside their bodies in the external world. As 'more and more relationships come to be seen as contractual and therefore legitimately amoral, the family with wife and mother as its core carries an even heavier burden in upholding both intimacy and morality'.[54] A chaste and tender wife with a baby at her breast was supposed to be for her husband 'the most exquisitely enchanting object on earth'.[55] She inspired 'the standing admiration of some great and noble work of Nature'[56] – reiterating the notion that she was there to be improved, protected and perfected, and reinforcing her association with the natural, unintended actions and bodily practices. Men's identities as subjects with rights, as rational masters and dutiful stewards, depended on establishing stable identities for women as wives and mothers in need of protection, fixing them in their dependence on men. For this to be effective, the binary opposition between men and women needed to be constructed and fixed as the most important difference.[57] To paraphrase C. B. Macpherson, it cannot be said that the nineteenth-century concept of gender difference was entirely derived from the concept of possession, but it was powerfully shaped by it.[58] The possessive assumptions are there in the opposition between subjects and non-subjects, in the ideas about chastity and distrust and in the notion of rational subjection as opposed to unlimited liberty. Women were not to be left in a state of nature, understood as a state of licence, but needed to be partially incorporated into civil society and the state as subordinates and as partial self-owners.

– MAKESHIFTS AND MERCENARIES –

This partial incorporation was differentiated not only by gender, but also by class. Sustaining the appearances and illusions of property involved performing gender and class together, and middle-class women were deeply invested in marking the boundaries of both. They carried their class status on their bodies, in their hands and clothes. Their social rounds, philanthropy, charity and cross-class interactions with their servants were all part of the moral enterprise of building reputation and status for the family, and at the same time consolidating their own feminine status within the familial context. Privatised family life came to be associated with order, rationality and usefulness, and with sustaining the moral space of property. Striving to live untouched by 'clinging stuff' and uncorrupted by sinful humours meant that white middle-class women needed to keep their distance from the reality of household labour. The institution of service was central to upper- and middle-class identity, and to their notions of civilisation, hearth and rootedness. From the second half of the nineteenth century, the code of domesticity constructed specific ideas about womanhood that were tied to class and to race and ethnicity as well as to gender, and were 'invented and enacted in everyday interactions between mistresses and workers'.[59] Belonging and exclusion were layered, and constantly reinforced by social practices, rather than fixed and ossified.

Middle-class women, figured as refuges and guardians, were supposed to remain in the private sphere, not to labour in the outside world. Men as active proprietors of themselves and of their labour struggled with the external world and fought their way to improving their property in their persons by owning their actions. Men's work represented their agency and their personhood. Through the sale of his labour power a man made himself a free worker and distinguished himself from an unfree labourer or a slave by exercising dominion over himself within his sphere of discretion. Living and surviving as independent beings in a free and industrious society required a full property in the person, significant self-ownership, rather than the partial version. Wages were paid 'to the male worker as a husband/breadwinner to maintain himself *and* his dependants, not merely in exchange for the sale of his labour power.'[60] Husbands became bread-winners and wives became economic dependants, whose earnings were understood to be supplementary. Women were assumed to be wives 'and wives are assumed to be economically dependent on their husbands, obtaining their subsistence in return for domestic service.'[61] Women who worked for wages claimed a property in their own person and so threat-ened both the domesticity of the private sphere and the masculine order of the workplace.

The connections between labour and self-ownership were not straight-forward for women living and working in the nineteenth century, or easily disentangled from their 'natural' roles as wives and mothers. While some wives worked with their husbands at the same trade, and carried on their trade as widows, most women did 'women's work' – domestic service, laundry, nursing, needlework, spinning, cleaning and midwifery. A high proportion of women's occupations were casual, intermittent and seasonal. Sara Horrell and Jane Humphries argue that the chronic under-reporting of women's occupations reflects the 'essentially opportunist and fragmented character of married women's work'.[62] This fragmentation created a different relationship to women's ownership of themselves and to their membership of the public sphere. Working women's property in their person and their citizenship were brought together in ways that were different from working men's and from bourgeois women's. The differential incorporation of working women reflected their qualified self-ownership and maintained the distinction between (male) honourable labour and (female) drudgery.

The great majority of women were unable to work in 'male' trades organised by guilds or livery companies. This meant that there was intense competition between women for the casual and poorly paid work that was left. Domestic service was the commonest occupation for women working in London, with most staying in one place for about a year. Women worked taking in washing, starching linen, cleaning silks and gloves, in needle trades, baking oatcakes for sale, as well as taking in lodgers, making flannel shirts and 'keeping a mangle'.[63] Their labour was intermittent and varied, and remained embedded within the household economy, en-twined with their domestic work and responsibilities. Women's work is best characterised as part of a broader 'economy of expedients' or an 'economy of makeshifts'.[64] These poor and plebeian women were part of the market place, and so were immediately suspect both as market actors and as women. They transgressed the boundaries of alienating market relations rather than marking them, but their work for wages was not understood as enhancing their moral and political agency, or as making them industrious and rational. Poor women's work was stigmatised as merely contingent and necessary, and understood as connecting them back to their bodies and to their 'natural' roles as domestic servants and mothers, rather than taking them out into the external world and the public sphere. Women (and men) who worked to serve others within an economy of expedients were not understood to be appropriating and improving the external world, and so could not make and remake the bases of their self-ownership as active proprietors. They were not linked into the chain of social connections, the reciprocity of production and exchange, the web of social relations that underpinned the version of civil society open to men as active proprietors of themselves and others. Women were not understood to be able to live as independent beings in a free, industrious society. Middle-class women were excluded from the amorality of market bargaining because they were assumed to lack mercenary instincts and self-interest, while working-class women were excluded from the morality of the market and the active proprietorship, the righteous labour and the industriousness that could underpin improvement and productivity.

The traps created for women by the fiction of self-ownership and the problems of fully integrating themselves into the fuller version of market and civil society have not disappeared in the modern world. Women still have problems constructing for themselves an abstract, dispassionate individuality and continue to be understood as inescapably woven into the fabric of their bodies. As Leonora Davidoff argues, the categories of 'men' and 'women' are part of a status system that attributes certain identities to some people and precludes them from others. Women are defined as women by being outside the realm of marketable skills.[65] Their outsider status, however, is mediated by class and race as well as by gender. Not all women have the same status, and their 'outsiderness' is not only regulated by being the reflections of men, but also refracted through their relationships with other women. The emphasis on women as property or as slaves draws attention to male privilege and 'total domination' and tends to imply that all women have the same relationship to domestic and reproductive labour, and 'that it is therefore a universal female experience'.[66]

Once reproductive labour is seen as gendered, and only as gendered, domestic labour is assumed to be identical for all women, and so is sometimes taken as the basis for a shared identity. Women as a group are expected, by this discourse, to have the same relationship to the imagined community, and the same experience of relative powerlessness.

The idea that all women have the same relationship to domestic work relies on an assumption similar to the doctrine of marital unity, the notion that women can become 'one person', merged or incorporated into one another. Some twentieth-century and early twenty-first-century middle-class women come close to becoming 'unowned' by detaching themselves from their 'natural' roles as care givers and 'works of nature'. Often, they achieve this by employing other women to carry the burden of embodiment. Nicky Gregson and Michelle Lowe's work focuses on the ways in which nannies are understood as mother substitutes. Their labour is primarily construed as care-related, and the nanny herself is described by her employers as the 'next best thing' to the mother, a woman who provides the forms of support service conventionally associated with the housewife, or the woman-as-refuge.[67] Nicky Gregson and Michelle Lowe's study involved interviewing middle-class dual-career householders whose way of life implicitly suggested a rejection of 'natural' mothering and of the ideology of 'exclusive motherhood'.

However, their respondents' comments on their nannies suggest that they saw childcare as a 'natural' role for 'other' women – those with the right temperament and the right bust size as well as the right training. One couple interviewed by Gregson and Lowe described their nanny as 'the archetypal mother figure': 'She was as wide as she was tall – 52DD!! Very placid, very calm, very relaxed'.[68] In his book *The Rise and Fall of the British Nanny*, Jonathan Gathorne-Hardy emphasises the 'humbleness' and 'simplicity' of the nanny in contrast to the upper-class mother, and remarks: 'Nannies frequently shared Simpson's [Gathorne-Hardy's nanny's] simple shape, as though like lilo's [sic] they inflated the better to comfort.'[69] Linda Blum identifies a similar, but more racialised, discourse informing the La Leche League in the contemporary US. She describes how, in the early twentieth-century US, white middle-class mothers who stayed at home to breastfeed and exclusively mother their children were constructed as the owners of 'pure' and 'civilized' bodies in contrast to the 'suspect' bodies of black women, loaded with sexuality and the dangers of 'pollution'.[70]

The bodies of women, black people, children and the 'lower' classes were all eroticised in this discourse, and constructed as closer to nature, 'dangerous and irresponsible, as against those who could be trusted to control themselves and others.'[71] We can see in this the different layers of lacking self-ownership, the degrees of partial incorporation: not being trusted by others to control yourself is different from being exhorted to 'own a humble distrust' of yourself. Honour and degradation, belonging and exclusion, labour and drudgery are all inflected by class, and by power relations between women. They involve different degrees of self-government, and women's statuses are implicated in each other and defined in contrast to each other, not just in contrast to men's trustworthiness and despotic dominion as men.

The employment of a nanny, for example, is not only a physical substitution, but an 'ideological substitution' as well.[72] This ideological substitution is a particular way of negotiating the underlying equation of women with reproduction and bodies, and trying to overcome the suspicion that many men still distrust women in the public realm 'in case they bring their bodies with them'.[73] The 'natural', maternal mother is left intact, embodied by the nanny, while the middle-class woman can enter the workplace without trailing her maternity with her. Gregson and Lowe point out that nanny employment is structured and arranged between women, and understood (by both men and women) as a way of substituting specifically for the mother's labour, and as a strategy that 'enables' women to go out to work. They quote from one of their female respondents, a PR consultant: 'The nannies come out of my salary … And I suppose the nanny was to help me so I could work, not really for both of us.'[74] In this situation, the nanny is understood to be acting as a direct substitute for the female partner, but it is important that she is not a mirror image. It is her difference that makes her a successful substitute. This substitution process confirms the disruption between women, the market and self-ownership. The 'working mother', by employing a nanny to care on her behalf, resists being constructed as a refuge, but reveals herself to be a 'mercenary', capable of pursuing her self-interest and of 'disengaging' herself. She is constituted as a particular kind of subject by what she chooses not to do, she is seen as denying her 'nature', and understood to be attempting to construct herself as disembodied. In this sense, the exchange with her substitute allows the middle-class woman to attempt to effect self-ownership by copying the disembodiment of her husband, trespassing on the 'masculine presumption' that her body is separable from her self.[75] The woman she employs enters into a market exchange like any other, and so she too is constructed as a 'mercenary', but the basis of the transaction means that she cannot leave her body or her maternity behind. Women's self-ownership is fractured and rucked by care, by class and by different embodiments.

The idea of women (and especially mothers) providing a 'forcible contrast' to the amorality and self-interest of market society has not disappeared entirely. Blum analyses the ideology of intensive motherhood: 'Good mothers, in this view, not only put their children's needs first, but provide labor- and emotion-intensive care to protect them from the harsh, impersonal market-driven society.'[76] Women, as mothers, continue to be constructed as unmotivated by mercenary self-interest. They are expected to preserve the integrity of the domestic sphere as a refuge from market relations, and when they do so they continue to risk economic dependence and invisibility. Other women, those who enter the market place, find that their 'ability to sell is no guarantee of personhood'.[77] Women, and especially working mothers, still often find themselves part of an economy of makeshifts rather than active self-proprietors and full members of civil society. They are understood to be both 'impaired market actors' and not 'good' mothers.[78] The central difficulty for women was, and remains, how to negotiate their female 'nature'. The idea of a gender-neutral 'person' whose ownership can be read back into his or her nature without reference to gender is deeply problematic. It carries with it the assumption that men are free to escape their bodies into autonomy, freedom, rationality, productive work and a sense of belonging to the political community and civil society. Raia Prokhovnik contrasts this direct transition to women's indirect and more cumbersome transition, their partial incorporation and their relation to property as a site of struggle. Women as a group are seen to have reproductive capacity and 'it is women as a group who take on the burden of the body defined according to this one narrow and specific capacity'.[79] This is very different from the idea of owning your own person and capacities and owing nothing to society for them, the defining features of men's self-ownership.

– CONCLUSION –

The connections between gender and property draw out the question of who can own property and who can be property, and the problems of negotiating how to do both. For women, property involves a constant effort at reconciliation and at managing the conflicts of private property and the morality of *Recht*. The tensions within property as simultaneously contingent and permanent, unstable and authentic are particularly clear in the ways in which property is caught up with gender. Despotic dominion is not easily extended to women, and their anchorage to the imagined community often proves fragile, and as disorientating as individualism. The intangible interest of the right to exclude, and the value that people place on the kind of power relations in which they stand to others, are clear in the relationship between gender and property, and the ways in which it is inflected by class and race. Gender, like race, is a complicated marker of possession and dispossession, inclusion and exclusion. The complex relationship between gender and property draws out the connections between freedom and belonging, and the entanglement of honour, belonging and labour in defining possession of the self. The final chapter returns to these themes in the context of defining possession of the earth and membership of the nation.

– NOTES –

1. Margaret Davies, 'Queer Property, Queer Persons: Self-ownership and Beyond', *Social and Legal Studies* 8:3, 1999, p. 329.
2. Patrick Day, 'The Self-Ownership Thesis: a Critique', *Philosophical Notes* 19, http://www.libertarian.co.uk/lapubs/philn/philn019.pdf, p. 1.
3. Ibid. p. 1.
4. C. B. Macpherson, *The Political Theory of Possessive Individualism* (Oxford: Oxford University Press, 1962), p. 3.
5. Ibid. p. 3.
6. Ibid. p. 141.
7. Ibid. p. 142.
8. Day, 'The Self-Ownership Thesis', p. 2
9. Macpherson, *Political Theory of Possessive Individualism*, p. 142.
10. Ian Shapiro, 'Resources, Capacities and Ownership: the Workmanship Ideal and Distributive Justice', in John Brewer and Susan Staves (eds), *Early Modern Conceptions of Property* (London and New York: Routledge, 1996), p. 25.
11. Charles Taylor, *Sources of the Self* (Cambridge: Cambridge University Press, 1989), p. 159.
12. Raia Prokhovnik, *Rational Woman: a Feminist Critique of Dichotomy* (London and New York: Routledge, 1999), p. 65.
13. Taylor, *Sources of the Self*, p. 159.
14. Mary Poovey, *Uneven Developments: the Ideological Work of Gender in Mid-Victorian England* (London: Virago, 1989), p. 75.
15. Ibid. p. 80.
16. Ibid. p. 52.
17. Ibid. p. 68.
18. Sir William Blackstone, *Commentaries on the Laws of England* (Oxford: Oxford University Press, 1765–9), http://www.yale.edu/lawweb/avalon/blackstone/bk2ch29.htm, p. 4.

19. Amy Louise Erickson, *Women and Property in Early Modern England* (London and New York: Routledge, 1993), p. 25.
20. Carole Pateman, *The Sexual Contract* (Cambridge: Polity Press, 1988), p. 159.
21. Ibid. p. 158.
22. Ibid. passim.
23. Alexandra Wald, 'What's Rightfully Ours: toward a Property Theory of Rape', *Columbia Journal of Law and Social Problems*, 30:3, Spring 1997, p. 466.
24. G. A. Cohen, *Self-ownership, Freedom and Equality* (Cambridge: Cambridge University Press, 1995), p. 100.
25. Ibid. p. 101.
26. Pateman, *Sexual Contract*, p. 181.
27. Ibid. p. 145.
28. Ursula Vogel, 'Private Contract and Public Institution: the Peculiar Case of Marriage', in Maurizio Passerin d'Entrèves and Ursula Vogel (eds), *Public and Private: Legal, Political and Philosophical Perspectives* (London and New York: Routledge, 2000), p. 189.
29. Ibid. p. 193.
30. Erickson, *Women and Property*, p. 235.
31. Pateman, *Sexual Contract*, p. 131.
32. Ibid. p. 185.
33. Donna Dickenson, *Property, Women and Politics* (Cambridge: Polity, 1997), p. 89.
34. Ibid. p. 76.
35. Ibid. p. 88.
36. Ibid. p. 80.
37. Erickson, *Women and Property*, pp. 225–6.
38. James Fordyce, *The Character and Conduct of the Female Sex* (London, 1776), p. 40.
39. *The Lady's New-years Gift: or, Advice to a Daughter* (London, 1688), p. 31.
40. Samuel Clark, *The Lives of Sundry Eminent Persons in this Later Age* (London, 1693), Part II, p. 140.
41. *The Art of Governing a Wife* (London, 1747), pp. 41–3.
42. *Lady's New-years Gift*, p. 61.
43. William Foster, *Thoughts on the Times but Chiefly on the Profligacy of our Women* (London, 1779), p. 8.
44. Ibid. p. 74.
45. William Fleetwood, *The Relative Duties of Parents and Children, Husbands and Wives, Masters and Servants* (London, 1705), p. 179.
46. *Lady's New-years Gift*, p. 34.
47. *Art of Governing a Wife*, p. 12.
48. Davies, 'Queer Property, Queer Persons', p. 336.
49. Oliver Heywood, *Advice to an only Child: or, Excellent Counsel to All Young Persons* (London, 1700), pp. 55, 56.
50. *The Whole Duty of a Woman: or a Guide to the Female Sex Written by a Lady* (London, 1701), p. 9.
51. Ann Laura Stoler, *Race and the Education of Desire* (Durham, NC and London: Duke University Press, 1995), p. 17. Stoler is quoting Henry Mayhew's 1851 work, *London Labour and the London Poor*.
52. *Whole Duty of a Woman*, p. 15.
53. Leonore Davidoff et al., *The Family Story: Blood, Contract and Intimacy, 1830–1960* (London and New York: Longman, 1999), p. 73.

54. Ibid. p. 97.
55. Hugh Smith, *Letters to Married Women* (London, 1748), p. 83.
56. Fleetwood, *Relative Duties*, p. 264.
57. Poovey, *Uneven Developments*, pp. 80–5.
58. Macpherson, *Political Theory of Possessive Individualism*, p. 5.
59. Evelyn Nakano Glenn, 'From Servitude to Service Work: Historical Continuities in the Racial Division of Paid Reproductive Labor', *Signs* 18:1, 1992, p. 32.
60. Pateman, *Sexual Contract*, p. 137.
61. Ibid. p. 138.
62. Sara Horrell and Jane Humphries, 'Women's Labour Force Participation and the Transition to the Male-breadwinner Family, 1790–1865', *Economic History Review* XLVII: I, 1996, p. 104.
63. Shani D'Cruze, 'Care, Diligence and "Usfull pride" [*sic*]: Gender, Industrialisation and the Domestic Economy, c. 1770 to c. 1840', *Women's History Review* 3:3 1994, p. 320.
64. Ibid. p. 318. See also Olwen Hufton, *The Prospect Before Her* (London: HarperCollins, 1995) and Sara Mendelson and Patricia Crawford, *Women in Early Modern England* (Oxford: Clarendon Press, 1998).
65. Leonore Davidoff, 'Regarding Some "Old Husbands' Tales": Public and Private in Feminist History', in Joan B. Landes (ed.), *Feminism: the Public and the Private* (Oxford: Oxford University Press, 1998), p. 185.
66. Glenn, 'From Servitude to Service Work', p. 2.
67. Nicky Gregson and Michelle Lowe, *Servicing the Middle Classes: Class, Gender and Waged Domestic Labour in Contemporary Britain* (London: Routledge, 1994), p. 119.
68. Ibid. p. 181.
69. Jonathan Gathorne-Hardy, *The Rise and Fall of the British Nanny* (London: Hodder and Stoughton, 1972), p. 117.
70. Linda M. Blum, *At the Breast: Ideologies of Breastfeeding and Motherhood in the Contemporary United States* (Boston: Beacon, 1999), pp. 22, 182.
71. Pam Carter, *Feminism, Breasts and Breast-Feeding* (London: Palgrave, 1995), p. 118.
72. Gregson and Lowe, *Servicing the Middle Classes*, p. 182.
73. Prokhovnik, *Rational Woman*, p. 121.
74. Gregson and Lowe, *Servicing the Middle Classes*, p. 187.
75. Judith Butler, *The Psychic Life of Power* (Palo Alto, CA: Stanford University Press, 1997), p. 37.
76. Blum, *At the Breast*, p. 5.
77. Wald, 'What's Rightfully Ours', p. 498.
78. Ibid. p. 488.
79. Prokhovnik, *Rational Woman*, p. 127.

CHAPTER 10

Lost Lands:
Property and Postcolonialism

This chapter explores the unequal possession of the earth by focusing on some of the ways in which property, belonging and exclusion intersected with notions of civilisation and progress beyond the seventeenth century. It looks at how the myths of states of nature and vacant lands developed in modernity, becoming entangled with notions of property rights, individual liberty and the development of human character. The colonial legacy brought into focus the struggle for self-ownership and how to fit the self into the nation, and the conflicts within the growing market system as it enriched some and dispossessed others. While it is unlikely that there have been circumstances under which absolute ownership has existed, the nineteenth century witnessed a growing cultural and political gulf between the land-owning elite and the land-occupying masses, reflecting the polarity between the propertied members of civil society and the proletarian outsiders. This polarising process had the effect of obscuring the varieties of ownership and property rights at work in different contexts, giving private property the appearance and illusion of universality. It also helped to reconfigure the notions of citizen and subject and to demarcate some of the boundaries of nation and empire. Some of these boundaries were constructed through racial and ethnic categories and political and cultural identities emerged as part of 'an imagined nation and empire with its hierarchical forms of belonging.'[1] Property, especially in land, was central to these identities, to the imagined nation and to belonging. Nation and empire expanded the fraught and contested moral space of property.

Land became, and continues to be, a particular focus of confrontation. Property rights in land are central to nationhood in terms of both territory and identity. They work as a means of defining who may control valuable objects and the conditions under which this power may be exercised. The elements of ownership vary in definition and range. Who can own property, what they may do with it, which interests are recognised and what can be owned are not fixed and immutable categories. In the debates over property ownership in the nineteenth, twentieth and twenty-first centuries, class, race, ethnicity and gender have all been significant and enmeshed in each other. Freedom and belonging reemerge as inseparable, and the colonial context draws us back to the oppositions between honour and degradation, belonging and exclusion, and labour and drudgery that structure property history. Questions about whose labour and whose honour count as significant underpin not only self- and property-ownership, but also the sense of belonging to the nation and to the imagined community. The Irish context draws out the connections between land and nationality, the cultural diversity of property rights and the role of the state in the system of property rights. The same issues resurface in the drive towards segregation in nineteenth- and early twentieth-century Rhodesia and in the current conflicts over land redistribution and resettlement in Zimbabwe. In the colonial contexts of Ireland and Rhodesia, the notion that the poor were like the 'untutored natives of distant lands' took on a new resonance, and the conflict between civil society and proletarian outsiders became a conflict between 'colonisers' and 'natives'.

From the late eighteenth and early nineteenth centuries onwards, the second phase of European colonialism moved away from the 'empty spaces' and vacant lands of the seventeenth century and into heavily populated countries, emphasising trade, commerce and political control.[2] In 1797, for example, Napoleon's foreign minister, Charles-Maurice de Talleyrand, recognised the distinction between the old settlements in America and Britain's new colonies in India. America was a place of conquest and settlement, whereas India was a place of exploitation, cultivation and dependency. British India, and the rest of the empire, was 'the creation of an essentially commercial society'.[3] Bhikhu Parekh sketches the broad outlines of this imperial project. Africa was understood as a continent without a history, and non-Europeans were figured as moral and political infants, unable to engage with the key notions of reason, progress, liberty, autonomy and civilisation. This meant that customary laws and practices could be ignored by the colonial institutions, which could then present imperialism as a civilising process. Parekh argues that neither John Locke nor John Stuart Mill 'recognised the natives as self-determining subjects entitled to define their true interests themselves and to lead their preferred ways of life'.[4] Property, especially in land and the self, was central to the notion of a self-determining subject, and to the division between the civilised and the primitive. This chapter seeks to interrogate how the self-determining subject was expressed through property in the colonial context. Imagining the nation, and especially the colonial nation, involved imagining ownership of land.

The colonial encounter was part of a complex and contested process of legitimisation and social acceptance. Ideas about property and civilisation are often fitted into an overarching 'transition narrative', a story about the shift from the primitive to the civilised and from feudalism into capitalism.[5] It is part of a heavily ideological narrative about transformation, as subordinate peoples were expected simply to give up their attachments to static and 'primitive' ways of life and systems of property rights in recognition of the overwhelming superiority of modern, flexible, private property. The transition narrative underpinned the institutions of industry, technology, the legal system and the modern nation state 'and to think the modern or the nation state was to think a history whose theoretical subject was Europe'.[6] Dipesh Chakrabarty argues that this is a metanarrative that celebrates the nation state, and keeps constructing and reconstructing the idea of Europe through 'the tales that both imperialism and nationalism have told the colonized'.[7] The modern state is positioned as the end of transition, and the relationship between the state and the citizen is presented as the 'ultimate construction of sociality'.[8] One of the most important elements of the transition narrative is the tale of property, told to the colonised as a single, straightforward story about the modernising potential of exclusive ownership and the commodification of land. The colonised themselves were fitted into a story that always privileged the modern by invoking the concepts of citizenship, self-ownership and the nation state. The model for the modern was Europe, its original home. Others, those outside Europe, were given a history that was made to look like 'yet another episode in the universal and (... the ultimately victorious) march of citizenship'.[9]

Within the transition narrative, the modern individual is situated 'at the very end of history'.[10] The modern individual is the figure of the citizen, and the citizen is European. The histories and the stories are dominated by Europe, and the modern is understood as an already-known history, 'something which has *already happened elsewhere*, and which is to be reproduced, mechanically or otherwise, with a local content'.[11] This seems to me to be exactly the case with the story of property and colonialism. Property had already happened elsewhere, at the heart of Europe, and it needed to reproduced in the colonies with a kind of 'positive unoriginality'. Like reason in Chakrabarty's account, private property, 'which was not always self-evident to everyone, has been made to look "obvious" far beyond the ground where it originated'.[12] The self-evidence and unoriginality of the Western system of private property required 'property' not to be happening independently in the colonies. The varieties of forms of land tenure and the range of property rights operating outside the 'hyperreal' Europe had to be effaced and covered over, in order not to trouble or unsettle the obviousness of colonial, commercial, private property.

In order to reproduce its unoriginality effectively, property required not only the legal and economic structures of the nation state, but also the conscious, rational, self-constituting human subject embodied in the notion of self-ownership and in the figure of the citizen. Such an individual found their fullest expression in civil society, separated from the state. Property relationships, as we have seen, are central to this intermediary sphere and to the contests over power that take place on this battlefield. Rosalind O'Hanlon points out the 'legitimating power of the sphere of civil society itself, the symbol in all its inviolability of the achievements of the western political tradition'.[13] It is within civil society that the sovereign subject emerges as an individual invested with liberties, rights, independence and happiness, able to exercise despotic dominion. This same subject is a citizen, able to move between the private and the public spheres, with a legitimate presence in both. O'Hanlon argues that it is this 'through this double characteristic that the marginalization of the subaltern acquires its particular character' rooted in inability, poverty, inarticulacy and lack of political participation.[14] Those who lived outside Europe found that their traditions, customs and cultures were not given a history. The subordinated peoples, those who were colonised in various ways, were rendered marginal by being excluded from the possibility of being self-determining individuals, without honour, belonging or righteous labour. They were understood to be subjects rather than citizens, regarded as fugitives and exiles, and so as having 'a weaker ability to articulate civil society's self-sustaining myth'.[15]

– IRELAND –

Ireland became part of the United Kingdom through the Act of Union in 1800, and all of Ireland was ruled from Westminster between 1801 and 1922. It was represented by 100 MPs in the House of Commons, and its landowners were a substantial force in the House of Lords. The landlord class tended to hold aristocratic attitudes towards their property, and traditionally these attitudes had included connecting property to paternalism, but this model of the landlord as paternalist, and hierarchy softened by neighbourliness, broke down in the face of the harsh and competitive conditions that came to prevail in Ireland. There was a clear perception that landlords in Ireland failed to protect their tenants, steward their property or reform their estates to make them productive and profitable. Irish aristocratic landlords were understood to be wasteful and exploitative, rather than industrious. There was a prevailing, and critical, sense that they had gone to Ireland to occupy and to benefit from the labour of others rather than to cultivate and to improve. As Peter Childs and Patrick Williams argue, Irishness was often defined as diametrically opposed to Englishness.[16] From the 1830s onwards, the indigenous Irish developed an alternative model of land tenure in opposition to the aristocratic settler values of the English landlords. Irish farmers insisted that the right of the landlord to his property and a fair return for its use needed to be balanced against the tenants' right to undisturbed cultivation, as long as the rent was paid. This system of tenant rights and custom was carefully contrasted to the competitive model based on laissez-faire economic ideology that was seen as emanating from Westminster, embodying Englishness and colonial oppression. The Irish model that arose in opposition drew on indigenous patterns of land ownership, and on a broader sense of the real, authentic, anti-colonial Ireland as an agricultural community with a rural identity.[17]

Settler attitudes towards ownership of the land in both Ireland and Rhodesia operated at a particular level, tying land into the free-trade model and the colonising interest. Land was treated as a commodity, available for exclusive ownership and exploitation. William Conner argued that this was an attitude that encouraged landlords to charge exorbitant rents, exacerbated poverty, reinforced insecurity of tenure and intensified competition for land. It did not, however, exhaust systems of land tenure and property rights. One of the features of the transition narrative is its incompleteness. One system never simply gives way to another. Land ownership reflects the cultural diversity of property rights and the historical variability of ownership, a diversity and a variability that undermine the 'obviousness' of exclusive ownership. In Ireland, when a tenancy was transferred from one farmer to another, the incoming tenant made a payment to the vacating tenant, treating the tenancy as a property right in itself.[18] The tenancy was transferred on the basis that tenure was permanent, that it could be passed on not only between owners but also through the generations. This was supplemented by the 'Ulster custom': Irish tenants who carried out improvements on their land were entitled to compensation if their landlords interfered and disturbed their improvements. Irish tenants treated their farms as perpetual tenancies that could be transferred, bequeathed and inherited 'and in every respect dealt with them as if they were their property'.[19] Their model of ownership included the rights to possess, use, manage, modify and transmit and so came close to fulfilling all the elements of full ownership. However, the tenants' security and immunity from expropriation were contested by the landlords. Their property rights were enough to underpin only a contingent sense of belonging, rather than a permanent interest, and were insufficient to provide the grounds for living and surviving as independent beings in a free, industrious society.

Irish farming was based on a system of scattered fields, and 'each tenant's land was intermingled with that of others', making exclusive ownership difficult to sustain.[20] Rent was determined by competition rather than by custom, so that families had to compete with each other for land. They made every effort to obtain land by taking on smallholdings and promising to rent them at a price they were incapable of paying. As a result, rents were forced up 'to the highest point consistent with keeping the population alive'.[21] As soon as the tenants took possession, they were in debt to their landlords, and found themselves paying more in rent than the market value of the whole produce of their land. They agreed to pay a money rent, but in practice the debt was worked out in labour, putting the tenants into the position identified by Pierre-Joseph Proudhon. The labourers lived off a subsistence crop of potatoes, and everything the land produced beyond subsistence went to the landlord to pay off the debt. Since even giving up the whole produce was often still less than the promised rent, tenants found themselves not only constantly in debt but also without any incentive to increase the value of the land they worked. William Thomas Thornton argued that these terms of land tenure prevented the peasantry from increasing their resources, and worked to encourage them to have more children. For Mill, the existing cottier-tenant system was an economic and moral evil, encouraging over-population and a 'savage competition for subsistence'.[22] As it stood, the system in Ireland militated against the tenant improving the land and himself: 'if he were industrious or prudent, nobody but his landlord would gain, if he is lazy or intemperate, it is at his landlord's expense'.[23] Tenants were fixed in their dependence on the landlords, and caught in a precarious and shifting balance of power.

Mill sought to overcome the fragility and vulnerability of use rights in his proposals for reform in Ireland in the mid-1840s. He argued for a major state-sponsored scheme to reclaim the wastes and settle the peasants on small freehold plots in order to 'begin the reconstruction of Irish rural society'.[24] For Mill, property owning was central to the process of civilisation and to the construction of a self-determining subject. The narrative of transformation and reconstruction was impossible without property rights. Irish society needed to be reformed to become a civil society, and active peasant proprietorship was essential for moral and economic regeneration. Mill insisted on the importance of peasant ownership in Ireland, and on the potential of the wastelands to generate wealth and improvement. His proposals for reform rested on a dual scheme of fixed rents set by the state accompanied by the reclamation of the wastelands. He saw the wastelands not as reserves of idleness but as tools for funda-mental reform, relieving immediate distress and creating a class of yeomanry, turning the peasants into 'proprietors of the soil which they cultivate.'[25] He expected this form of proprietorship to help to improve the plots and make them profitable and productive, so grounding the possibility of living as independent beings in a free and industrious society.

In 1847 the Waste Lands Bill was passed, earmarking one million pounds for the project of reclamation, introducing compulsory-purchase powers over the wastes and transferring the lands to the state via the Board of Works, which would undertake drainage and road building. Plots of 25–50 acres would then be either sold or let to tenants for a fixed period, under a system enabling them to purchase their plot by instal-ments. Mill argued that Irish tenants could not be expected to take on a capitalist, improving role unless their property interest was recognised. Property was 'essential to achieving and maintaining civilization'[26] and the possession of property would make the Irish peasant an orderly citizen and a self-determining subject, industrious, active and self-reliant. Mill argued: 'Property in the soil has a sort of magic power of engendering industry, perseverance, forethought in an agricultural people.'[27]

The logic of Mill's argument required some acknowledgement in Ireland that the customary rights of the native occupiers should have been counted as property rights.[28] The essence of the debate was how far this acknowledgement could be allowed to encroach on the rights of landlords as landowners without unsettling the inviolability of property rights in England and Scotland. In the 1840s, challenging the free-trade model that protected the possibility of full exclusive ownership 'struck at the heart of British conceptions of the state' and at the idea of Britain as a single, unified market and political unit.[29] Free-trade radicals opposed the Waste Lands Bill, arguing that the measures would encumber Ireland by making her too reliant on government assistance from Westminster. For those interested in protecting England's identity as a free trading nation, the implication of Karl Marx's problematic, the relationship of differentiation, was clear: 'Every claim by a tenant farmer to proprietorial right would have necessarily involved a diminution in the rights attached to another person's title.'[30] Property was a zero-sum game.

The free traders insisted that projects for reclaiming the wastes would be undertaken by private enterprise if they were likely to prove profitable. For them, private property and free trade had their own modernising impetus built into them. Free-trade radicals pronounced peasant proprietorship 'a delusion' and certainly not applicable to Irish conditions; instead 'emulation of English social models should be the aim of all policy'.[31] In Ireland, one suggested free-trade solution was to increase capital investment in land, and instigate large-scale capitalist farming to increase productivity, employment and wages and guarantee secure returns to investors. The model was based on the 'Anglicization of Irish society', replicating England's conditions for progress and agricultural improvement.[32] Free trade and progress went together; it was a story that had already happened elsewhere and simply needed to be transplanted to a new context where it could be made to look obvious and unoriginal, and to reinforce England's identity.

In contrast to this free-trade model, Mill insisted on the moral imperative of bringing together ownership and improvement and stressed the importance of being an improver rather than a landlord. Mill's approach should remind us of property as a contested moral space; he was arguing for a different constellation of freedom and belonging by insisting on the importance of righteous labour, and the honour of improvement. For him, the situation in Ireland represented a specific example of abuse. The owners of the Irish estates had drained the land of its produce and its resources, taking no responsibility for improvement and raising rents to make a cash profit, leaving the tenants to beg and starve. The liberal reformers began to argue that free trade, free contract and absolute control over property should be understood as the product of English customs rather than as universal principles. They challenged the self-evidence of the laissez-faire narrative by emphasising the morality, and not just the economics, of the history that had already happened elsewhere. Full exclusive private property was re-presented by them as a modern, local tradition, as one possibility amongst others. It was possible for alternative systems of land tenure not only to exist, but to be judged legitimate on the grounds that they brought benefits to the community.[33]

During the nineteenth century, thinkers like Mill, Herbert Spencer and Henry George began to argue that land needed to be treated as a special kind of property to which the normal justifications of exclusive ownership did not apply. Its origins were natural, it was necessary to life and it was scarce. Liberal land reformers were prepared to understand land as common property, and developed a liberal theory of common ownership and 'a distinctively liberal conception of exploitation which casts the landlord, not the capitalist, in the role of the class enemy – as the parasite on society's collectively produced wealth'.[34] As Ursula Vogel argues, these liberal thinkers borrowed the socialist language of land robbery, slavery and unearned income, but confined their critique of property to the issue of rent, leaving unlimited capital accumulation intact. The aim was not to achieve collective ownership or to abolish private property in land, but to protect both society's right to the value of raw land and the individual's right to the value of all improvements. These liberal reformers campaigned for the abolition of feudal land laws and for an end to aristocratic attitudes to property that underpinned 'the unassailable power base of a closed, parasitic ruling class' who were idle rather than industrious and immune to market competition.[35] For these thinkers, the land question was a political question requiring the active intervention of the state to tax rents, protect tenants' rights, prohibit enclosures and sponsor agricultural co-operatives, and to shift the balance of power between classes.

This transition narrative in property history required the state. The tenants themselves were treated as if they had no ability to make their own history. Few people had faith in a vision of an emancipated and moralised peasantry in any of the colonies. Peasants were expected to be unable to halt economic decline or their own descent into barbarism and superstition. As we saw in our discussion of Jeremy Bentham, property was equated with civilisation, subsistence with savagery. Catherine Hall makes clear how this equation worked in the Irish context. James Phillips Kay, a senior physician working as secretary to the Manchester Board of Health in 1832, identified the Irish as savage hordes. Living on the margins of subsistence left them without access to the pleasures of civilisation and its commodities and so turned them into barbarians without properly furnished houses, a varied diet or decent clothes. Without artificial wants to allow them to think beyond their immediate preservation, they were fundamentally uncivilised.[36] Thomas Carlyle described the miserable Irish as 'there to undertake all work that can be done by mere strength of hand and back; for wages that will purchase him potatoes.'[37] The Irish were considered to be excessively dependent on the potato, and many British government officials were convinced that potato cultivation was 'morally debilitating', and so dishonouring, because it required little industry or skill to produce a prolific crop.[38] Robert Peel's Irish relief policy based on free-trade principles included importing maize from America to feed the poor, so that Ireland could export the bulk of its produce. Corn was expected to form the basis of Irish 'regeneration': the taste for a higher kind of food would introduce habits of industry and improvement.

During the nineteenth century, imperial discourse shifted away from an emphasis on diet, constitutions and cultural adaptations to climate and place, towards a more biological and physical understanding of race. This biologising and essentialising of race invested power in one self-defined racial group, and fixed race as a profound and unbridgeable gap.[39] The language and sentiments of race that developed in the Atlantic world were fitted into the story of citizenship, and 'race' became a part of history that had already happened elsewhere and could be reproduced with a local content, and a positive unoriginality. The process of reproduction was complicated in Ireland by the whiteness of the Irish, and racial theorists had to work hard to fit them into the hierarchy of empire. In the late nineteenth-century the Irish were constructed as simianised and degenerate, 'a kind of white negroes'.[40] Anne McClintock argues that where skin colour as a marker of power proved to be imprecise and unstable, 'the iconography of *domestic degeneracy* was widely used to mediate the manifold contradictions in imperial hierarchy'.[41] Irish men were figured as slothful, slovenly domestic barbarians. Their unfixed, unstable, contradictory whiteness became 'the warning sign, for the English, of possible degradation'.[42] One of the consequences of understanding whiteness as property is to make clear that it is an insecure status, not a fixed marker of belonging, and that it carries with it a fear of invasion. The Irish, working for subsistence and potatoes, were savages, but they also belonged to the nation. This ambiguity meant that they could slip between race and nation, whiteness and property. Their position within the transition narrative drew attention to its incompleteness, and to the difficulties of reproducing positive unoriginality both in property and in race.

– Rhodesia/Zimbabwe –

The colonial scheme as a civilising mission worked differently in Africa. Cecil Rhodes aimed to bring about the end of all wars and to place the greater part of the world under British law. The first phase of his grand scheme involved the submission of Africa to Anglo-Saxon civilisation and the accumulation of land, dispossessing the native occupiers and forcing their descendants to work in the mines.[43] In Rhodesia, the scramble for land in the 1890s meant that the settlers felt that they had conquered the land by appropriating it. Like the elites in Ireland, they claimed exclusive ownership on the basis of conquest, and they treated land as a cheap and abundant commodity. Until 1918, the land in Rhodesia was owned by the British South Africa Company. It confiscated the mineral resources and the land, and then distributed and sold them to settlers, Africans and missionaries. Pioneer land rights ended up in the hands of syndicates, vested interests and fortune hunters. These European immigrants were absentee landlords with very little interest in commercial farming. They needed a labour force, and the indigenous people living on European farms rented land from the settlers and paid either in cash or in labour. Indigenous people found that their own imagined communities disappeared, 'the land on which their ancestors had been born had suddenly become a white man's farm' and they had become a source of revenue for their landlord.[44] Europeans bought the land and disappeared, leaving agents to collect their rents, discipline their labour force and tax their workers. The landowners were part of the new commercial society, and they tied their ideas about property to the wider, global economy of free trade rather than to principles of cultivation and improvement.

In Rhodesia, the settlers presented indigenous cultivation methods as aimed at subsistence and no more, and drew the same equation as was made in Ireland between subsistence and savagery. Nineteenth-century indigenous Shona farmers in Rhodesia cultivated the land by clearing an acre, digging and fertilising the ground and planting crops as soon as the rains began. The following year another acre would be brought under cultivation in the same way until about three or four acres were in use, when the land first used was allowed to revert to fallow for several years to recover its fertility. The system helped the soils to retain their fertility and worked to prevent soil erosion. The end of the nineteenth and the beginning of the twentieth century was a time of prosperity for the indigenous farmers. As new markets opened up and the mine workers demanded more food and beer, the Shona were producing surplus crops for sale to the Europeans. They diversified into new crops and vegetables, including beans, monkey nuts and maize, and increased their cattle numbers. Some found themselves employing other indigenous people as wage labourers and trading in African products rather than farming themselves. In the face of this evidence of prosperity and innovation, the settlers clung to the myth of subsistence and savagery to sustain the appearances and illusions of private property and to fix the criteria of belonging and exclusion.

The settlers denigrated indigenous land tenure in Rhodesia, seeing it as a relic of barbarism and contrasting it to individual freehold title as the highest form of evolution in land tenure. Traditional views of property rights worked on the assumption that indigenous social and economic organisation was based on 'primitive communism' characterised by common possession and use of valuables rather than by individual, joint or common ownership. Settlers tended to characterise indigenous notions of ownership as 'communal', implying that the indigenous population lacked the civilised qualities needed to recognise the superiority of individual property rights, and that dispossession would (conveniently) be less of a hardship, since their occupancy was only ever temporary and piecemeal. Where elements of the notion of full ownership were missing, settlers concluded that ownership itself was absent.[45] The transition narrative was used to characterise communal, blurry-edged property rights as barbarous and sustainable only within a subsistence economy. As Edward Mlambo points out, 'it was correct that the Africans never had a title, in the European sense, but not that Africans never had any right to their land'.[46]

In Shona society, the moral space of property operated differently and rested on alternative notions of belonging. No one could dispose of their rights in land to a third party, except to the next of kin in the case of senility or death. Land was held by an extended group, as members of the ward and the chiefdom. The land and resources belonged to the community, and every individual had 'an inalienable right to a reasonable share according to his requirements'.[47] Rather as Gerrard Winstanley proposed, the Shona people operated a system of land tenure based on use and communal obligations. The traditional system of property rights was based on communal tenure with usufructuary rights allocated to individual peasant cultivators by chiefs and headmen. Farm owners allocated cultivation rights to 'squatters', or to additional cultivators who worked the land for subsistence. These cultivation rights involved various degrees of permanence and independence. Some additional cultivators managed the whole farm, while others had a much more limited responsibility for a particular section of a field. These additional cultivators laboured on the land, planting, weeding and reaping their own crops without gaining any right to the land itself. This split between labour and the land meant that it was difficult to fit indigenous land rights into the story of improvement and progress, and the role of the chief and the community in the process meant that property rights were about government and society, but not about the state.[48] Rights and responsibilities were not allocated from the centre, so that a sense of belonging was not mediated by the nation state, and additional cultivators were unable to use their property to forge an identity as citizens. The collective traditions of the Shona as a subordinate group could be positioned within the transition narrative not only as timeless and primordial, but also as incomplete and lacking.[49]

By insisting on the incompleteness of the indigenous system of land tenure, the settlers refused to recognise that indigenous property rights carried immunities, or any right to exclude others. Indigenous property rights, not recognised as titles, were too weak to impose correlative duties on others not to encroach upon them. The settlers subjected the indigenous farmers to arbitrary taxation in the form of a hut tax, collected by confiscating cattle or in the form of cash, grain, alluvial gold or labour. The settlers pegged the price of grain and cattle at below its market value to encourage the indigenous people to pay them in cash or in labour. Indigenous farmers were also forced to pay a dog tax, extortionate grazing fees and compulsory dipping fees for cattle. As part of the hedging out process effected through the white agricultural policy, settler farmers began to impose high rents and other burdens in order to evict indigenous people from their farms and force them into reserves, away from the main markets.[50] The structure of indigenous rights proved to be weak in the face of such assaults because as individuals they were not assigned a despotic dominion that could be effective against the rights of the white settlers. They were excluded from the legitimating power of the sphere of civil society, and from the inviolability that is part of its self-sustaining myth. Public discourse determined that settler privileges were non-negotiable, and indigenous property rights did not carry secure expectations with them. This insecurity and precariousness of their property undermined their ability to live and survive in a free, industrious society. As Lawrence Becker argues, any right that is not secured does not count as a private property right. Full ownership by an individual or group can only operate 'in cases where no other individual or group has any form of ownership in the same thing'.[51] By insisting on compulsory fees and taxes, the settlers asserted a form of ownership in the grain, cattle and land that belonged to the indigenous people, and so unsettled and 'uncivilised' their ownership.

This disregard for the property rights of indigenous peoples fitted easily into the self-serving transition narrative and the dichotomy between the 'civilised' and the 'primitive'. In Rhodesia, the colonial mind was able to create a state-of-nature myth for itself in a way which proved more difficult in Ireland because of its ambiguous status as a colony that was part of the United Kingdom, with a white population. The complex and contested process of legitimising Rhodesia as a nation state was made to look self-evident and obvious. The dispossession and destruction of the first peoples was made to appear 'natural', the first stage in the modernisation process. Douglas Reed, for example, a former *Times* journalist, wrote in 1966: 'At the start the land was scrub, constantly impoverished by the tribal method of farming and by erosion.' It was not a vacant land, an uninhabited desert, but it was a lonely, savage place: 'disease, tribal raids and wild beasts ravaged the people and the land'. a world of wild beasts and 'timid and harried but not unkindly men'.[52] In this colonial discourse, the white settlers had transformed this troubled wilderness into a land of plenty, saving the indigenous people from themselves, from disease and killing. Race, property and civilisation worked together as explanatory categories. Anthony Marx argues that white unity and loyalty required a formally unified state and the centralisation of power. The development of the state, the escape from the state of nature, involved the white elites enforcing racial segregation, restricting the purchase of land by native peoples and co-ordinating transport and fiscal policy from the centre. Racial domination was used as 'a strategy for encouraging white unity and state building'.[53]

This strategy worked not only at the level of state building, but also at the level of the racial contract, the establishment of personhood and subpersonhood and the invention of whiteness. The construction of the self-determining subject, being fitted for full personhood and full membership, was connected to land, righteous labour and the honour of improvement.[54] The white colonisers contrasted themselves carefully to the indigenous farmers, and they took care to stress that it was settlers' cultivation, their methods of improvement, that made the difference. Colonial farming methods were based on deep ploughing and on constantly rotating crops rather than leaving the land fallow. They boasted of their productivity, their capacity to overcome the limitations of Africa and to participate and compete in the world economy. The white farming areas, they claimed, 'show crops, the equal of those in the Mid West or anywhere in the world'.[55] This economic success was opposed to the insignificance of indigenous subsistence farming, characterised as 'the tribesman cling[ing] to his immemorial custom of growing just enough to eat'. Belonging to the imagined community was about economic participation in the market, and so about not only the nation state but also the global economy. Those on the white commercial farming side of the fence grew endless crops, while the other side of the fence was 'tribal land, bare and denuded, where, one might say, nothing would grow'. The land was the same; only the method was different.[56] The settlers' language clearly reflects Locke's preoccupations with improvement, productivity and waste and draws similar contrasts between land, labour and value. In fact, white farming methods depleted the soils and their yields were lower than those of the indigenous farmers until the introduction of fertilisers, herbicides, pesticides, new crop strains and machinery after the Second World War, an agricultural revolution that brought with it an influx of new white settlers.

Since within this narrative it was white farming methods that effected the transformation of the state of nature, the Rhodesia that emerged from the mythical state of nature needed new inhabitants. It was presented to potential immigrants as a land of plenty, overflowing with water, cattle, corn, wood, gold, copper and iron and needing only 'more British blood' to fertilise it.[57] Colonists with more than £700 capital were welcomed and given access to credit and loans for purchase and improvement through the Land Bank. The white agricultural policy encouraged the European settlers to compete with the indigenous farmers by growing tobacco, citrus crops and maize, and by ranching cattle. European farmers growing maize for export were a direct threat to the peasant farmers; their ranching intensified competition for grazing land, and their tobacco was grown on the sandy soils favoured by the Shona. The white agricultural policy challenged the Africans for markets, cattle and land. It was a process of disqualification that left many of the indigenous people effectively propertyless. By 1913, the Belgian Henri Rolin saw Southern Rhodesia as divided into two castes: property owners and white capitalists who owned the natural resources, and a black proletariat who had been turned into their hired servants. The system of labour relations was almost feudal, based on personalistic power, drawing the workers into relationships based on debt and dependence, and then fixing that relationship. Forced labour was widespread, workers were whipped both by their employers and by the Native Reserves Commissioners, and sometimes forced to flee without being paid.[58] As Benedict Anderson argues, late colonial empires tended to reinforce 'antique conceptions of power and privilege' by dressing up capitalism in 'feudal-aristocratic drag'.[59] Like slaves, black workers were understood to have no moral impulse to labour and to need direction to perform particular tasks.

As Anthony Marx argues about South Africa, Africans in Rhodesia were forced off the land where they could be self-sufficient, ensuring a large supply of cheap labour. Those people who were not employed by the settlers were moved into reserve lands. The settlers and the farmers, in a clear echo of the enclosure debates in seventeenth-century England, argued that the reserves (like the commons) encouraged idleness and should be provided only for those whose labour was not required. The Native Reserves Commission recommended smaller reserves as easier to supervise, and a more effective mechanism for breaking up tribal loyalties. The commission argued that the country and soil should be more equitably divided according to the 'differing needs' of 'natives' and settlers. The idea of differing needs resulted in the distribution of sandy, rocky, dry, barren and fly-infested areas to the indigenous people and 'rich red soils' near the railways to the European settlers. Black, fertile soil was declared too heavy for 'the present primitive native method of cultivation', and so much better suited to the Europeans, who would also appreciate being close to the railways and mining centres.[60] The imagined nation had its contours defined by race, and intrawhite tensions were appeased by segregation. The discourse of biologised and scientific racism meant that the racial division between Africans and Europeans was understood to be unbridgeable, precluding any sense of shared identity or a common future, and property was used to help fix these racialised identities.

In 1923, with the introduction of responsible government and an end to the era of company rule, Southern Rhodesia became a 'self-governing colony' and political power passed to the white settlers.[61] At the same time, European agriculture was expanding and the settlers' economic power was growing, culminating in the demand for segregation of land ownership. White farmers were almost unanimously opposed to an open land market, and terrified of a mixed rural population of land owners. Robin Palmer argues that the basic driving force behind the movement to segregation 'was the intense hatred displayed by the overwhelming majority of European farmers at the idea of Africans buying land in their midst'.[62] Land-owning indigenous people had the potential to become neighbours, legal equals and economic competitors rather than labourers or rent-paying tenants. They might be able to live and survive as independent beings in a free, industrious society, and to exercise despotic dominion over themselves. Living amongst the settlers they would find themselves with equal access to better soils and to markets, and with property rights that carried immunities and correlative duties. The settlers concluded that constant close proximity between the different races was bound to create irritations and conflicts.[63] An open land market would inevitably increase racial friction. It was presented as 'the immutable African truth' that the points of contact between indigenous people and settlers should be reduced 'until the Native has advanced very much farther on the paths of civilization'.[64] Racial domination worked as a strategy by fixing differences and making 'truths' immutable.

White farmers protested whenever indigenous farmers bought farms, arguing that the value of neighbouring property would depreciate, future white settlement would suffer and eventually the indigenous farmers would buy up all the land. The idea of indigenous landowners was clearly deeply threatening to the settlers, who experienced it as a threat to their full ownership, their secure expectations and so to their sense of themselves, nation and future. The myth of civil society could only sustain itself effectively if it remained exclusive. Property, again, is at the heart of how people connect and recognise one another and of how white people see themselves as white. If whiteness was a property, it made sense to the settlers to see property as whiteness, and both as marks of a status to which black people could not aspire. The settlers used race as a means of defining who could control the land and the conditions under which this power could be exercised. The imperatives of nation state consolidation rested on 'vicious demarcations that solidified those included by distinguishing those

excluded'.[65] The obvious answer was a total ban on indigenous land ownership, but the white farmers settled for a separate purchase areas policy.[66]

African purchase of land was restricted to designated areas close to the
reserves, since, as H. J. Taylor, a member of the Land Commission,
remarked, 'in the interests of all it is not desirable that natives should
acquire land indiscriminately'.[67] The Native Purchase Areas were set
aside as 'freehold havens' for 'advanced' Africans retiring from the civil
service or the missions and not wishing to move to the Communal Areas.
As Angela Cheater argues, the purchase areas were not designed to promote economically viable farming, but established to restrict indigenous
land ownership. They were 'a political move, which explicitly differentiated freehold among Blacks from the same pattern of land tenure among
Whites' in order to diminish the threat of eventual black majority rule.[68]
The purchase lands were as far as possible adjacent to the reserves and
were carefully regulated. Failure to occupy the land or subletting to others
risked forfeiting the land. Failure to make improvements could delay the
grant of a title. Once again, indigenous property rights were not absolute,
but blurred and hedged about with conditions imposed to protect the
settlers' privileges and their whiteness. These conditions explicitly excluded
black people from living and surviving independently, and from participating in the market and the wider economy.

In Rhodesia, the Land Apportionment Act of 1930 reflected the new
concern to extend the white areas and protect the land from what was
regarded as black encroachment. The expectation that inevitable economic integration would bring civilising values with it was replaced by a new
segregationist ideology that saw separation as the only way to protect
European values from African invasion. The legislation was reinforced by
the Native Land Husbandry Act of 1951 and the Land Tenure Act of
1969. Indigenous farmers found their property rights severely curtailed:
they had no right to transfer their grazing or cultivation rights without the
permission of the district commissioner, who also had the right to interfere in their inheritance arrangements. The nation was imagined as
belonging to the white elite. The new forms of prohibition of land tenure
and differential treatment helped to rationalise and fix the 'order of
difference' and to define membership of the body politic.[69] Property in
land was central to the racially created and managed nation state, and to
Rhodesia's vision of itself as a white nation. Race and property also served
to define the capacity for self-ownership and self-direction. The division
between the industrious and the idle reinserted itself into the transition

narrative as a clear demarcation between the 'primitive' and the 'civilised'. Those indigenous people who were not designated as 'advanced', and so not capable of being freeholders, were forced to live in the reserve areas.

The reserve areas went through several incarnations as 'native reserves', tribal trust lands and communal areas. These communal areas were made up of arable land under fairly constant cultivation, without many fallow periods, decreasing fertility and increasing erosion. New families in need of plots encroached upon the land for common grazing so that the grazing areas deteriorated from congestion and over-use. The system of land use and the farming techniques were, and are, unsustainable, contributing to deforestation, soil erosion and declining soil fertility. About three-quarters of the communal lands are semi-arid, with no more than marginal agricultural potential. They are in regions with the least reliable rainfall, rocky landscape, steep slopes and shallow, infertile soils. As people living on the reserves struggled to cultivate the unproductive land, white farming expanded as the infrastructure was improved by increased investment in road building and maintenance and a move into producing more maize, cattle and tobacco. Indigenous farmers 'faced the full blast of competition from heavily subsidized European farmers while simultaneously being pushed away from easy access to markets'.[70]

In 1969, there were on average 3.6 hectares per capita for those living on African land, and 61 hectares per capita for those on European land.[71] After the imposition of sanctions in 1965, commercial white farmers were encouraged to diversify out of tobacco and into maize, cattle and cotton. In the early 1970s, the state gave white farmers annual subsidies and loans of 8,000 Rhodesian dollars per person, compared to sixty cents each for indigenous cultivators.[72] In the 1960s, white commercial agriculture provided 30 per cent of domestic food production. By 1979, this number had risen to 75 per cent, increasing the absolute poverty of the poor peasants and generating landlessness and unemployment, especially among the young. The white nation was tied to the global economy and the market, while its black members were not 'invited in', but instead were shut out of the earth and the imagined nation. Like the English in Ireland in the mid-nineteenth century, mid-twentieth-century white Rhodesians saw progress as being part of a single, unified market and a centralised political unit. For them, as well as for the free-trade radicals, peasant proprietorship was a delusion. The only way they saw to escape the state-of-nature fantasy they had created for themselves was to instigate intensive capitalist farming and tie the white, trading part of the nation to the global economy.

– 1980 AND BEYOND –

At independence in 1980, the issue of the 'lost lands' and the question of redistribution were high on the political agenda. They were dealt with through the 'willing seller, willing buyer' clause, which was the cornerstone of the Lancaster House Agreement, put there to ensure that white farmers would not find their land expropriated by the incoming government based on black majority rule. It was a classic expression of the fear felt by those with property towards the dispossessed and those without property. In the Zimbabwean situation, there are no willing sellers and no able buyers. Market forces in Zimbabwe only ever applied to the commercial sector; those forced to live in the communal areas could not participate in the market. The 'willing seller, willing buyer' clause rested on the same assumptions as were made by the free traders in 1840s Ireland, that progress was only possible through the mechanisms of the market. It also captures the double-edgedness of a colonial project that relied on the legitimating power of civil society and on the universal march of citizenship, without extending membership of either civil society or the body politic beyond the white elite. The narrative that celebrates the nation state risks celebrating the role of force, and it was this story that was taken on by Robert Mugabe.

Since 1980, Mugabe and Zanu (PF) have been committed to various programmes of land reform, most of which have proved disastrous. In 1990 the white commercial farmers still held nearly 60 per cent of the fertile land. In 1992 the government removed the 'willing seller, willing buyer' clause. The programme intensified to allow compulsory land acquisition by the state in 1998. By 2002, nearly two-thirds of the three million hectares bought from white farmers and distributed to landless black people had reverted mainly to subsistence plots, with no money available to install the roads, water pipes and other infrastructure needed to make the plots profitable. Unlike the white farmers, who can use their land as collateral for bank loans, resettled black farmers do not own their farms. The state holds the deeds and gives them farming rights. The indigenous farmers work with fragile use rights, vulnerable to more or less continuous redefinition. In this sense, very little has changed for the indigenous farmers since independence. Peasant proprietorship continues to be a delusion, and the 'magic power' of property has failed to do its work. They may now be tied into a different transition narrative, and a different myth, but even as citizens they are treated like subjects, and their 'invitation' to join the nation still comes from the centre. The poor in Zimbabwe have been subject to 'the ambivalences, contradictions, the use of force, and the tragedies and the ironies' that attend the history of modernity.[73]

The mechanisms of exclusion operate at the level of participation in the global economy and the international market. The Economic Structural Adjustment Programme introduced in Zimbabwe in 1991 was based on deregulation, privatisation and the reduction of government subsidies, bringing Zimbabwe into line with the trading preoccupations of the wider world economy. The model is close to the 'westernisation' of Zimbabwean society, mimicking the developed world's conditions for progress and improvement. Land reform was not integrated into the process, and only the large-scale commercial farmers benefited from the reforms promoting agricultural exports.[74] The results of the Economic Structural Adjustment Programme meant that large-scale commercial farmers remained the most politically influential segment of the white population. Large-scale commercial farms had access to good soils and climate, to mechanisation, and to the extensive use of fertilisers, pesticides and hybrid seed. Tobacco, cotton, sugar, tea, coffee and beef were all linked to foreign-exchange earnings, but the system relied on an extensive system of land use with millions of hectares of the best land in the country being grazed or not used at all.[75] Most large-scale commercial farming land is used for ranching in some areas. Rather as Mill and Thornton argued for the reclamation of the wastelands in Ireland, reformers in Zimbabwe argue that using the land for mixed husbandry instead of grazing could double the area under cultivation and increase employment fivefold. The peasant alternative might produce more food for subsistence and sale. The argument is that high-potential land needs to be farmed intensively and improved, with more crops and wider access to markets. As the situation in Zimbabwe stands at the moment, high potential land is under-utilised while low-potential land is over-utilised. The problem is not the farming system itself, but 'the constraints of land pressure under which people farm'.[76] The challenge facing Zimbabwe is the same as faced Ireland in the 1840s, 'to gain access to more high-potential land and then redistribute it in a manner that is less wasteful'.[77] About 60 per cent of the households in the communal lands do not have enough food, and between one-fifth and one-quarter of Zimbabwean children suffer from malnutrition, especially in the communal areas and on the large-scale commercial farms.[78] In 2002, the Department for International Development (DFID) estimated that 49 per cent of the Zimbabwean population, 6.7 million people, were in need of food aid. From September 2002 to March 2003, DFID estimated that Zimbabwe needed 486,000 tonnes of food aid, and would need to import 1.5 million tonnes of cereals for the year.

In his analysis of the prospects for agricultural transformation in Zimbabwe, Lionel Cliffe distinguishes between three alternative futures that entail three ways of imagining the nation and of constructing belonging and exclusion: capitalist, statist and populist. The capitalist strand focuses on improvement in the communal areas based on individual title to holdings, and echoes the insistence that where improvement is necessary it will be undertaken for profit, regardless of the system of land tenure, even in the context of land hunger. The 'statist' approach is based on resettlement with an emphasis on state farms and top-down plans for land use, while the 'populist' version demands expanded resettlement, the redrawing of the boundaries between the communal areas and the large-scale commercial farms, and the evolution of the communal areas farming system to take into account the interests of women and the poor. All three of these alternative futures disrupt the traditional transition narrative based on modernisation and development. Cliffe describes a 'modernisation world view' that sees commercial farms as a more productive use of land than resettlement, an orthodoxy upheld by the World Bank and Western experts who are not attuned to the realities of peasant agriculture.[79] The dominant liberal discourse assumes, as it did in its promotion of free trade in the 1840s, that market forces will result in the optimal allocation of resources and in the creation of a civil society.

The struggle to imagine and define the Zimbabwean nation since 1980 has taken place against a complicated colonial backdrop, and property and land, coupled with race, have once again proved central to the process. Landless peasants responded to the failure of the resettlement exercise by occupying and using land belonging to the white large-scale commercial farmers, to politicians and to the black elite. Human-rights organisations are concerned by the party political control of access to the forms for applying for land and by the key role of the war veterans and Zanu (PF) militias in distributing and allocating the land. They argue that the outside world's reaction to the crisis has been distorted through the prism of property fetishism. The external focus on the injustice of expropriation of the white-owned farms worked (to an extent) to reinforce a sense of the inviolability of private property rights. It was, perhaps, property and not morality that was held sacred. The fast-track land reform process was presented as an attempt to reverse the universal march of citizenship, to undo the self-determining sovereign subject and to take apart civil society's self-sustaining myth. The result was a discourse that equated 'rights', and in particular 'human rights', with property rights, and then assumed that only property-owning, self-determining citizens could be having their rights violated. State intervention in Zimbabwean land redistribution is condemned 'because it encroaches upon the sanctity of private property in general', and not just the property rights of the white farmers.[80] The conflict between civil society and proletarian outsiders, between 'colonisers' and 'natives', reemerged in a new guise. While

> international attention has focused on the plight of the white farm owners and on the consequences of illegal expropriations of land for property rights and the macro-economy, it is poor, rural, black people who have suffered most from the violence that has accompanied the fast-track process.[81]

To correct the distorting focus on property rights, and to imagine the nation in a different way, rights discourse needs to take account of the inclusive elements of the 'populist' future discussed by Cliffe. As Anne Hellum and Bill Derman argue, the Zimbabwean case 'epitomizes the tension between human rights instruments that oblige the state to protect established property rights and those that oblige the state to ensure people's right to livelihood'.[82] Article 17 of the Universal Declaration of Human Rights states that everyone has the right to own property, alone and in association with others, and the right not to be arbitrarily deprived of their property. Article 11 of the International Covenant on Economic, Social and Cultural Rights obliges the state to recognise the right of everyone to an adequate standard of living including adequate food, clothing and housing and to the improvement of their living conditions. The answer might be to expand rights beyond those guaranteed by exclusive ownership to include 'rights to livelihood brought by farm workers; the right of equal protection of tenure and access to resettlement land for women; the right of farm workers' children to education, health and physical security'.[83] The process of expanding rights involves reimagining the community and the boundaries of belonging and exclusion. It means returning to property as a moral space and a site of struggle, and to the connections between insecurity and unfreedom.

One example of this expansion of rights beyond established property rights and into the protection of a right to livelihood would be the recognition of the rights of squatters and additional cultivators. In Zimbabwe, male migration patterns have resulted in an increase in female-headed households, and these now account for 60 per cent of the house-holds in the communal areas. Female-headed households are likely to be allocated smaller parcels of land than those headed by men, and so are 40 per cent poorer than rural male-headed households. Customary law gives the husband status as head of household, including the right to hold property on behalf of his family. In communal areas, land rights are usually conferred on the husband and women's access to loans is thereby severely hampered. Crops are marketed in the husband's name and he receives the payments in his name. The Women and Land Lobby Group argues that women need 'inviting in' to the imagined nation through recognition of their rights as additional cultivators and 'squatters' who have access to and work the land without necessarily owning or controlling it. The lobby group proposes that 30 per cent of the land allocated under the fast-track process should be registered to women, regardless of marital status. Focusing on the right to livelihood, the Women and Land group is lobbying for adequate health services, schools, water sources, credit schemes and agricultural extension services. These services are ways of increasing security and connecting women to the nation and to the imagined com-munity. Land allocation returns us to the question of women's differential incorporation and suggests a new way of imagining belonging and com-bating exclusion.

The distorting focus on the white-owned farms has been made possible, and perhaps inevitable, by a narrow definition of what counts as a pro-perty right, who can own property, and which interests are recognised. In the Irish context, Philip Bull argues that capitalist ideologues and free-trade radicals were confused about property rights. Their theory of capital-ism was 'distorted by the prism of English practice and colonising interest'.[84] Polarisation over tenure damaged Irish agriculture's capacity to respond to the demands of capitalist competition and the long conflict over land led to the 'idealisation of its possession, even in unsustainably small parcels'.[85] It also fixed the identities of 'natives' and 'occupiers' and their role in the imagined nation. The historical circumstances of the conquest of Ireland meant that the tenant class was continuously associated with the land, and with 'backwardness'.[86] They were fitted into the transition narrative as 'primitive' rather than 'civilised' and so as subjects rather than citizens.

In Zimbabwe, the prism of capitalism and the colonising interest has associated human rights with land ownership, and fundamentally with the state. In this broadened context, the land invasions raise a range of human rights concerns that take the ideas of property and rights beyond land ownership. The transition from Rhodesia to Zimbabwe has failed to tackle the problem of an uncivil civil society based on force and violent exclusion. The poor in Zimbabwe remain marginalised by inability, poverty, inarticulacy and a lack of political participation. They are still no more than shadow members of society. A forced, statist, resettlement programme that fails to account for the complex tangle of property, class, race, ethnicity and gender is unlikely to succeed in resolving the conflict between 'natives' and 'occupiers', however constituted or reconstituted. The oppositions between honour and degradation, belonging and exclusion, labour and drudgery remain unresolved, and continue to underpin unequal possession of the earth, the nation and the self.

– NOTES –

1. Catherine Hall et al., *Defining the Victorian Nation: Class, Race, Gender and the Reform Act of 1867* (Cambridge: Cambridge University Press, 2000), p. 180.
2. Bhikhu Parekh, 'Liberalism and Colonialism: a Critique of Locke and Mill', in Jan Nederveen Pietersen and Bhikhu Parekh (eds), *The Decolonization of the Imagination: Culture, Knowledge and Power* (London: Zed Books, 1995).
3. Anthony Pagden, *Lords of All the World: Ideologies of Empire in Spain, Britain and France* (New Haven and London: Yale University Press, 1995), pp. 6–7.
4. Parekh, 'Liberalism and Colonialism', p. 96.
5. Dipesh Chakrabarty, 'Postcoloniality and the Artifice of History: Who Speaks for "Indian" Pasts?' *Representations* 37, Winter 1992, p. 4.
6. Ibid. p. 8.
7. Ibid. p. 18.
8. Ibid. p. 10.
9. Ibid. p. 17.
10. Ibid. p. 10.
11. Ibid. p. 17, quoting from Meaghan Morris 'Metamorphoses at Sydney Tower', *New Formations* 11, Summer 1990, p. 10.
12. Ibid. p. 20.
13. Rosalind O'Hanlon, 'Recovering the Subject: *Subaltern Studies* and Histories of Resistance in Colonial South Asia', *Modern Asian Studies* 22:1, 1988, p. 220.
14. Ibid. p. 220.
15. Ibid. p. 221.
16. Peter Childs and Patrick Williams, *An Introduction to Post-Colonial Theory* (Hemel Hempstead: Harvester Wheatsheaf, 1997), p. 68.
17. Ibid. p. 68.
18. Philip Bull, *Land, Politics and Nationalism: a Study of the Irish Land Question* (Dublin: Gill & Macmillan, 1996), p. 36.
19. Ibid. p. 51.
20. Ibid. p. 14.
21. John Stuart Mill, *Principles of Political Economy* (Oxford: Oxford University Press, [1848] 1994), p. 319.

22. Peter Gray, *Famine, Land and Politics: British Government and Irish Society, 1843–1850* (Dublin: Irish Academic Press, 1999), p. 156.
23. Mill, *Principles of Political Economy*, p. 323.
24. Gray, *Famine, Land and Politics*, p. 156.
25. Bull, *Land, Politics and Nationalism*, p. 31.
26. John Robson, 'Civilization and Culture as Moral Concepts', in John Skorupski (ed.), *The Cambridge Companion to Mill* (Cambridge: Cambridge University Press, 1998), p. 357.
27. Gray, *Famine, Land and Politics*, p. 157, quoting John Stuart Mill in the *Morning Chronicle*, 14 October 1846.
28. Bull, *Land, Politics and Nationalism*, p. 46.
29. Ibid. p. 55.
30. Ibid. p. 52.
31. Gray, *Famine, Land and Politics*, p. 163.
32. Ibid. p. 9.
33. Ursula Vogel, 'The Land Question: a Liberal Theory of Communal Property', *History Workshop*. 27, Spring 1989, p. 117.
34. Ibid. p. 108.
35. Ibid. p. 110.
36. Hall et al., *Defining the Victorian Nation*, p. 210.
37. Quoted in Hall et al., *Defining the Victorian Nation*, p. 212.
38. Gray, *Famine, Land and Politics*, p. 119.
39. David Arnold, 'Corporeality and Colonialism: Race, Place and Bodily Difference in Early Nineteenth-century India', Plenary Lecture, Anglo-American Conference 2003, Institute of Historical Research, London.
40. Anne McClintock, *Imperial Leather: Race, Gender and Sexuality in the Colonial Contest* (London: Routledge, 1997), p. 52. McClintock is quoting from Gustave de Molinari, and the phrase appeared in a leader in *The Times* in 1880.
41. Ibid. p. 53.
42. Hall et al., *Defining the Victorian Nation*, p. 213.
43. Marc Ferro, *Colonization: a Global History* (London and New York: Routledge, 1997), pp. 81–2.
44. Eshmael Mlambo, *Rhodesia: the Struggle for a Birthright* (London: C. Hurst and Company, 1972), p. 28.
45. Lawrence C. Becker, 'The Moral Basis of Property Rights', in J. Roland Pennock and John W. Chapman (eds), *Nomos XXII: Property* (New York: New York University Press, 1980), p. 198.
46. Mlambo, *Rhodesia*, p. 39.
47. Robin Palmer, *Land and Racial Domination in Rhodesia* (London: Heinemann, 1977), p. 17, quoting the Report of the Mangwende Reserve Commission of Inquiry, Salisbury, 1961.
48. For further discussion of this distinction between government and the state, see John Hoffman, *Sovereignty* (Buckingham: Open University Press, 1998), pp. 50–2.
49. For further discussion of the themes of 'lack' and 'inadequacy', see Chakrabarty, 'Postcoloniality'.
50. Palmer, *Land and Racial Domination*, passim.
51. Becker, 'Moral Basis of Property Rights', p. 192.
52. Douglas Reed, *The Battle for Rhodesia* (Cape Town: Haumm, 1966), p. 24.
53. Anthony W. Marx, *Making Race and Nation: a Comparison of South Africa, the United*

States and Brazil (Cambridge: Cambridge University Press, 1998), p. 101.

54. Charles W. Mills, *The Racial Contract* (Ithaca, NY and London: Cornell University Press, 1997), p. 54.

55. Reed, *Battle for Rhodesia*, p. 24.

56. Ibid. pp. 24–5.

57. Mlambo, *Rhodesia*, p. 14.

58. Palmer, *Land and Racial Domination*, p. 43.

59. Benedict Anderson, *Imagined Communities* (London: Verso, 1991), pp. 150, 151.

60. Palmer, *Land and Racial Domination*, p. 118. Quotation from Holland's Diary, 1915, Hist.MSS. HO 7/2/1.

61. Ibid. p. 132.

62. Ibid. p. 136.

63. Reed, *Battle for Rhodesia*, p. 26.

64. Ibid. p. 26.

65. Marx, *Making Race and Nation*, p. 275.

66. Palmer, *Land and Racial Domination*, p. 139.

67. Ibid. p. 140.

68. Angela P. Cheater, *Idioms of Accumulation: Rural Development and Class Formation among Freeholders in Zimbabwe* (Gweru: Mambo Press, 1984), p. 7.

69. David Theo Goldberg, *Racist Culture: Philosophy and the Politics of Meaning* (Oxford: Blackwell, 1993, p. 81.

70. Palmer, *Land and Racial Domination*, p. 147.

71. James R. Scarritt, 'Zimbabwe: Revolutionary Violence Resulting in Reform', in Jack A. Goldstone et al. (eds), *Revolutions of the late Twentieth Century* (Boulder, CO: Westview Press, 1991).

72. Ian Phimister, 'The Combined and Contradictory Inheritance of the Struggle Against Colonialism', in Colin Stoneman (ed.), *Zimbabwe's Prospects* (Basingstoke: Macmillan, 1988), p. 8.

73. Chakrabarty, 'Postcoloniality', p. 21.

74. Chris Talbot, 'Zimbabwe faces acute famine', World Socialist Web Site, 27 July 2002, www.wsws.org/articles/2002/jul2002/zimb-j27.shtml

75. Daniel Weiner, 'Land and Agricultural Development', in Stoneman, *Zimbabwe's Prospects*.

76. Lionel Cliffe, 'The Prospects for Agricultural Transformation in Zimbabwe', in Stoneman, *Zimbabwe's Prospects*, p. 320.

77. Weiner, 'Land and Agricultural Development', p. 84.

78. Food and Agriculture Organization, 'Women's Rights', in *Zimbabwe – Women, Agriculture and Rural Development* (Rome: Food and Agriculture Organization, 1995), http://www.fao.org/docrep/V9101e/v9101e04.htm

79. Cliffe, 'Prospects for Agricultural Transformation', p. 324.

80. M. Baregu, 'The Third Chimurenga: Human and Social Rights Confront Individual and Property Rights in Zimbabwe', paper presented to Rethinking Land, State and Citizenship. through the Zimbabwe Crisis, Centre for Development Research, Copenhagen, September 2001.

81. Human Rights Watch, 'Fast Track Land Reform in Zimbabwe', *Human Rights Watch* 14:1(A), March 2002, p. 4.

82. Anne Hellum and Bill Derman, 'Land Reform and Human Rights in Contemporary Zimbabwe: Balancing Individual and Social Justice through an Integrated Human

Rights Framework', African Studies Association Annual Meeting, Nashville, TN, November 2000, p. 5.

83. Ibid. p. 3.
84. Bull, *Land, Politics and Nationalism*, p. 184.
85. Ibid. p. 192.
86. Ibid. p. 46.

Bibliography

Anon. (1747), *The Art of Governing a Wife*, London.

Anon. (1688), *The Lady's New-years Gift: or, Advice to a Daughter*, London.

Anon., *A Rawls Glossary*. <http://www.infro.bris.ac.uk/~plcdib/rglos.html>

Anon. (1653), *The Waste Land's Improvement*, London.

Anon. (1701), *The Whole Duty of a Woman: or a Guide to the Female Sex Written by a Lady*, London.

Anderson, B. (1991), *Imagined Communities*, London: Verso.

Arneil, B. (1996), *John Locke and America: the Defence of English Colonialism*, Oxford: Clarendon Press.

Arnold, D. (2003) 'Corporeality and Colonialism: Race, Place and Bodily Difference in Early Nineteenth-century India', Plenary Lecture, Anglo-American Conference 2003, Institute of Historical Research, London.

Aughey, A. (1989), 'The Moderate Right: the Conservative Tradition in America and Britain', in R. Eatwell and N. Sullivan (eds), *The Nature of the Right: European and American Politics and Political Thought since 1789*, London: Pinter.

Avnon, D. and de-Shalit, A. (1999), 'Introduction: Liberalism between Promise And Practice', in D. Avnon and A. de-Shalit (eds), *Liberalism and its Practice*, London and New York: Routledge.

Baregu, M. (2001), 'The Third Chimurenga: Human and Social Rights Confront Individual and Property Rights in Zimbabwe', paper presented to Rethinking Land, State and Citizenship through the Zimbabwe Crisis, Centre for Development Research, Copenhagen.

Becker, L. C. (1980), 'The Moral Basis of Property Rights', in J. R. Pennock and J. W. Chapman (eds), *Nomos XXII: Property*, New York: New York University Press.

Beckles, H. (1996), 'The Concept of "White Slavery" in the English Caribbean during the Early Seventeenth Century', in J. Brewer and S. Staves (eds), *Early Modern Conceptions of Property*, London and New York: Routledge.

Bellamy, R. (1992), *Liberalism and Modern Society: an Historical Argument*, Cambridge: Polity.

Benhabib, S. (1984), 'Obligation, Contract and Exchange: on the Significance of Hegel's Abstract Right', in Z. A. Pelczynski (ed.), *The State and Civil Society*, Cambridge: Cambridge University Press.

Bentham, J. (1907), *An Introduction to the Principles of Morals and Legislation*, Oxford: Clarendon Press.

Berki, R. N. (1981), *On Political Realism*, London: J. M. Dent and Sons.

Bernstein, J. M. (1984), 'From Self-consciousness to Community: Act and Recognition in the Master–Slave Relationship', in Z. A. Pelczynski (ed.), *The State and Civil Society*, Cambridge: Cambridge University Press.

Blackburn, R. (1988), 'Defining slavery – Its Special Features and Social Role', in L. Archer (ed.), *Slavery and Other Forms of Unfree Labour*, London and New York: Routledge.

Blackstone, Sir W. (1765–9), *Commentaries on the Laws of England*, Oxford: Oxford University Press. <http://www.yale.edu/lawweb/avalon/blackstone/bk2ch29.htm>

Blith, W. (1649), *The English Improver: or, a New Survey of Husbandry*, London.

Blum, L. M. (1999), *At the Breast: Ideologies of Breastfeeding and Motherhood in the Contemporary United States*, Boston: Beacon.

Boralevi, L. C. (1987), 'Utilitarianism and Feminism', in E. Kennedy and S. Mendus (eds), *Women in Western Political Philosophy*, Brighton: Wheatsheaf.

Brace, L. (1997), 'Imagining the Boundaries of a Sovereign Self', in L. Brace and J. Hoffman (eds), *Reclaiming Sovereignty*, London: Cassell.

Bull, P. (1996), *Land, Politics and Nationalism: a Study of the Irish Land Question*, Dublin: Gill & Macmillan.

Burbach, R. et al. (1997), *Globalization and its Discontents*, London and Chicago: Pluto.

Burke, E. [1790] (1969), *Reflections on the Revolution in France*, ed. C. C. O'Brien, Harmondsworth: Penguin.

Butler, J. (1997), *The Psychic Life of Power*, Stanford: Stanford University Press.

Carter, P. (1995), *Feminism, Breasts and Breast-feeding*, London: Palgrave.

Chakrabarty, D. (1992), 'Postcoloniality and the Artifice of History: Who Speaks for "Indian" Pasts?', *Representations* 37, pp. 1–27.

Cheater, A. P. (1984), *Idioms of Accumulation: Rural Development and Class Formation among Freeholders in Zimbabwe*, Gweru: Mambo.

Childs, P. and P. Williams, (1997), *An Introduction to Post-colonial Theory*, Hemel Hempstead: Harvester Wheatsheaf.

Christi, F. R. (1978), 'Hegel on Possession and Property', *Canadian Journal of Social and Political Theory* 2, pp. 111–24.

Claeys, G. (ed.) (1994), *Utopias of the British Enlightenment*, Cambridge: Cambridge University Press.

Clark, J. P. (1977), *The Philosophical Anarchism of William Godwin*, Princeton: Princeton University Press.

Clark, S. (1693), *The Lives of Sundry Eminent Persons in This Later Age*, London.

Cliffe, L. (1988) 'The Prospects for Agricultural Transformation in Zimbabwe', in C. Stoneman (ed.), *Zimbabwe's Prospects*, Basingstoke: Macmillan.

Cohen, G. A. (1995), *Self-ownership, Freedom and Equality*, Cambridge: Cambridge University Press.

Cohen, G. A. (2000), *If You're an Egalitarian, How Come You're So Rich?*, Cambridge, MA: Harvard University Press.

Cohen, J. (1998), 'The Arc of the Moral Universe', in T. L. Lott (ed.), *Subjugation and Bondage: Critical Essays on Slavery and Social Philosophy*, Boulder, CO and Oxford: Rowman and Littlefield.

Cole, D. H. (1999), '"An Unqualified Human Good": E. P. Thompson and the Rule of Law'. <http://www.iulaw.indy.indiana.edu/instructors/cole/THOMPSON.pdf>

Connolly, W. E. (1988), *Political Theory and Modernity*, Oxford: Blackwell.

Crowder, G. (1991), *Classical Anarchism*, Oxford: Clarendon Press.

Cullen, B. (1987), 'Hegel's Historical Phenomenology and Social Analysis', in D. Lamb (ed.), *Hegel and Modern Philosophy*, London: Croom Helm.

Daunton, M. and R, Halpern (eds.) (1999), *Empire and Others: British Encounters with Indigenous Peoples, 1600–1850*, London: UCL Press.

Davidoff, L. (1998), 'Regarding Some "Old Husbands' Tales": Public and Private in Feminist History', in J. B. Landes (ed.), *Feminism: the Public and the Private*, Oxford: Oxford University Press.

Davidoff, L. et al., (1999), *The Family Story: Blood, Contract and Intimacy, 1830–1960*, London and New York: Longman.

Davies, M. (1999), 'Queer Property, Queer Persons: Self-ownership and Beyond', *Social and Legal Studies* 8:3, pp. 327–52.

Davis, D. B. (1966), *The Problem of Slavery in Western Culture*, Ithaca, NY: Cornell University Press.

Davis, D. B. (1986), *Slavery and Human Progress*, Oxford: Oxford University Press.

Day, J. (1993). 'John Stuart Mill: *On Liberty*', in M. Forsyth et al., (eds), *The Political Classics: Hamilton to Mill*, Oxford: Oxford University Press.

Day, P. (1992), 'The Self-ownership Thesis: a Critique', *Philosophical Notes* 19. <http://www.libertarian.co.uk/lapubs/philn/philn019.pdf>

D'Cruze, S. (1994), 'Care, Diligence and 'Usfull pride' [*sic*]: Gender, Industrialisation and the Domestic Economy, c. 1770 to c. 1840', *Women's History Review* 3:3, pp. 315–45.

Dickenson, D. (1997), *Property, Women and Politics*, Cambridge: Polity Press.

Dinwiddy, J. R. (1992), *Radicalism and Reform in Britain, 1780–1850*, London: Hambledon.

Drayton, R. (1998), 'Knowledge and Empire', in P. J. Marshall (ed.), *The Oxford History of the British Empire: the Eighteenth Century*, Oxford: Oxford University Press.

Dworkin, R. (1975), 'The Original Position', in N. Daniels (ed.), *Reading Rawls*, Oxford: Blackwell.

Dworkin, R. (1986), *A Matter of Principle*, Oxford: Clarendon Press.

Eatwell, R. (1989), 'The Nature of the Right, 1: Is There an "Essentialist" Philosophical Core', in R. Eatwell and N. Sullivan (eds), *The Nature of the Right: European and American Politics and Political Thought since 1789*, London: Pinter.

Edgeworth, B. (1988), 'Post-property? A Postmodern Conception of Private Property', *University of New South Wales Law Journal* 11, pp. 87–116.

Erickson, A. L. (1993), *Women and Property in Early Modern England*, London and New York: Routledge.

Ferro, M. (1997), *Colonization: a Global History*, London and New York: Routledge.

Fitzpatrick, M. (1979), 'William Godwin and the Rational Dissenters', *Price-Priestley Newsletter* 3, pp. 4–28.

Fleetwood, W. (1705), *The Relative Duties of Parents and Children, Husbands and Wives, Masters and Servants*, London.

Food and Agriculture Organization (1995), 'Women's Rights', in *Zimbabwe – Women, Agriculture and Rural Development*, Rome: Food and Agriculture Organization. <http://www.fao.org/docrep/v9101e/v9101e.04.htm>

Fordyce, J. (1776), *The Character and Conduct of the Female Sex*, London.

Foster, W. (1779), *Thoughts on the Times but Chiefly on the Profligacy of our Women*, London.

Freeden, M. (1996), *Ideologies and Political Theory: a Conceptual Approach*, Oxford: Clarendon Press.

Gathorne-Hardy, J. (1972), *The Rise and Fall of the British Nanny*, London: Hodder and Stoughton.

Geras, N. (1997), *The Contract of Mutual Indifference*, London: Verso.

Glenn, E. N. (1992), 'From Servitude to Service Work: Historical Continuities in the Racial Division of Paid Reproductive Labor', *Signs* 18:1.

Godwin, W. [1798] (1971), *Enquiry Concerning Political Justice*, ed. K. C. Carter, Oxford: Clarendon Press.

Goldberg, D. T. (1993), *Racist Culture: Philosophy and the Politics of Meaning*, Oxford: Blackwell.

Gould, C. C. (2001), 'Democratic Egalitarianism', in J. P. Sterba (ed.), *Social and Political Philosophy: Contemporary Perspectives*, London and New York, Routledge.

Gray, P. (1999), *Famine, Land and Politics: British Government and Irish Society, 1843–1850*, Dublin: Irish Academic Press.

Green, E. H. H. (2002), *Ideologies of Conservatism: Conservative Political Ideas in the Twentieth Century*, Oxford: Oxford University Press.

Gregson, N. and Lowe, M. (1994), *Servicing the Middle Classes: Class, Gender and Waged Domestic Labour in Contemporary Britain*, London: Routledge.

Gutmann, A. (1980), *Liberal Equality*, Cambridge: Cambridge University Press.

Halevy, E. (1972), *The Growth of Philosophical Radicalism*, London: Faber & Faber.

Hall, C. et al., (2000), *Defining the Victorian Nation: Class, Race, Gender and the Reform Act of 1867*, Cambridge: Cambridge University Press.

Hampsher-Monk, I. (1992), *A History of Modern Political Thought*, Oxford: Blackwell.

Hare, R. M. (1998), 'What Is Wrong with Slavery?' in T. L. Lott (ed.), *Subjugation and Bondage: Critical Essays on Slavery and Social Philosophy*, Boulder, CO and Oxford: Rowman and Littlefield.

Harris, C. I. (1993), 'Whiteness as Property', *Harvard Law Review* 106, pp. 1707–91.

Hart, H. L. A. (1975), 'Rawls on Liberty and its Priority', in N. Daniels (ed.), *Reading Rawls*, Oxford: Blackwell.

Hayes, T. W. (1979), *Winstanley the Digger*, Cambridge, MA: Harvard University Press.

Hegel, G. W. F. [1807] (1977), *Phenomenology of Spirit*, tr. A. V. Miller, Oxford: Clarendon Press.

Hegel, G. W. F. [1821] (1967), *The Philosophy of Right*, tr. T. M. Cox, Oxford: Oxford University Press.

Heilbroner, R. (1988), *The Worldly Philosophers*, Harmondsworth: Penguin.

Hellum, A. and B. Derman, (2000), 'Land Reform and Human Rights in Contemporary Zimbabwe: Balancing Individual and Social Justice through an Integrated Human Rights Framework', African Studies Association Annual Meeting, Nashville.

Herzog, D. (1998), *Poisoning the Minds of the Lower Orders*, Princeton: Princeton University Press.

Heywood. O. (1700), *Advice to an Only Child: or, Excellent Counsel to All Young Persons*, London.

Hill, C. (1967), *Reformation to Industrial Revolution*, London: Weidenfeld and Nicolson.

History Guide (2000), 'The French Revolution and the Socialist Tradition: Early French Communists (1)'. <http://www.historyguide.org/intellect/lecture19a.html>

Hoffman, J. (1998), *Sovereignty*, Buckingham: Open University Press.

Holmes, S. (1999), 'Can Weak-state Liberalism survive?' in D. Avnon and A. De-Shalit (eds), *Liberalism and its Practice*, London and New York: Routledge.

Honderich, T. (1990), *Conservatism*, London: Hamish Hamilton.

Horrell, S. and J. Humphries (1996), 'Women's Labour Force Participation and the Transition to the Male-breadwinner Family, 1790–1865', *Economic History Review* XLVII:I, pp. 89–117.

Hudson, W. S. (1946), 'Economic and Social Thought of Gerrard Winstanley', *Journal of Modern History* 18.

Hufton, O. (1995), *The Prospect before Her*, London: HarperCollins.

Human Rights Watch (2002), 'Fast Track Land Reform in Zimbabwe', *Human Rights Watch* 14:1(A).

Hyde, A. (1997), *Bodies of Law*, Princeton: Princeton University Press.

Jacobson, M. F. (1998), *Whiteness of a Different Color: European Immigrants and the Alchemy of Race*, Cambridge, MA and London: Harvard University Press.

Jameson, F. (1996), 'Actually Existing Marxism', in S. Makdisi et al. (eds), *Marxism beyond Marxism*, New York and London: Routledge.

Keane, J. (1988), 'Despotism and Democracy: the Origins and Development of the Distinction Between Civil Society and the State, 1750–1850', in J. Keane (ed.), *Civil Society and the State*, London: Verso.

Kenyon, T. (1985), 'Labour–Natural, Property–Artificial: the Radical Insights of Gerrard Winstanley', *History of European Ideas* 6:2.

Kenyon, T. (1989), *Utopian Communism and Political Thought in Early Modern England*, London: Pinter.

Kramer, M. H. (1997), *John Locke and the Origins of Private Property: Philosophical Explorations of Individualism, Community and Equality*, Cambridge: Cambridge University Press.

Kukathas, C. (1997), 'Liberalism, Multiculturalism, Oppression', in A. Vincent (ed.), *Political Theory: Tradition and Diversity*, Cambridge: Cambridge University Press.

Landes, J. B. (1981), 'Hegel's Conception of the Family', *Polity* 14, pp. 5–28.

Laslett, P. (1991), Introduction in J. Locke, *Two Treatises of Government*, Cambridge: Cambridge University Press.

Lessnoff, M. H. (1999), *Political Philosophers of the Twentieth Century*, Oxford: Blackwell.

Li X. (2001), 'The Market–Democracy Conundrum', *Journal of Political Ideologies* 6:1, pp. 75–94.

Locke, D. (1980), *A Fantasy of Reason: the Life and Thought of William Godwin*, London: Routledge and Kegan Paul.

Locke, J. [1698] (1991), *Two Treatises of Government*, Cambridge: Cambridge University Press.

Loomba, A. (1998), *Colonialism/Postcolonialism*, London and New York: Routledge.

Lott, T. L. (1998), 'Early Enlightenment Conceptions of the Rights of Slaves', in T. L. Lott (ed.), *Subjugation and Bondage: Critical Essays on Slavery and Social Philosophy*, Boulder, CO and Oxford: Rowman and Littlefield.

Lubasz, H. (1977), 'Marx's Initial Problematic: the Problem of Poverty', *Political Studies* XXIV:1, pp.24–42.

Lukes, S. (1985), *Marxism and Morality*, Oxford: Oxford University Press.

McClintock, A. (1997), *Imperial Leather: Race, Gender and Sexuality in the Colonial Contest*, London: Routledge.

Macfarlane, A. (1978), *The Origins of English Individualism: the Family, Property and Social Transition*, Oxford: Blackwell.

Macpherson, C. B. (1962), *The Political Theory of Possessive Individualism*, Oxford: Oxford University Press.

Macpherson, C. B. (1978), *Property: Mainstream and Critical Positions*, Oxford: Blackwell.

Mannheim, K. (1986), *Conservatism: a Contribution to the Sociology of Knowledge*, London and New York: Routledge and Kegan Paul.

Marx, A. W. (1998), *Making Race and Nation: a Comparison of South Africa, the United States and Brazil*, Cambridge: Cambridge University Press.

Marx, K. [1890–4] (1976), *Capital*, Vol. I, Harmondsworth: Penguin.

Marx, K. (2000), 'Economic and Philosophical Manuscripts', in D. McLellan (ed.), *Karl Marx: Selected Writings*, Oxford: Oxford University Press.

Marx, K. (2000), 'On James Mill', in D. McLellan (ed.), *Karl Marx: Selected Writings*, Oxford: Oxford University Press.

Marx, K. (2000), 'Private Property and Communism', in D. McLellan (ed.), *Karl Marx: Selected Writings*, Oxford: Oxford University Press.

Meek, N. (1998), '"Society" Does Not Exist (and If It Did It Shouldn't)', *Political Notes* 144. <http://www.libertarian.co.uk/lapubs/polin/polin144.pdf>

Mehta, U. S. (1990), 'Liberal Strategies of Exclusion', *Politics and Society* 18:4, pp. 427–54.

Mendelson, S. and P. Crawford (1998), *Women in Early Modern England*, Oxford: Clarendon Press.

Miles, R. (1987), *Capitalism and Unfree Labour*, London: Tavistock.

Mill, J. S. [1848] (1994), *Principles of Political Economy*, Oxford: Oxford University Press.

Mill, J. S. [1859] (1991) 'On Liberty', in J. S. Mill and J. Bentham, *Utilitarianism and Other Essays*, ed. H. B. Acton, London: Penguin.

Miller, W. I. (1993), *Humiliation: and Other Essays on Honor, Social Discomfort and Violence*, Ithaca, NY and London: Cornell University Press.

Mills, C. W. (1997), *The Racial Contract*, Ithaca, NY and London: Cornell University Press.

Mills, C. W. (1998), *Blackness Visible: Essays on Philosophy and Race*, Ithaca, NY and London: Cornell University Press.

Minogue, K. (1968), 'Revolution, Tradition and Political Continuity', in P. King and B. Parekh (eds), *Politics and Experience*, Cambridge: Cambridge University Press.

Minogue, K. (1980), 'The Concept of Property and its Contemporary Significance', in J. R. Pennock and J. W. Chapman (eds), *Nomos XXII: Property*, New York: New York University Press.

Mlambo, E. (1972), *Rhodesia: the Struggle for a Birthright*, London: C. Hurst and Company.

Moore, A. (1653), *Bread for the Poor*, London.

Münkler, H. and K. Fischer (2002), 'Common Good and Civic Spirit in the Welfare State: Problems of Societal Self-description', *Journal of Political Philosophy* 10:4, pp. 416–38.

Nagel, T. (1975), 'Rawls on Justice', in N. Daniels (ed.), *Reading Rawls*, Oxford: Blackwell.

Nedelsky, J. (1990), 'Law, Boundaries and the Bounded Self', *Representations* 30, pp. 162–89.

Nielsen, K. (2001), 'Socialism and Egalitarian Justice', in J. P. Sterba (ed.), *Social and Political Philosophy: Contemporary Perspectives*, London and New York: Routledge.

Nisbet, R. (1986), *Conservatism*, Milton Keynes: Open University Press.

Nozick, R. (1974), *Anarchy, State and Utopia*, Oxford: Blackwell.

Oakeshott, M. (1991), *Rationalism in Politics and Other Essays*, Indianapolis: Liberty Press.

O'Brien, J. (1999), '"They Are So Frequently Shifting Their Place of Residence": Land and the Construction of Social Place of Indians in Colonial Massachusetts', in M. Daunton and R. Halpern (eds), *Empire and Others: British Encounters with Indigenous Peoples, 1600–1850*, London: UCL Press.

O'Hanlon, R. (1988), 'Recovering the Subject: *Subaltern Studies* and Histories of Resistance in Colonial South Asia', *Modern Asian Studies* 22:1, pp. 189–224.

Pagden, A. (1995), *Lords of All the World: Ideologies of Empire in Spain, Britain and France*, New Haven and London: Yale University Press.

Palmer, R. (1977), *Land and Racial Domination in Rhodesia*, London: Heinemann.

Parekh, B. (1995), 'Liberalism and Colonialism: a Critique of Locke and Mill', in J. N. Pietersen and B. Parekh (eds), *The Decolonization of the Imagination: Culture, Knowledge and Power*, London: Zed.

Parry, G. (1978), *John Locke*, London: Allen and Unwin.

Parry, G. (1992), 'John Evelyn as Hortulan Saint', in M. Leslie and T. Raylor (eds), *Culture and Cultivation in Early Modern England: Writing and the Land*, Leicester: Leicester University Press.

Pateman, C. (1988), *The Sexual Contract*, Cambridge: Polity Press.

Patterson, O. (1982), *Slavery and Social Death: a Comparative Study*, Cambridge, MA and London: Harvard University Press.

Petergorsky, D. W. [1940] (1972), *Left-wing Democracy in the English Civil War*, New York: Gollancz.

Phillips, A. (1997), 'What Has Socialism to Do with Sexual Equality?', in J. Franklin (ed.), *Equality*, London: IPPR.

Philp, M. (1986), *Godwin's Political Justice*, London: Duckworth.

Phimister, I. (1988), 'The Combined and Contradictory Inheritance of the Struggle against Colonialism', in C. Stoneman (ed.), *Zimbabwe's Prospects*, Basingstoke: Macmillan.

Pipes, R. (1999), *Property and Freedom*, London: Harvill.

Plant, R. (1977), 'Hegel and Political Economy', *New Left Review* 103, pp. 79–92.

Plant, R. (1977), 'Hegel and Political Economy II', *New Left Review* 104, pp. 103–13.

Poovey, M. (1989), *Uneven Developments: the Ideological Work of Gender in Mid-Victorian England*, London: Virago.

Prokhovnik, R. (1999), *Rational Woman: a Feminist Critique of Dichotomy*, London and New York: Routledge.

Proudhon, P.-J. [1840] (1994), *What is Property?*, ed. and tr. D. R. Kelley and B. G. Smith, Cambridge: Cambridge University Press.

Quinton, A. (1999), 'Conservatism', in R. E. Goodin and P. Pettit (eds), *A Companion to Political Philosophy*, Oxford: Blackwell.

Raven, J. (1996), 'Defending Conduct and Property: the London Press and the Luxury Debate', in J. Brewer and S. Staves (eds), *Early Modern Conceptions of Property*, London and New York: Routledge.

Rawls, J. (1993), *Political Liberalism*, New York: University of Columbia Press.

Reed, D. (1966), *The Battle for Rhodesia*, Cape Town: Haumm.

Richardson, R. (1987), *Death, Dissection and the Destitute*, London: Routledge and Kegan Paul.

Robson, J. (1998), 'Civilization and Culture as Moral Concepts', in J. Skorupski (ed.), *The Cambridge Companion to Mill*, Cambridge: Cambridge University Press.

Rosen, F. (1983), *Jeremy Bentham and Representative Democracy*, Oxford: Clarendon Press.

Rousseau, J.-J. (1973) *Social Contract and Discourses*, tr. G. D. H. Cole, London: Dent.

Ryan, A. (1984), 'Hegel on Work, Ownership and Citizenship', in Z. A. Pelczynski (ed.), *The State and Civil Society*, Cambridge: Cambridge University Press.

Ryan, A. (1987), *Property*, Milton Keynes: Open University Press.

Ryan, A. (1993), 'Liberalism', in R. E. Goodin and P. Pettit (eds), *A Companion to Contemporary Political Philosophy*, Oxford: Blackwell.

Ste. Croix, G. E. M. de (1988), 'Slavery and Other Forms of Unfree Labour', in L. Archer (ed.), *Slavery and Other Forms of Unfree Labour*, London and New York: Routledge.

Sandel, M. J. (1992), 'The Procedural Republic and the Unencumbered Self', in T. B. Strong (ed.), *The Self and the Political Order*, Oxford: Blackwell.

Sawyer, R. (1986), *Slavery in the Twentieth Century*, London and New York: Routledge and Kegan Paul.

Sayer, D. (1991), *Capitalism and Modernity*, London and New York: Routledge.

Scanlon, T. M. (1975), 'Nozick on Rights, Liberty and Property', in N. Daniels (ed.), *Reading Rawls*, Oxford: Blackwell.

Scanlon, T. M. (1975), 'Rawls' Theory of Justice', in N. Daniels (ed.), *Reading Rawls*, Oxford: Blackwell.

Scarritt, J. R. (1991), 'Zimbabwe: Revolutionary Violence Resulting in Reform', in J. A. Goldstone et al. (eds), *Revolutions of the Late Twentieth Century*, Boulder, CO: Westview Press.

Scruton, R. (1989), *The Meaning of Conservatism*, 2nd ed., London and Basingstoke: Macmillan.

Scruton, R. (2000), *England: an Elegy*, London: Pimlico.

Self, P. (1993), 'Socialism', in R. E. Goodin and P. Pettit (eds), *A Companion to Contemporary Political Philosophy*, Oxford: Blackwell.

Shapiro, I. (1996), 'Resources, Capacities and Ownership: the Workmanship Ideal and Distributive Justice', in J. Brewer and S. Staves (eds), *Early Modern Conceptions of Property*, London and New York: Routledge.

Singer, J. W. (1992), 'Re-reading Property', *New England Law Review* 26, pp. 711–30.

Singer, P. (1975), 'The right to be rich or poor', *New York Review of Books* 22:3, 6 March. <http://www.nybooks.com/articles/9252>

Sivanandan, A. (1990), *Communities of Resistance: Writings on Black Struggles for Socialism*, London and New York: Verso.

Smith, Hugh (1748), *Letters to Married Women*, London.

Smith, Rogers M. (1997), *Civic Ideals: Conflicting Visions of Citizenship in U.S. History*, New Haven and London: Yale University Press.

Somers, M. R. (1996), 'The "Misteries" of Property: Relationality, Rural-industrialization, and Community in Chartist Narratives of Political Rights', in J. Brewer and S. Staves (eds), *Early Modern Conceptions of Property*, London and New York: Routledge.

Sperling, L. (2001), *Women, Political Philosophy and Politics*, Edinburgh: Edinburgh University Press.

Squires, J. (2000), *Gender in Political Theory*, Cambridge: Polity Press.

Sreenivisan, G. (1995), *The Limits of Lockean Rights in Property*, New York and Oxford: Oxford University Press.

Steiner, H. (1980), 'Slavery, Socialism, and Private Property', in J. R. Pennock and J. W. Chapman (eds), *Nomos XXII: Property*, New York: New York University Press.

Steintrager, J. (1977), *Bentham*, London: Allen and Unwin.

Stillman, P. G. (1980), 'Property, Freedom and Individuality in Hegel's and Marx's Political Thought', in J. R. Pennock and J. W. Chapman (eds), *Nomos XXII: Property*, New York: New York University Press.

Stoler, A. L. (1995), *Race and the Education of Desire*, Durham, NC and London: Duke University Press.

Surin, K. (1996), '"The Continued Relevance of Marxism" as a Question: Some Propositions', in S. Makdisi et al. (eds), *Marxism beyond Marxism*, New York and London: Routledge.

Sutherland, D. R. (1990–1), 'The Religion of Gerrard Winstanley and Digger Communism', *Essays in History* 33. <http://etext.lib.virginia.edu/journals/EH/EH33/suther33.html>

Takaki, R. T. (1979), *Iron Cages: Race and Culture in Nineteenth-century America*, New York: Knopf.

Talbot, C. (2002), 'Zimbabwe faces acute famine', World Socialist Web Site, 27 July. <http://www.wsws.org/articles/2002/jul2002/zimb-j27.shtml>

Tawney, R. H. [1931] (1979), *Equality*, London: George Allen and Unwin.

Taylor, C. (1989), *Sources of the Self*, Cambridge: Cambridge University Press.

Taylor, K. (1982), *The Political Ideas of the Utopian Socialists*, London: Frank Cass.

Thirsk, J. (1984), *The Rural Economy of England*, London: Hambledon.

Thompson, E. P. [1975] (1990), *Whigs and Hunters*, Harmondsworth: Penguin.

Turley, D. (2000), *Slavery*, Oxford: Blackwell.

Underkuffler, L. (1990), 'On Property: an Essay', *Yale Law Journal* 100:127, pp. 127–49.

Veblen, T. [1899] (1994), *The Theory of the Leisure Class*, New York: Dover Publications.

Vogel, U. (1989), 'The Land Question: a Liberal Theory of Communal Property', *History Workshop* 27, pp. 106–36.

Vogel, U. (2000), 'Private Contract and Public Institution: the Peculiar Case of Marriage', in M. Passerin d'Entrèves and U. Vogel (eds), *Public and Private: Legal, Political and Philosophical Perspectives*, London and New York: Routledge.

Wald, A. (1997), 'What's Rightfully Ours: toward a Property Theory of Rape', *Columbia Journal of Law and Social Problems* 30:3, pp. 459–502.

Waldron, J. (1988), *The Right to Private Property*, Oxford: Clarendon Press.

Walvin, J. (1996), *Questioning Slavery*, London: Routledge.

Warner, M. (1998), 'Is there a place from which the dickhead's self can speak?', *London Review of Books* 20:19, 1 October.

Warrender, H. (1983), *The Clarendon Edition of the Philosophical Works of Thomas Hobbes*, Vol. III: 'De Cive', English version, Oxford: Clarendon Press.

Weeks, K. (1996), 'Subject for a Feminist Standpoint', in S. Makdisi et al. (eds), *Marxism beyond Marxism*, New York and London: Routledge.

Weiner, D. (1988), 'Land and Agricultural Development', in C. Stoneman (ed.), *Zimbabwe's Prospects*, Basingstoke: Macmillan.

Willett, C. (1995), *Maternal Ethics and Other Slave Moralities*, New York and London: Routledge.

Willett, C. (1998), 'The Master–Slave Dialectic: Hegel vs. Douglass', in T. L. Lott (ed.), *Subjugation and Bondage: Critical Essays on Slavery and Social Philosophy*, Boulder, CO and Oxford: Rowman and Littlefield.

Williams, B. (1998), 'Necessary Identities', in T. L. Lott (ed.), *Subjugation and Bondage: Critical Essays on Slavery and Social Philosophy*, Boulder, CO and Oxford: Rowman and Littlefield.

Williams, R. A. (1990), *The American Indian in Western Legal Thought: the Discourses of Conquest*, New York and Oxford: Oxford University Press.

Williams, R. R. (1997), *Hegel's Ethics of Recognition*, Berkeley: University of California Press.

Winstanley, G. (1973), 'An Appeal to the House of Commons', in C. Hill, *Winstanley: the Law of Freedom*, Harmondsworth: Penguin.

Winstanley, G. (1973), 'A Declaration from the Poor Oppressed People of England', in C. Hill, *Winstanley: the Law of Freedom*, Harmondsworth: Penguin.

Winstanley, G. (1973), 'Fire in the Bush', in C. Hill, *Winstanley: the Law of Freedom*, Harmondsworth: Penguin.

Winstanley, G. (1973), 'The Law of Freedom in a Platform', in C. Hill, *Winstanley: the Law of Freedom*, Harmondsworth: Penguin.

Winstanley, G. (1973), 'The Law of Freedom in a Platform or True Magistracy Restored', in C. Hill, *Winstanley: the Law of Freedom*, Harmondsworth: Penguin.

Winstanley, G. (1973), 'A Letter to Lord Fairfax', in C. Hill, *Winstanley: the Law of Freedom*, Harmondsworth: Penguin.

Winstanley, G. (1973), 'The New Law of Righteousness', in C. Hill, *Winstanley: the Law of Freedom*, Harmondsworth: Penguin.

Winstanley, G. (1973), 'True Levellers' Standard', in C. Hill, *Winstanley: the Law of Freedom*, Harmondsworth: Penguin.

Wood, A. W. (1990), *Hegel's Ethical Thought*, Cambridge: Cambridge University Press.

Wood, N. (1984), *John Locke and Agrarian Capitalism*, Berkeley: University of California Press.

Wright, A. (1986), *Socialisms*, Oxford: Oxford University Press.

Further Reading

Allen, A. L. (1990), 'Surrogacy, Slavery and the Ownership of Life', *Harvard Journal of Law and Public Policy* 13, pp. 139–50.

Appleby, J. O. (1978), *Economic Thought and Ideology in Seventeenth-Century England*, Princeton: Princeton University Press.

Becker, L. C. (1977), *Property Rights*, London: Routledge and Kegan Paul.

Brace, L. (1998), *The Idea of Property in Seventeenth-century England*, Manchester: Manchester University Press.

Brace, L. (2002), 'The Tragedy of the Freelance Hustler: Hegel, Gender and Civil Society', *Contemporary Political Theory* 1:3, pp. 329–49.

Buck, A. R. et al., (eds) (2001), *Land and Freedom: Law, Property Rights and the British Diaspora*, Aldershot: Ashgate.

Carter, A. (1989), *The Philosophical Foundations of Property Rights*, London: Harvester Wheatsheaf.

Glausser, W. (1990), 'Three Approaches to Locke and the Slave Trade', *Journal of the History of Ideas* 51:2.

Grunebaum, J. O. (1987), *Private Ownership*, London: Routledge and Kegan Paul.

Herzog, D. (1989), *Happy Slaves: a Critique of Consent Theory*, Chicago and London: University of Chicago Press.

Horne, T. A. (1990), *Property Rights and Poverty: Political Argument in Britain, 1605–1834*, Chapel Hill, NC and London: University of North Carolina Press.

Nursey-Bray, P. (1996), 'Autonomy and Community: William Godwin and the Anarchist Project', *Anarchist Studies* 4:2, pp. 97–113.

Olivecrona, K. (1974), 'Appropriation in the State of Nature: Locke on the Origin of Property', *Journal of the History of Ideas* 35.

Pateman, C. (2002), 'Self-ownership and Property in the Person: Democratization and a Tale of Two Concepts', *Journal of Political Philosophy* 10:1, pp. 20–53.

Radin, M. J. (1982), 'Property and Personhood', *Stanford Law Review* 34, pp. 957–1015.

Radin, M. J. (1991), 'Reflections on Objectification', *Southern California Law*

Review 65, pp. 341–55.

Rawls, J. (1972), *A Theory of Justice*, Oxford: Oxford University Press.

Reeve, A. (1986), *Property*, London: Macmillan.

Ryan, A. (1984), *Property and Political Theory*, Oxford: Blackwell.

Singer, J. W. (1991), 'Sovereignty and Property', *Northwestern University Law Review* 86:1, pp. 1–56.

Tully, J, (1993), *An Approach to Political Philosophy: Locke in Contexts*, Cambridge: Cambridge University Press.

Index